Book 5: Fixed Income, Derivatives, and Alternative Investments

SchweserNotes™ 2019

Level I CFA®

SCHWESERNOTES™ 2019 LEVEL I CFA® BOOK 5: FIXED INCOME, DERIVATIVES, AND ALTERNATIVE INVESTMENTS

©2018 Kaplan, Inc. All rights reserved.

Published in 2018 by Kaplan, Inc.

Printed in the United States of America.

ISBN: 978-1-4754-7834-1

CONTENTS

STUDY SESSION 19—Alternative Investments

READING 58

LEARNING OUTCOME STATEMENTS (LOS)

STUDY SESSION 16

The topical coverage corresponds with the following CFA Institute assigned reading:
50. Fixed-Income Securities: Defining Elements
The candidate should be able to:
a. describe basic features of a fixed-income security. (page 2)
b. describe content of a bond indenture. (page 3)
c. compare affirmative and negative covenants and identify examples of each. (page 3)
d. describe how legal, regulatory, and tax considerations affect the issuance and trading of fixed-income securities. (page 4)
e. describe how cash flows of fixed-income securities are structured. (page 8)
f. describe contingency provisions affecting the timing and/or nature of cash flows of fixed-income securities and identify whether such provisions benefit the borrower or the lender. (page 11)

The topical coverage corresponds with the following CFA Institute assigned reading:
51. Fixed-Income Markets: Issuance, Trading, and Funding
The candidate should be able to:
a. describe classifications of global fixed-income markets. (page 19)
b. describe the use of interbank offered rates as reference rates in floating-rate debt. (page 20)
c. describe mechanisms available for issuing bonds in primary markets. (page 21)
d. describe secondary markets for bonds. (page 22)
e. describe securities issued by sovereign governments. (page 22)
f. describe securities issued by non-sovereign governments, quasi-government entities, and supranational agencies. (page 23)
g. describe types of debt issued by corporations. (page 24)
h. describe structured financial instruments. (page 26)
i. describe short-term funding alternatives available to banks. (page 28)
j. describe repurchase agreements (repos) and the risks associated with them. (page 29)

The topical coverage corresponds with the following CFA Institute assigned reading:
52. Introduction to Fixed-Income Valuation
The candidate should be able to:
a. calculate a bond's price given a market discount rate. (page 35)
b. identify the relationships among a bond's price, coupon rate, maturity, and market discount rate (yield-to-maturity). (page 37)
c. define spot rates and calculate the price of a bond using spot rates. (page 40)
d. describe and calculate the flat price, accrued interest, and the full price of a bond. (page 41)
e. describe matrix pricing. (page 42)
f. calculate and interpret yield measures for fixed-rate bonds, floating-rate notes, and money market instruments. (page 44)

g. define and compare the spot curve, yield curve on coupon bonds, par curve, and forward curve. (page 50)
h. define forward rates and calculate spot rates from forward rates, forward rates from spot rates, and the price of a bond using forward rates. (page 52)
i. compare, calculate, and interpret yield spread measures. (page 56)

The topical coverage corresponds with the following CFA Institute assigned reading:

53. Introduction to Asset-Backed Securities

The candidate should be able to:

a. explain benefits of securitization for economies and financial markets. (page 65)
b. describe securitization, including the parties involved in the process and the roles they play. (page 66)
c. describe typical structures of securitizations, including credit tranching and time tranching. (page 68)
d. describe types and characteristics of residential mortgage loans that are typically securitized. (page 69)
e. describe types and characteristics of residential mortgage-backed securities, including mortgage pass-through securities and collateralized mortgage obligations, and explain the cash flows and risks for each type. (page 71)
f. define prepayment risk and describe the prepayment risk of mortgage-backed securities. (page 71)
g. describe characteristics and risks of commercial mortgage-backed securities. (page 77)
h. describe types and characteristics of non-mortgage asset-backed securities, including the cash flows and risks of each type. (page 79)
i. describe collateralized debt obligations, including their cash flows and risks. (page 81)

STUDY SESSION 17

The topical coverage corresponds with the following CFA Institute assigned reading:

54. Understanding Fixed-Income Risk and Return

The candidate should be able to:

a. calculate and interpret the sources of return from investing in a fixed-rate bond. (page 89)
b. define, calculate, and interpret Macaulay, modified, and effective durations. (page 95)
c. explain why effective duration is the most appropriate measure of interest rate risk for bonds with embedded options. (page 98)
d. define key rate duration and describe the use of key rate durations in measuring the sensitivity of bonds to changes in the shape of the benchmark yield curve. (page 100)
e. explain how a bond's maturity, coupon, and yield level affect its interest rate risk. (page 100)
f. calculate the duration of a portfolio and explain the limitations of portfolio duration. (page 101)
g. calculate and interpret the money duration of a bond and price value of a basis point (PVBP). (page 102)

h. calculate and interpret approximate convexity and distinguish between approximate and effective convexity. (page 103)
i. estimate the percentage price change of a bond for a specified change in yield, given the bond's approximate duration and convexity. (page 105)
j. describe how the term structure of yield volatility affects the interest rate risk of a bond. (page 106)
k. describe the relationships among a bond's holding period return, its duration, and the investment horizon. (page 107)
l. explain how changes in credit spread and liquidity affect yield-to-maturity of a bond and how duration and convexity can be used to estimate the price effect of the changes. (page 109)

The topical coverage corresponds with the following CFA Institute assigned reading:
55. Fundamentals of Credit Analysis
The candidate should be able to:
a. describe credit risk and credit-related risks affecting corporate bonds. (page 117)
b. describe default probability and loss severity as components of credit risk. (page 117)
c. describe seniority rankings of corporate debt and explain the potential violation of the priority of claims in a bankruptcy proceeding. (page 118)
d. distinguish between corporate issuer credit ratings and issue credit ratings and describe the rating agency practice of "notching." (page 119)
e. explain risks in relying on ratings from credit rating agencies. (page 121)
f. explain the four Cs (Capacity, Collateral, Covenants, and Character) of traditional credit analysis. (page 121)
g. calculate and interpret financial ratios used in credit analysis. (page 124)
h. evaluate the credit quality of a corporate bond issuer and a bond of that issuer, given key financial ratios of the issuer and the industry. (page 124)
i. describe factors that influence the level and volatility of yield spreads. (page 127)
j. explain special considerations when evaluating the credit of high yield, sovereign, and non-sovereign government debt issuers and issues. (page 128)

STUDY SESSION 18

The topical coverage corresponds with the following CFA Institute assigned reading:
56. Derivative Markets and Instruments
The candidate should be able to:
a. define a derivative and distinguish between exchange-traded and over-the-counter derivatives. (page 143)
b. contrast forward commitments with contingent claims. (page 144)
c. define forward contracts, futures contracts, options (calls and puts), swaps, and credit derivatives and compare their basic characteristics. (page 144)
d. describe purposes of, and controversies related to, derivative markets. (page 149)
e. explain arbitrage and the role it plays in determining prices and promoting market efficiency. (page 149)

The topical coverage corresponds with the following CFA Institute assigned reading:

57. Basics of Derivative Pricing and Valuation

The candidate should be able to:

a. explain how the concepts of arbitrage, replication, and risk neutrality are used in pricing derivatives. (page 155)

b. distinguish between value and price of forward and futures contracts. (page 158)

c. explain how the value and price of a forward contract are determined at expiration, during the life of the contract, and at initiation. (page 159)

d. describe monetary and nonmonetary benefits and costs associated with holding the underlying asset and explain how they affect the value and price of a forward contract. (page 160)

e. define a forward rate agreement and describe its uses. (page 161)

f. explain why forward and futures prices differ. (page 163)

g. explain how swap contracts are similar to but different from a series of forward contracts. (page 163)

h. distinguish between the value and price of swaps. (page 163)

i. explain how the value of a European option is determined at expiration. (page 165)

j. explain the exercise value, time value, and moneyness of an option. (page 165)

k. identify the factors that determine the value of an option and explain how each factor affects the value of an option. (page 167)

l. explain put–call parity for European options. (page 168)

m. explain put–call–forward parity for European options. (page 170)

n. explain how the value of an option is determined using a one-period binomial model. (page 171)

o. explain under which circumstances the values of European and American options differ. (page 174)

STUDY SESSION 19

The topical coverage corresponds with the following CFA Institute assigned reading:

58. Introduction to Alternative Investments

The candidate should be able to:

a. compare alternative investments with traditional investments. (page 183)

b. describe categories of alternative investments. (page 184)

c. describe potential benefits of alternative investments in the context of portfolio management. (page 185)

d. describe hedge funds, private equity, real estate, commodities, infrastructure, and other alternative investments, including, as applicable, strategies, sub-categories, potential benefits and risks, fee structures, and due diligence. (page 185)

e. describe, calculate, and interpret management and incentive fees and net-of-fees returns to hedge funds. (page 199)

f. describe issues in valuing and calculating returns on hedge funds, private equity, real estate, commodities, and infrastructure. (page 185)

g. describe risk management of alternative investments. (page 201)

READING 50

Fixed-Income Securities: Defining Elements

EXAM FOCUS

Here your focus should be on learning the basic characteristics of debt securities and as much of the bond terminology as you can remember. Key items are the coupon structure of bonds and options embedded in bonds: call options, put options, and conversion (to common stock) options.

MODULE 50.1: BOND INDENTURES, REGULATION, AND TAXATION

Video covering this content is available online.

There are two important points about fixed-income securities that we will develop further along in the Fixed Income study sessions but may be helpful as you read this topic review.

- The most common type of fixed-income security is a bond that promises to make a series of interest payments in fixed amounts and to repay the principal amount at maturity. When market interest rates (i.e., yields on bonds) *increase*, the value of such bonds *decreases* because the present value of a bond's promised cash flows decreases when a higher discount rate is used.

- Bonds are rated based on their relative probability of default (failure to make promised payments). Because investors prefer bonds with lower probability of default, bonds with lower credit quality must offer investors higher yields to compensate for the greater probability of default. Other things equal, a decrease in a bond's rating (an increased probability of default) will decrease the price of the bond, thus increasing its yield.

LOS 50.a: Describe basic features of a fixed-income security.

CFA® Program Curriculum: Volume 5, page 299

The features of a fixed-income security include specification of:

- The issuer of the bond.

- The maturity date of the bond.

- The par value (principal value to be repaid).

- Coupon rate and frequency.

- Currency in which payments will be made.

Issuers of Bonds

There are several types of entities that issue bonds when they borrow money, including:

- **Corporations.** Often corporate bonds are divided into those issued by financial companies and those issued by nonfinancial companies.

- **Sovereign national governments.** A prime example is U.S. Treasury bonds, but many countries issue sovereign bonds.

- **Non-sovereign governments.** Issued by government entities that are not national governments, such as the state of California or the city of Toronto.

- **Quasi-government entities.** Not a direct obligation of a country's government or central bank. An example is the Federal National Mortgage Association (Fannie Mae).

- **Supranational entities.** Issued by organizations that operate globally such as the World Bank, the European Investment Bank, and the International Monetary Fund (IMF).

Bond Maturity

The maturity date of a bond is the date on which the principal is to be repaid. Once a bond has been issued, the time remaining until maturity is referred to as the **term to maturity** or **tenor** of a bond.

When bonds are issued, their terms to maturity range from one day to 30 years or more. Both Disney and Coca-Cola have issued bonds with original maturities of 100 years. Bonds that have no maturity date are called **perpetual bonds**. They make periodic interest payments but do not promise to repay the principal amount.

Bonds with original maturities of one year or less are referred to as **money market securities**. Bonds with original maturities of more than one year are referred to as **capital market securities**.

Par Value

The **par value** of a bond is the **principal amount** that will be repaid at maturity. The par value is also referred to as the *face value*, *maturity value*, *redemption value*, or *principal value* of a bond. Bonds can have a par value of any amount, and their prices are quoted as a percentage of par. A bond with a par value of $1,000 quoted at 98 is selling for $980.

A bond that is selling for more than its par value is said to be trading at a **premium** to par; a bond that is selling at less than its par value is said to be trading at a **discount** to par; and a bond that is selling for exactly its par value is said to be trading **at par**.

Coupon Payments

The coupon rate on a bond is the annual percentage of its par value that will be paid to bondholders. Some bonds make coupon interest payments annually, while others make semiannual, quarterly, or monthly payments. A $1,000 par value semiannual-pay bond with a 5% coupon would pay 2.5% of $1,000, or $25, every six months. A bond with a fixed coupon rate is called a **plain vanilla** bond or a **conventional** bond.

Some bonds pay no interest prior to maturity and are called **zero-coupon bonds** or **pure discount bonds**. *Pure discount* refers to the fact that these bonds are sold at a discount to their par value and the interest is all paid at maturity when bondholders receive the par value. A 10-year, $1,000, zero-coupon bond yielding 7% would sell at about $500 initially and pay $1,000 at maturity. We discuss various other coupon structures later in this topic review.

Currencies

Bonds are issued in many currencies. Sometimes borrowers from countries with volatile currencies issue bonds denominated in euros or U.S. dollars to make them more attractive to a wide range investors. A **dual-currency bond** makes coupon interest payments in one currency and the principal repayment at maturity in another currency. A **currency option bond** gives bondholders a choice of which of two currencies they would like to receive their payments in.

LOS 50.b: Describe content of a bond indenture.

LOS 50.c: Compare affirmative and negative covenants and identify examples of each.

CFA® Program Curriculum: Volume 5, page 305

The legal contract between the bond issuer (borrower) and bondholders (lenders) is called a **trust deed**, and in the United States and Canada, it is also often referred to as the **bond indenture**. The indenture defines the obligations of and restrictions on the borrower and forms the basis for all future transactions between the bondholder and the issuer.

The provisions in the bond indenture are known as *covenants* and include both *negative covenants* (prohibitions on the borrower) and *affirmative covenants* (actions the borrower promises to perform).

Negative covenants include restrictions on asset sales (the company can't sell assets that have been pledged as collateral), negative pledge of collateral (the company can't claim that the same assets back several debt issues simultaneously), and restrictions on additional borrowings (the company can't borrow additional money unless certain financial conditions are met).

Negative covenants serve to protect the interests of bondholders and prevent the issuing firm from taking actions that would increase the risk of default. At the same time, the covenants must not be so restrictive that they prevent the firm from taking advantage of opportunities that arise or responding appropriately to changing business circumstances.

Affirmative covenants do not typically restrict the operating decisions of the issuer. Common affirmative covenants are to make timely interest and principal payments to bondholders, to insure and maintain assets, and to comply with applicable laws and regulations.

LOS 50.d: Describe how legal, regulatory, and tax considerations affect the issuance and trading of fixed-income securities.

CFA® Program Curriculum: Volume 5, page 313

Bonds are subject to different legal and regulatory requirements depending on where they are issued and traded. Bonds issued by a firm domiciled in a country and also traded in that country's currency are referred to as **domestic bonds**. Bonds issued by a firm incorporated in a foreign country that trade on the **national bond market** of another country in that country's currency are referred to as **foreign bonds**. Examples include bonds issued by foreign firms that trade in China and are denominated in yuan, which are called *panda bonds*, and bonds issued by firms incorporated outside the United States that trade in the United States and are denominated in U.S. dollars, which are called *Yankee bonds*.

Eurobonds are issued outside the jurisdiction of any one country and denominated in a currency different from the currency of the countries in which they are sold. They are subject to less regulation than domestic bonds in most jurisdictions and were initially introduced to avoid U.S. regulations. Eurobonds should not be confused with bonds denominated in euros or thought to originate in Europe, although they can be both. Eurobonds got the "euro" name because they were first introduced in Europe, and most are still traded by firms in European capitals. A bond issued by a Chinese firm that is denominated in yen and traded in markets outside Japan would fit the definition of a Eurobond. Eurobonds that trade in the national bond market of a country other than the country that issues the currency the bond is denominated in, and in the Eurobond market, are referred to as **global bonds**.

Eurobonds are referred to by the currency they are denominated in. Eurodollar bonds are denominated in U.S. dollars, and euroyen bonds are denominated in yen. The majority of Eurobonds are issued in **bearer** form. Ownership of bearer bonds is evidenced simply by possessing the bonds, whereas ownership of **registered bonds** is recorded. Bearer bonds may be more attractive than registered bonds to those seeking to avoid taxes.

Other legal and regulatory issues addressed in a trust deed include:

- Legal information about the entity issuing the bond.
- Any assets (collateral) pledged to support repayment of the bond.
- Any additional features that increase the probability of repayment (credit enhancements).
- Covenants describing any actions the firm must take and any actions the firm is prohibited from taking.

Issuing Entities

Bonds are issued by several types of legal entities, and bondholders must be aware of which entity has actually promised to make the interest and principal payments. Sovereign bonds are most often issued by the treasury of the issuing country.

Corporate bonds may be issued by a well-known corporation such as Microsoft, by a subsidiary of a company, or by a holding company that is the overall owner of several operating companies. Bondholders must pay attention to the specific entity issuing the bonds because the credit quality can differ among related entities.

Sometimes an entity is created solely for the purpose of owning specific assets and issuing bonds to provide the funds to purchase the assets. These entities are referred to as **special purpose entities** (SPEs) in the United States and special purpose vehicles (SPVs) in Europe. Bonds issued by these entities are called **securitized bonds**. As an example, a firm could sell loans it has made to customers to an SPE that issues bonds to purchase the loans. The interest and principal payments on the loans are then used to make the interest and principal payments on the bonds.

Often, an SPE can issue bonds at a lower interest rate than bonds issued by the originating corporation. This is because the assets supporting the bonds are owned by the SPE and are used to make the payments to holders of the securitized bonds even if the company itself runs into financial trouble. For this reason, SPEs are called **bankruptcy remote vehicles** or entities.

Sources of Repayment

Sovereign bonds are typically repaid by the tax receipts of the issuing country. Bonds issued by non-sovereign government entities are repaid by either general taxes, revenues of a specific project (e.g., an airport), or by special taxes or fees dedicated to bond repayment (e.g., a water district or sewer district).

Corporate bonds are generally repaid from cash generated by the firm's operations. As noted previously, securitized bonds are repaid from the cash flows of the financial assets owned by the SPE.

Collateral and Credit Enhancements

Unsecured bonds represent a claim to the overall assets and cash flows of the issuer. **Secured bonds** are backed by a claim to specific assets of a corporation, which reduces their risk of default and, consequently, the yield that investors require on the bonds. Assets pledged to support a bond issue (or any loan) are referred to as **collateral**.

Because they are backed by collateral, secured bonds are *senior* to unsecured bonds. Among unsecured bonds, two different issues may have different priority in the event of bankruptcy or liquidation of the issuing entity. The claim of senior unsecured debt is below (after) that of secured debt but ahead of *subordinated*, or junior, debt.

Sometimes secured debt is referred to by the type of collateral pledged. **Equipment trust certificates** are debt securities backed by equipment such as railroad cars and oil drilling rigs. **Collateral trust bonds** are backed by financial assets, such as stocks and (other) bonds. Be aware that while the term **debentures** refers to unsecured debt in the United States and elsewhere, in Great Britain and some other countries the term refers to bonds collateralized by specific assets.

The most common type of securitized bond is a **mortgage-backed security** (MBS). The underlying assets are a pool of mortgages, and the interest and principal payments from the mortgages are used to pay the interest and principal on the MBS.

In some countries, especially European countries, financial companies issue **covered bonds**. Covered bonds are similar to asset-backed securities, but the underlying assets (the cover pool), although segregated, remain on the balance sheet of the issuing corporation (i.e., no SPE is created). Special legislation protects the assets in the cover pool in the event of firm insolvency (they are bankruptcy remote). In contrast to an SPE structure, covered bonds also provide recourse to the issuing firm that must replace or augment non-performing assets in the cover pool so that it always provides for the payment of the covered bond's promised interest and principal payments.

Credit enhancement can be either internal (built into the structure of a bond issue) or external (provided by a third party). One method of internal credit enhancement is *overcollateralization*, in which the collateral pledged has a value greater than the par value of the debt issued. One limitation of this method of credit enhancement is that the additional collateral is also the underlying assets, so when asset defaults are high, the value of the excess collateral declines in value.

Two other methods of internal credit enhancement are a *cash reserve fund* and an *excess spread account*. A cash reserve fund is cash set aside to make up for credit losses on the underlying assets. With an excess spread account, the yield promised on the bonds issued is less than the promised yield on the assets supporting the ABS. This gives some protection if the yield on the financial assets is less than anticipated. If the assets perform as anticipated, the excess cash flow from the collateral can be used to retire (pay off the principal on) some of the outstanding bonds.

Another method of internal credit enhancement is to divide a bond issue into *tranches* (French for *slices*) with different seniority of claims. Any losses due to poor performance of the assets supporting a securitized bond are first absorbed by the bonds with the lowest seniority, then the bonds with the next-lowest priority of claims. The most senior tranches in this structure can receive very high credit ratings because the probability is very low that losses will be so large that they cannot be absorbed by the subordinated tranches. The subordinated tranches must have higher yields to compensate investors for the additional risk of default. This is sometimes referred to as *waterfall structure* because available funds first go to the most senior tranche of bonds, then to the next-highest priority bonds, and so forth.

External credit enhancements include surety bonds, bank guarantees, and letters of credit from financial institutions. *Surety bonds* are issued by insurance companies and are a promise to make up any shortfall in the cash available to service the debt. *Bank guarantees* serve the same function. A *letter of credit* is a promise to lend money to the issuing entity if it does not have enough cash to make the promised payments on the covered debt. While all three of these external credit enhancements increase the credit quality of debt issues and decrease their yields, deterioration of the credit quality of the guarantor will also reduce the credit quality of the covered issue.

Taxation of Bond Income

Most often, the interest income paid to bondholders is taxed as ordinary income at the same rate as wage and salary income. The interest income from bonds issued by municipal governments in the United States, however, is most often exempt from national income tax and often from any state income tax in the state of issue.

When a bondholder sells a coupon bond prior to maturity, it may be at a gain or a loss relative to its purchase price. Such gains and losses are considered capital gains income (rather than ordinary taxable income). Capital gains are often taxed at a lower rate than ordinary income. Capital gains on the sale of an asset that has been owned for more than some minimum amount of time may be classified as *long-term* capital gains and taxed at an even lower rate.

Pure-discount bonds and other bonds sold at significant discounts to par when issued are termed **original issue discount** (OID) bonds. Because the gains over an OID bond's tenor as the price moves towards par value are really interest income, these bonds can generate a tax liability even when no cash interest payment has been made. In many tax jurisdictions, a portion of the discount from par at issuance is treated as taxable interest income each year. This tax treatment also allows that the tax basis of the OID bonds is increased each year by the amount of interest income recognized, so there is no additional capital gains tax liability at maturity.

Some tax jurisdictions provide a symmetric treatment for bonds issued at a premium to par, allowing part of the premium to be used to reduce the taxable portion of coupon interest payments.

 MODULE QUIZ 50.1

To best evaluate your performance, enter your quiz answers online.

1. A dual-currency bond pays coupon interest in a currency:
    A. of the bondholder's choice.
    B. other than the home currency of the issuer.
    C. other than the currency in which it repays principal.

2. A bond's indenture:
   A. contains its covenants.
   B. is the same as a debenture.
   C. relates only to its interest and principal payments.

3. A clause in a bond indenture that requires the borrower to perform a certain action is *most accurately* described as:
   A. a trust deed.
   B. a negative covenant.
   C. an affirmative covenant.

4. An investor buys a pure-discount bond, holds it to maturity, and receives its par value. For tax purposes, the increase in the bond's value is *most likely* to be treated as:
   A. a capital gain.
   B. interest income.
   C. tax-exempt income.

MODULE 50.2: BOND CASH FLOWS AND CONTINGENCIES

Video covering this content is available online.

LOS 50.e: Describe how cash flows of fixed-income securities are structured.

CFA® Program Curriculum: Volume 5, page 318

A typical bond has a **bullet** structure. Periodic interest payments (coupon payments) are made over the life of the bond, and the principal value is paid with the final interest payment at maturity. The interest payments are referred to as the bond's **coupons**. When the final payment includes a lump sum in addition to the final period's interest, it is referred to as a **balloon payment**.

Consider a $1,000 face value 5-year bond with an annual coupon rate of 5%. With a bullet structure, the bond's promised payments at the end of each year would be as follows.

Year	1	2	3	4	5
PMT	$50	$50	$50	$50	$1,050
Principal remaining	$1,000	$1,000	$1,000	$1,000	$0

A loan structure in which the periodic payments include both interest and some repayment of principal (the amount borrowed) is called an **amortizing loan**. If a bond (loan) is **fully amortizing**, this means the principal is fully paid off when the last periodic payment is made. Typically, automobile loans and home loans are fully amortizing loans. If the 5-year, 5% bond in the previous table had a fully amortizing structure rather than a bullet structure, the payments and remaining principal balance at each year-end would be as follows (final payment reflects rounding of previous payments).

Year	1	2	3	4	5
PMT	$230.97	$230.97	$230.97	$230.97	$230.98
Principal remaining	$819.03	$629.01	$429.49	$219.99	$0

A bond can also be structured to be **partially amortizing** so that there is a balloon payment at bond maturity, just as with a bullet structure. However, unlike a bullet structure, the final payment includes just the remaining unamortized principal amount rather than the full principal amount. In the following table, the final payment includes $200 to repay the remaining principal outstanding.

Year	1	2	3	4	5
PMT	$194.78	$194.78	$194.78	$194.78	$394.78
Principal remaining	$855.22	$703.20	$543.58	$375.98	$0

Sinking fund provisions provide for the repayment of principal through a series of payments over the life of the issue. For example, a 20-year issue with a face amount of $300 million may require that the issuer retire $20 million of the principal every year beginning in the sixth year.

Details of sinking fund provisions vary. There may be a period during which no sinking fund redemptions are made. The amount of bonds redeemed according to the sinking fund provision could decline each year or increase each year.

The price at which bonds are redeemed under a sinking fund provision is typically par but can be different from par. If the market price is less than the sinking fund redemption price, the issuer can satisfy the sinking fund provision by buying bonds in the open market with a par value equal to the amount of bonds that must be redeemed. This would be the case if interest rates had risen since issuance so that the bonds were trading below the sinking fund redemption price.

Sinking fund provisions offer both advantages and disadvantages to bondholders. On the plus side, bonds with a sinking fund provision have less credit risk because the periodic redemptions reduce the total amount of principal to be repaid at maturity. The presence of a sinking fund, however, can be a disadvantage to bondholders when interest rates fall.

This disadvantage to bondholders can be seen by considering the case where interest rates have fallen since bond issuance, so the bonds are trading at a price above the sinking fund redemption price. In this case, the bond trustee will select outstanding bonds for redemption randomly. A bondholder would suffer a loss if her bonds were selected to be redeemed at a price below the current market price. This means the bonds have more *reinvestment risk* because bondholders who have their bonds redeemed can only reinvest the funds at the new, lower yield (assuming they buy bonds of similar risk).

PROFESSOR'S NOTE

The concept of reinvestment risk is developed more in subsequent topic reviews. It can be defined as the uncertainty about the interest to be earned on cash flows from a bond that are reinvested in other debt securities. In the case of a bond with a sinking fund, the greater probability of receiving the principal repayment prior to maturity increases the expected cash flows during the bond's life and, therefore, the uncertainty about interest income on reinvested funds.

There are several coupon structures besides a fixed-coupon structure, and we summarize the most important ones here.

Floating-Rate Notes

Some bonds pay periodic interest that depends on a current market rate of interest. These bonds are called **floating-rate notes** (FRN) or **floaters**. The market rate of interest is called the **reference rate**, and an FRN promises to pay the reference rate plus some interest margin. This added margin is typically expressed in **basis points**, which are hundredths of 1%. A 120 basis point margin is equivalent to 1.2%.

As an example, consider a floating-rate note that pays the London Interbank Offered Rate (LIBOR) plus a margin of 0.75% (75 basis points) annually. If 1-year LIBOR is 2.3% at the beginning of the year, the bond will pay 2.3% + 0.75% = 3.05% of its par value at the end of the year. The new 1-year rate at that time will determine the rate of interest paid at the end of the next year. Most floaters pay quarterly and are based on a quarterly (90-day) reference rate. A **variable-rate note** is one for which the margin above the reference rate is not fixed.

A floating-rate note may have a **cap**, which benefits the issuer by placing a limit on how high the coupon rate can rise. Often, FRNs with caps also have a **floor**, which benefits the bondholder by placing a minimum on the coupon rate (regardless of how low the reference rate falls). An **inverse floater** has a coupon rate that increases when the reference rate decreases and decreases when the reference rate increases.

OTHER COUPON STRUCTURES

Step-up coupon bonds are structured so that the coupon rate increases over time according to a predetermined schedule. Typically, step-up coupon bonds have a *call feature* that allows the firm to redeem the bond issue at a set price at each step-up date. If the new higher coupon rate is greater than what the market yield would be at the call price, the firm will call the bonds and retire them. This means if market yields rise, a bondholder may, in turn, get a higher coupon rate because the bonds are less likely to be called on the step-up date.

Yields could increase because an issuer's credit rating has fallen, in which case the higher step-up coupon rate simply compensates investors for greater credit risk. Aside from this, we can view step-up coupon bonds as having some protection against increases in market interest rates to the extent they are offset by increases in bond coupon rates.

A **credit-linked coupon bond** carries a provision stating that the coupon rate will go up by a certain amount if the credit rating of the issuer falls and go down if the credit rating of the issuer improves. While this offers some protection against a credit downgrade of the issuer, the higher required coupon payments may make the financial situation of the issuer worse and possibly increase the probability of default.

A **payment-in-kind (PIK) bond** allows the issuer to make the coupon payments by increasing the principal amount of the outstanding bonds, essentially paying bond interest with more bonds. Firms that issue PIK bonds typically do so because they anticipate that firm cash flows may be less than required to service the debt, often because of high levels of debt financing (leverage). These bonds typically have higher yields because of a lower perceived credit quality from cash flow shortfalls or simply because of the high leverage of the issuing firm.

With a **deferred coupon bond**, also called a **split coupon bond**, regular coupon payments do not begin until a period of time after issuance. These are issued by firms that anticipate cash flows will increase in the future to allow them to make coupon interest payments.

Deferred coupon bonds may be appropriate financing for a firm financing a large project that will not be completed and generating revenue for some period of time after bond issuance. Deferred coupon bonds may offer bondholders tax advantages in some jurisdictions. Zero-coupon bonds can be considered a type of deferred coupon bond.

An **index-linked bond** has coupon payments and/or a principal value that is based on a commodity index, an equity index, or some other published index number. **Inflation-linked bonds** (also called **linkers**) are the most common type of index-linked bonds. Their payments are based on the change in an inflation index, such as the Consumer Price Index (CPI) in the United States. Indexed bonds that will not pay less than their original par value at maturity, even when the index has decreased, are termed **principal protected bonds**.

The different structures of inflation-indexed bonds include the following:

- **Indexed-annuity bonds.** Fully amortizing bonds with the periodic payments directly adjusted for inflation or deflation.

- **Indexed zero-coupon bonds.** The payment at maturity is adjusted for inflation.

- **Interest-indexed bonds.** The coupon rate is adjusted for inflation while the principal value remains unchanged.

- **Capital-indexed bonds.** This is the most common structure. An example is U.S. Treasury Inflation Protected Securities (TIPS). The coupon rate remains constant, and the principal value of the bonds is increased by the rate of inflation (or decreased by deflation).

To better understand the structure of capital-indexed bonds, consider a bond with a par value of $1,000 at issuance, a 3% annual coupon rate paid semiannually, and a provision that the principal value will be adjusted for inflation (or deflation). If six months after issuance the reported inflation has been 1% over the period, the principal value of the bonds is increased by 1% from $1,000 to $1,010, and the six-month coupon of 1.5% is calculated as 1.5% of the new (adjusted) principal value of $1,010 (i.e., $1,010 \times 1.5\% = \$15.15$).

With this structure we can view the coupon rate of 3% as a real rate of interest. Unexpected inflation will not decrease the purchasing power of the coupon interest payments, and the principal value paid at maturity will have approximately the same purchasing power as the $1,000 par value did at bond issuance.

LOS 50.f: Describe contingency provisions affecting the timing and/or nature of cash flows of fixed-income securities and identify whether such provisions benefit the borrower or the lender.

CFA® Program Curriculum: Volume 5, page 329

A **contingency provision** in a contract describes an action that may be taken if an event (the contingency) actually occurs. Contingency provisions in bond indentures are referred to as **embedded options**, embedded in the sense that they are an integral part of the bond contract and are not a separate security. Some embedded options are exercisable at the option of the issuer of the bond and, therefore, are valuable to the issuer; others are exercisable at the option of the purchaser of the bond and, thus, have value to the bondholder.

Bonds that do not have contingency provisions are referred to as **straight** or **option-free** bonds.

A **call option** gives the *issuer* the right to redeem all or part of a bond issue at a specific price (call price) if they choose to. As an example of a call provision, consider a 6% 20-year bond issued at par on June 1, 2012, for which the indenture includes the following *call schedule*:

■ The bonds can be redeemed by the issuer at 102% of par after June 1, 2017.

■ The bonds can be redeemed by the issuer at 101% of par after June 1, 2020.

■ The bonds can be redeemed by the issuer at 100% of par after June 1, 2022.

For the 5-year period from the issue date until June 2017, the bond is not callable. We say the bond has five years of *call protection*, or that the bond is *call protected* for five years. This 5-year period is also referred to as a *lockout period*, a *cushion*, or a *deferment period*.

June 1, 2017, is referred to as the *first call date*, and the *call price* is 102 (102% of par value) between that date and June 2020. The amount by which the call price is above par is referred to as the *call premium*. The call premium at the first call date in this example is 2%, or $20 per $1,000 bond. The call price declines to 101 (101% of par) after June 1, 2020. After, June 1, 2022, the bond is callable at par, and that date is referred to as the *first par call* date.

For a bond that is currently callable, the call price puts an upper limit on the value of the bond in the market.

A call option has value to the issuer because it gives the issuer the right to redeem the bond and issue a new bond (borrow) if the market yield on the bond declines. This could occur either because interest rates in general have decreased or because the credit quality of the bond has increased (default risk has decreased).

Consider a situation where the market yield on the previously discussed 6% 20-year bond has declined from 6% at issuance to 4% on June 1, 2017 (the first call date). If the bond did not have a call option, it would trade at approximately $1,224. With a call price of 102, the issuer can redeem the bonds at $1,020 each and borrow that amount at the current market yield of 4%, reducing the annual interest payment from $60 per bond to $40.80.

 PROFESSOR'S NOTE

This is analogous to refinancing a home mortgage when mortgage rates fall in order to reduce the monthly payments.

The issuer will only choose to exercise the call option when it is to their advantage to do so. That is, they can reduce their interest expense by calling the bond and issuing new bonds at a lower yield. Bond buyers are disadvantaged by the call provision and have more reinvestment risk because their bonds will only be called (redeemed prior to maturity) when the proceeds can be reinvested only at a lower yield. For this reason, a callable bond must offer a higher yield (sell at a lower price) than an otherwise identical noncallable bond. The difference in price between a callable bond and an otherwise identical noncallable bond is equal to the value of the call option to the issuer.

There are three *styles of exercise* for callable bonds:

1. American style—the bonds can be called anytime after the first call date.

2. European style—the bonds can only be called on the call date specified.

3. Bermuda style—the bonds can be called on specified dates after the first call date, often on coupon payment dates.

Note that these are only style names and are not indicative of where the bonds are issued.

To avoid the higher interest rates required on callable bonds but still preserve the option to redeem bonds early when corporate or operating events require it, issuers introduced bonds with **make-whole** call provisions. With a make-whole bond, the call price is not fixed but includes a lump-sum payment based on the present value of the future coupons the bondholder will not receive if the bond is called early.

With a make-whole call provision, the calculated call price is unlikely to be lower than the market value of the bond. Therefore the issuer is unlikely to call the bond except when corporate circumstances, such as an acquisition or restructuring, require it. The make-whole provision does not put an upper limit on bond values when interest rates fall as does a regular call provision. The make-whole provision actually penalizes the issuer for calling the bond. The net effect is that the bond can be called if necessary, but it can also be issued at a lower yield than a bond with a traditional call provision.

Putable Bonds

A **put option** gives the *bondholder* the right to sell the bond back to the issuing company at a prespecified price, typically par. Bondholders are likely to exercise such a put option when the fair value of the bond is less than the put price because interest rates have risen or the credit quality of the issuer has fallen. Exercise styles used are similar to those we enumerated for callable bonds.

Unlike a call option, a put option has value to the bondholder because the choice of whether to exercise the option is the bondholder's. For this reason, a putable bond will sell at a higher price (offer a lower yield) compared to an otherwise identical option-free bond.

Convertible Bonds

Convertible bonds, typically issued with maturities of 5–10 years, give bondholders the option to exchange the bond for a specific number of shares of the issuing corporation's common stock. This gives bondholders the opportunity to profit from increases in the value of the common shares. Regardless of the price of the common shares, the value of a convertible bond will be at least equal to its bond value without the conversion option. Because the conversion option is valuable to bondholders, convertible bonds can be issued with lower yields compared to otherwise identical straight bonds.

Essentially, the owner of a convertible bond has the downside protection (compared to equity shares) of a bond, but at a reduced yield, and the upside opportunity of equity shares. For this reason convertible bonds are often referred to as a *hybrid security*—part debt and part equity.

To issuers, the advantages of issuing convertible bonds are a lower yield (interest cost) compared to straight bonds and the fact that debt financing is converted to equity financing when the bonds are converted to common shares. Some terms related to convertible bonds are:

- **Conversion price.** The price per share at which the bond (at its par value) may be converted to common stock.

- **Conversion ratio.** Equal to the par value of the bond divided by the conversion price. If a bond with a $1,000 par value has a conversion price of $40, its *conversion ratio* is 1,000 / 40 = 25 shares per bond.

- **Conversion value.** This is the market value of the shares that would be received upon conversion. A bond with a conversion ratio of 25 shares when the current market price of a common share is $50 would have a conversion value of 25 × 50 = $1,250.

Even if the share price increases to a level where the conversion value is significantly above the bond's par value, bondholders might not convert the bonds to common stock until they must because the interest yield on the bonds is higher than the dividend yield on the common shares received through conversion. For this reason, many convertible bonds have a call provision. Because the call price will be less than the conversion value of the shares, by exercising their call provision, the issuers can force bondholders to exercise their conversion option when the conversion value is significantly above the par value of the bonds.

Warrants

An alternative way to give bondholders an opportunity for additional returns when the firm's common shares increase in value is to include **warrants** with straight bonds when they are issued. Warrants give their holders the right to buy the firm's common shares at a given price over a given period of time. As an example, warrants that give their holders the right to buy shares for $40 will provide profits if the common shares increase in value above $40 prior to expiration of the warrants. For a young firm, issuing debt can be difficult because the downside (probability of firm failure) is significant, and the upside is limited to the promised debt payments. Including warrants, which are sometimes referred to as a "sweetener," makes the debt more attractive to investors because it adds potential upside profits if the common shares increase in value.

Contingent Convertible Bonds

Contingent convertible bonds (referred to as *CoCos*) are bonds that convert from debt to common equity automatically if a specific event occurs. This type of bond has been issued by some European banks. Banks must maintain specific levels of equity financing. If a bank's equity falls below the required level, they must somehow raise more equity financing to comply with regulations. CoCos are often structured so that if the bank's equity capital falls below a given level, they are automatically converted to common stock. This has the effect of decreasing the bank's debt liabilities and increasing its equity capital at the same time, which helps the bank to meet its minimum equity requirement.

MODULE QUIZ 50.2

To best evaluate your performance, enter your quiz answers online.

1. A 10-year bond pays no interest for three years, then pays $229.25, followed by payments of $35 semiannually for seven years, and an additional $1,000 at maturity. This bond is:
   A. a step-up bond.
   B. a zero-coupon bond.
   C. a deferred-coupon bond.

2. Which of the following statements is *most accurate* with regard to floating-rate issues that have caps and floors?
   A. A cap is an advantage to the bondholder, while a floor is an advantage to the issuer.
   B. A floor is an advantage to the bondholder, while a cap is an advantage to the issuer.
   C. A floor is an advantage to both the issuer and the bondholder, while a cap is a disadvantage to both the issuer and the bondholder.

3. Which of the following *most accurately* describes the maximum price for a currently callable bond?
   A. Its par value.
   B. The call price.
   C. The present value of its par value.

KEY CONCEPTS

LOS 50.a

Basic features of a fixed income security include the issuer, maturity date, par value, coupon rate, coupon frequency, and currency.

■ Issuers include corporations, governments, quasi-government entities, and supranational entities.

■ Bonds with original maturities of one year or less are money market securities. Bonds with original maturities of more than one year are capital market securities.

■ Par value is the principal amount that will be repaid to bondholders at maturity. Bonds are trading at a premium if their market price is greater than par value or trading at a discount if their price is less than par value.

■ Coupon rate is the percentage of par value that is paid annually as interest. Coupon frequency may be annual, semiannual, quarterly, or monthly. Zero-coupon bonds pay no coupon interest and are pure discount securities.

■ Bonds may be issued in a single currency, dual currencies (one currency for interest and another for principal), or with a bondholder's choice of currency.

LOS 50.b

A bond indenture or trust deed is a contract between a bond issuer and the bondholders, which defines the bond's features and the issuer's obligations. An indenture specifies the entity issuing the bond, the source of funds for repayment, assets pledged as collateral, credit enhancements, and any covenants with which the issuer must comply.

LOS 50.c

Covenants are provisions of a bond indenture that protect the bondholders' interests. Negative covenants are restrictions on a bond issuer's operating decisions, such as prohibiting the issuer from issuing additional debt or selling the assets pledged as collateral. Affirmative covenants are administrative actions the issuer must perform, such as making the interest and principal payments on time.

LOS 50.d

Legal and regulatory matters that affect fixed income securities include the places where they are issued and traded, the issuing entities, sources of repayment, and collateral and credit enhancements.

■ Domestic bonds trade in the issuer's home country and currency. Foreign bonds are from foreign issuers but denominated in the currency of the country where they trade. Eurobonds are issued outside the jurisdiction of any single country and denominated in a currency other than that of the countries in which they trade.

■ Issuing entities may be a government or agency; a corporation, holding company, or subsidiary; or a special purpose entity.

Study Session 16
Cross-Reference to CFA Institute Assigned Reading #50 – Fixed-Income Securities: Defining Elements

Study Session 16

■ The source of repayment for sovereign bonds is the country's taxing authority. For non-sovereign government bonds, the sources may be taxing authority or revenues from a project. Corporate bonds are repaid with funds from the firm's operations. Securitized bonds are repaid with cash flows from a pool of financial assets.

■ Bonds are secured if they are backed by specific collateral or unsecured if they represent an overall claim against the issuer's cash flows and assets.

■ Credit enhancement may be internal (overcollateralization, excess spread, tranches with different priority of claims) or external (surety bonds, bank guarantees, letters of credit).

Interest income is typically taxed at the same rate as ordinary income, while gains or losses from selling a bond are taxed at the capital gains tax rate. However, the increase in value toward par of original issue discount bonds is considered interest income. In the United States, interest income from municipal bonds is usually tax-exempt at the national level and in the issuer's state.

LOS 50.e

A bond with a bullet structure pays coupon interest periodically and repays the entire principal value at maturity.

A bond with an amortizing structure repays part of its principal at each payment date. A fully amortizing structure makes equal payments throughout the bond's life. A partially amortizing structure has a balloon payment at maturity, which repays the remaining principal as a lump sum.

A sinking fund provision requires the issuer to retire a portion of a bond issue at specified times during the bonds' life.

Floating-rate notes have coupon rates that adjust based on a reference rate such as LIBOR.

Other coupon structures include step-up coupon notes, credit-linked coupon bonds, payment-in-kind bonds, deferred coupon bonds, and index-linked bonds.

LOS 50.f

Embedded options benefit the party who has the right to exercise them. Call options benefit the issuer, while put options and conversion options benefit the bondholder.

Call options allow the issuer to redeem bonds at a specified call price.

Put options allow the bondholder to sell bonds back to the issuer at a specified put price.

Conversion options allow the bondholder to exchange bonds for a specified number of shares of the issuer's common stock.

ANSWER KEY FOR MODULE QUIZZES

Module Quiz 50.1

1. **C** Dual-currency bonds pay coupon interest in one currency and principal in a different currency. These currencies may or may not include the home currency of the issuer. A currency option bond allows the bondholder to choose a currency in which to be paid. (LOS 50.a)

2. **A** An indenture is the contract between the company and its bondholders and contains the bond's covenants. (LOS 50.b)

3. **C** Affirmative covenants require the borrower to perform certain actions. Negative covenants restrict the borrower from performing certain actions. Trust deed is another name for a bond indenture. (LOS 50.c)

4. **B** Tax authorities typically treat the increase in value of a pure-discount bond toward par as interest income to the bondholder. In many jurisdictions this interest income is taxed periodically during the life of the bond even though the bondholder does not receive any cash until maturity. (LOS 50.d)

Module Quiz 50.2

1. **C** This pattern describes a deferred-coupon bond. The first payment of $229.25 is the value of the accrued coupon payments for the first three years. (LOS 50.e)

2. **B** A cap is a maximum on the coupon rate and is advantageous to the issuer. A floor is a minimum on the coupon rate and is, therefore, advantageous to the bondholder. (LOS 50.e)

3. **B** Whenever the price of the bond increases above the strike price stipulated on the call option, it will be optimal for the issuer to call the bond. Theoretically, the price of a currently callable bond should never rise above its call price. (LOS 50.f)

The following is a review of the Fixed Income (1) principles designed to address the learning outcome statements set forth by CFA Institute. Cross-Reference to CFA Institute Assigned Reading #51.

READING 51

Fixed-Income Markets: Issuance, Trading, and Funding

EXAM FOCUS

This topic review introduces many terms and definitions. Focus on different types of issuers, features of the various debt security structures, and why different sources of funds have different interest costs. Understand well the differences between fixed-rate and floating-rate debt and how rates are determined on floating-rate debt and for repurchase agreements.

MODULE 51.1: TYPES OF BONDS AND ISSUERS

LOS 51.a: Describe classifications of global fixed-income markets.

Video covering this content is available online.

CFA® Program Curriculum: Volume 5, page 348

Global bond markets can be classified by several bond characteristics, including type of issuer, credit quality, maturity, coupon, currency, geography, indexing, and taxable status.

Type of issuer. Common classifications are government and government related bonds, corporate bonds, and structured finance (securitized bonds). Corporate bonds are often further classified as issues from financial corporations and issues from nonfinancial corporations. The largest issuers by total value of bonds outstanding in global markets are financial corporations and governments.

Credit quality. Standard & Poor's (S&P), Moody's, and Fitch all provide credit ratings on bonds. For S&P and Fitch, the highest bond ratings are AAA, AA, A, and BBB, and are considered *investment grade bonds*. The equivalent ratings by Moody's are Aaa through Baa3. Bonds BB+ or lower (Ba1 or lower) are termed high-yield, speculative, or "junk" bonds. Some institutions are prohibited from investing in bonds of less than investment grade.

Original maturities. Securities with original maturities of one year or less are classified as **money market securities**. Examples include U.S. Treasury bills, commercial paper (issued by corporations), and negotiable certificates of deposit, or CDs (issued by banks). Securities with original maturities greater than one year are referred to as **capital market securities**.

Coupon structure. Bonds are classified as either floating-rate or fixed-rate bonds, depending on whether their coupon interest payments are stated in the bond indenture or depend on the level of a short-term market *reference rate* determined over the life of the bond. Purchasing floating-rate debt is attractive to some institutions that have variable-rate sources of funds (liabilities), such as banks. This allows these institutions to avoid the balance sheet effects of interest rate increases that would increase the cost of funds but leave the interest income at a fixed rate. The value of fixed-rate bonds (assets) held would fall in the value, while the value of their liabilities would be much less affected.

Currency denomination. A bond's price and returns are determined by the interest rates in the bond's currency. The majority of bonds issued are denominated in either U.S. dollars or euros.

Geography. Bonds may be classified by the markets in which they are issued. Recall the discussion in the previous topic review of domestic (or national) bond markets, foreign bonds, and eurobonds, and the differences among them. Bond markets may also be classified as **developed markets** or **emerging markets**. Emerging markets are countries whose capital markets are less well-established than those in developed markets. Emerging market bonds are typically viewed as riskier than developed market bonds and therefore have higher yields.

Indexing. As discussed previously, the cash flows on some bonds are based on an index (**index-linked bonds**). Bonds with cash flows determined by inflation rates are referred to as inflation-indexed or inflation-linked bonds. Inflation-linked bonds are issued primarily by governments but also by some corporations of high credit quality.

Tax status. In various countries, some issuers may issue bonds that are exempt from income taxes. In the United States, these bonds can be issued by municipalities and are called **municipal bonds**, or **munis**. Tax exempt bonds are sold with lower yields than taxable bonds of similar risk and maturity, to reflect the impact of taxes on the after-tax yield of taxable bonds.

LOS 51.b: Describe the use of interbank offered rates as reference rates in floating-rate debt.

CFA® Program Curriculum: Volume 5, page 352

The most widely used reference rate for floating-rate bonds is the London Interbank Offered Rate (LIBOR), although other reference rates, such as Euribor, are also used. LIBOR rates are published daily for several currencies and for maturities of one day (overnight rates) to one year. Thus, there is no single "LIBOR rate" but rather a set of rates, such as "30-day U.S. dollar LIBOR" or "90-day Swiss franc LIBOR."

Study Session 16
Cross-Reference to CFA Institute Assigned Reading #51 – Fixed-Income Markets: Issuance, Trading, and Funding

Study Session 16

The rates are based on expected rates for unsecured loans from one bank to another in the **interbank money market**. An average is calculated from a survey of 18 banks' expected borrowing rates in the interbank market, after excluding the highest and lowest quotes.

For floating-rate bonds, the reference rate must match the frequency with which the coupon rate on the bond is reset. For example, a bond denominated in euros with a coupon rate that is reset twice each year might use 6-month euro LIBOR or 6-month Euribor as a reference rate.

LOS 51.c: Describe mechanisms available for issuing bonds in primary markets.

CFA® Program Curriculum: Volume 5, page 359

Sales of newly issued bonds are referred to as **primary market** transactions. Newly issued bonds can be registered with securities regulators for sale to the public, a **public offering**, or sold only to qualified investors, a **private placement**.

A public offering of bonds in the primary market is typically done with the help of an investment bank. The investment bank has expertise in the various steps of a public offering, including:

- Determining funding needs.
- Structuring the debt security.
- Creating the bond indenture.
- Naming a bond trustee (a trust company or bank trust department).
- Registering the issue with securities regulators.
- Assessing demand and pricing the bonds given market conditions.
- Selling the bonds.

Bonds can be sold through an **underwritten offering** or a **best efforts offering**. In an underwritten offering, the entire bond issue is purchased from the issuing firm by the investment bank, termed the underwriter in this case. While smaller bond issues may be sold by a single investment bank, for larger issues, the *lead underwriter* heads a **syndicate** of investment banks who collectively establish the pricing of the issue and are responsible for selling the bonds to dealers, who in turn sell them to investors. The syndicate takes the risk that the bonds will not all be sold.

A new bond issue is publicized and dealers indicate their interest in buying the bonds, which provides information about appropriate pricing. Some bonds are traded on a *when issued* basis in what is called the **grey market**. Such trading prior to the offering date of the bonds provides additional information about the demand for and market clearing price (yield) for the new bond issue.

In a *best efforts* offering, the investment banks sell the bonds on a commission basis. Unlike an underwritten offering, the investment banks do not commit to purchase the whole issue (i.e., underwrite the issue).

Some bonds, especially government bonds, are sold through an auction.

PROFESSOR'S NOTE

Recall that auction procedures were explained in detail in the prerequisite readings for Economics.

U.S. Treasury securities are sold through single price auctions with the majority of purchases made by **primary dealers** that participate in purchases and sales of bonds with the Federal Reserve Bank of New York to facilitate the open market operations of the Fed. Individuals can purchase U.S. Treasury securities through the periodic auctions as well, but are a small part of the total.

In a **shelf registration**, a bond issue is registered with securities regulators in its aggregate value with a master prospectus. Bonds can then be issued over time when the issuer needs to raise funds. Because individual offerings under a shelf registration require less disclosure than a separate registration of a bond issue, only financially sound companies are granted this option. In some countries, bonds registered under a shelf registration can be sold only to qualified investors.

LOS 51.d: Describe secondary markets for bonds.

CFA® Program Curriculum: Volume 5, page 365

Secondary markets refer to the trading of previously issued bonds. While some government bonds and corporate bonds are traded on exchanges, the great majority of bond trading in the secondary market is made in the dealer, or over-the-counter, market. Dealers post bid (purchase) prices and ask or offer (selling) prices for various bond issues. The difference between the bid and ask prices is the dealer's spread. The average spread is often between 10 and 12 basis points but varies across individual bonds according to their liquidity and may be more than 50 basis points for an illiquid issue.[1]

Bond trades are cleared through a clearing system, just as equities trades are. Settlement (the exchange of bonds for cash) for government bonds is either the day of the trade (cash settlement) or the next business day (T + 1). Corporate bonds typically settle on T + 2 or T + 3, although in some markets it is longer.

LOS 51.e: Describe securities issued by sovereign governments.

CFA® Program Curriculum: Volume 5, page 367

National governments or their treasuries issue bonds backed by the taxing power of the government that are referred to as **sovereign bonds**. Bonds issued in the currency of the issuing government carry high credit ratings and are considered to be essentially free of default risk. Both a sovereign's ability to collect taxes and its ability to print the currency support these high credit ratings.

Sovereign nations also issue bonds denominated in currencies different from their own. Credit ratings are often higher for a sovereign's local currency bonds than for example, its euro or U.S. dollar-denominated bonds. This is because the national

---

1. Fixed Income Markets: Issuance, Trading, and Funding, Choudhry, M.; Mann, S.; and Whitmer, L.; in CFA Program 2019 Level I Curriculum, Volume 5 (CFA Institute, 2018).

Study Session 16
Cross-Reference to CFA Institute Assigned Reading #51 – Fixed-Income Markets: Issuance, Trading, and Funding

Study Session 16

government cannot print the developed market currency and the developed market currency value of local currency tax collections is dependent on the exchange rate between the two currencies.

Trading is most active and prices most informative for the most recently issued government securities of a particular maturity. These issues are referred to as **on-the-run** bonds and also as **benchmark** bonds because the yields of other bonds are determined relative to the "benchmark" yields of sovereign bonds of similar maturities.

Sovereign governments issue fixed-rate, floating-rate, and inflation-indexed bonds.

LOS 51.f: Describe securities issued by non-sovereign governments, quasi-government entities, and supranational agencies.

CFA® Program Curriculum: Volume 5, page 371

Non-sovereign government bonds are issued by states, provinces, counties, and sometimes by entities created to fund and provide services such as for the construction of hospitals, airports, and other municipal services. Payments on the bonds may be supported by the revenues of a specific project, from general tax revenues, or from special taxes or fees dedicated to the repayment of project debt.

Non-sovereign bonds are typically of high credit quality, but sovereign bonds typically trade with lower yields (higher prices) because their credit risk is perceived to be less than that of non-sovereign bonds.

PROFESSOR'S NOTE

We will examine the credit quality of sovereign and non-sovereign government bonds in our topic review of "Fundamentals of Credit Analysis."

Agency or **quasi-government** bonds are issued by entities created by national governments for specific purposes such as financing small businesses or providing mortgage financing. In the United States, bonds are issued by government-sponsored enterprises (GSEs), such as the Federal National Mortgage Association and the Tennessee Valley Authority.

Some quasi-government bonds are backed by the national government, which gives them high credit quality. Even those not backed by the national government typically have high credit quality although their yields are marginally higher than those of sovereign bonds.

Supranational bonds are issued by supranational agencies, also known as *multilateral agencies*. Examples are the World Bank, the IMF, and the Asian Development Bank. Bonds issued by supranational agencies typically have high credit quality and can be very liquid, especially large issues of well-known entities.

MODULE QUIZ 51.1
To best evaluate your performance, enter your quiz answers online.

1. An analyst who describes a fixed-income security as being a structured finance instrument is classifying the security by:
   A. credit quality.
   B. type of issuer.
   C. taxable status.

2. LIBOR rates are determined:
   A. by countries' central banks.
   B. by money market regulators.
   C. in the interbank lending market.

3. In which type of primary market transaction does an investment bank sell bonds on a commission basis?
   A. Single-price auction.
   B. Best-efforts offering.
   C. Underwritten offering.

4. Secondary market bond transactions *most likely* take place:
   A. in dealer markets.
   B. in brokered markets.
   C. on organized exchanges.

5. Sovereign bonds are described as on-the-run when they:
   A. are the most recent issue in a specific maturity.
   B. have increased substantially in price since they were issued.
   C. receive greater-than-expected demand from auction bidders.

6. Bonds issued by the World Bank would *most likely* be:
   A. quasi-government bonds.
   B. global bonds.
   C. supranational bonds.

Video covering this content is available online.

MODULE 51.2: CORPORATE DEBT AND FUNDING ALTERNATIVES

LOS 51.g: Describe types of debt issued by corporations.

CFA® Program Curriculum: Volume 5, page 373

Bank Debt

Most corporations fund their businesses to some extent with bank loans. These are typically LIBOR-based, variable-rate loans. When the loan involves only one bank, it is referred to as a **bilateral loan**. In contrast, when a loan is funded by several banks, it is referred to as a **syndicated loan** and the group of banks is the syndicate. There is a secondary market in syndicated loan interests that are also securitized, creating bonds that are sold to investors.

Study Session 16
Cross-Reference to CFA Institute Assigned Reading #51 – Fixed-Income Markets: Issuance, Trading, and Funding

Study Session 16

Commercial Paper

For larger creditworthy corporations, funding costs can be reduced by issuing short-term debt securities referred to as **commercial paper**. For these firms, the interest cost of commercial paper is less than the interest on a bank loan. Commercial paper yields more than short-term sovereign debt because it has, on average, more credit risk and less liquidity.

Firms use commercial paper to fund working capital and as a temporary source of funds prior to issuing longer-term debt. Debt that is temporary until permanent financing can be secured is referred to as **bridge financing**.

Commercial paper is a short-term, unsecured debt instrument. In the United States, commercial paper is issued with maturities of 270 days or less, because debt securities with maturities of 270 days or less are exempt from SEC registration. Eurocommercial paper (ECP) is issued in several countries with maturities as long as 364 days. Commercial paper is issued with maturities as short as one day (overnight paper), with most issues maturing in about 90 days.

Commercial paper is often reissued or *rolled over* when it matures. The risk that a company will not be able to sell new commercial paper to replace maturing paper is termed *rollover risk*. The two important circumstances in which a company will face rollover difficulties are (1) there is a deterioration in a company's actual or perceived ability to repay the debt at maturity, which will significantly increase the required yield on the paper or lead to less-than-full subscription to a new issue, and (2) significant systemic financial distress, as was experienced in the 2008 financial crisis, that may "freeze" debt markets so that very little commercial paper can be sold at all.

In order to get an acceptable credit rating from the ratings services on their commercial paper, corporations maintain **backup lines of credit** with banks. These are sometimes referred to as *liquidity enhancement* or *backup liquidity lines*. The bank agrees to provide the funds when the paper matures, if needed, except in the case of a *material adverse change* (i.e., when the company's financial situation has deteriorated significantly).

Similar to U.S. T-bills, commercial paper in the United States is typically issued as a pure discount security, making a single payment equal to the face value at maturity. Prices are quoted as a percentage discount from face value. In contrast, ECP rates may be quoted as either a discount yield or an *add-on yield*, that is, the percentage interest paid at maturity in addition to the par value of the commercial paper. As an example, consider 240-day commercial paper with a holding period yield of 1.35%. If it is quoted with a discount yield, it will be issued at 100 / 1.0135 = 98.668 and pay 100 at maturity. If it is quoted with an add-on yield, it will be issued at 100 and pay 101.35 at maturity.

PROFESSOR'S NOTE

Recall from Quantitative Methods that a 180-day T-bill quoted at a discount yield of 2% for the 180-day period is priced at $980 per $1,000 face value. The effective 180-day return is 1,000 / 980 − 1 = 2.041%. For ECP with a 180-day, add-on yield of 2%, the effective return is simply 2%.

Corporate Bonds

In the previous topic review, we discussed several features of corporate bonds. **Corporate bonds** are issued with various coupon structures and with both fixed-rate and floating-rate coupon payments. They may be secured by collateral or unsecured and may have call, put, or conversion provisions.

We also discussed a sinking fund provision as a way to reduce the credit risk of a bond by redeeming part of the bond issue periodically over a bond's life. An alternative to a sinking fund provision is to issue a **serial bond issue**. With a serial bond issue, bonds are issued with several maturity dates so that a portion of the issue is redeemed periodically. An important difference between a serial bond issue and an issue with a sinking fund is that with a serial bond issue, investors know at issuance when specific bonds will be redeemed. A bond issue that does not have a serial maturity structure is said to have a **term maturity structure** with all the bonds maturing on the same date.

In general, corporate bonds are referred to as short-term if they are issued with maturities of up to 5 years, medium-term when issued with maturities from 5 to 12 years, and long-term when maturities exceed 12 years.

Corporations issue debt securities called **medium-term notes** (MTNs), which are not necessarily medium-term in maturity. MTNs are issued in various maturities, ranging from nine months to periods as long as 100 years. Issuers provide *maturity ranges* (e.g., 18 months to two years) for MTNs they wish to sell and provide yield quotes for those ranges. Investors interested in purchasing the notes make an offer to the issuer's agent, specifying the face value and an exact maturity within one of the ranges offered. The agent then confirms the issuer's willingness to sell those MTNs and effects the transaction.

MTNs can have fixed- or floating-rate coupons, but longer-maturity MTNs are typically fixed-rate bonds. Most MTNs, other than long-term MTNs, are issued by financial corporations and most buyers are financial institutions. MTNs can be structured to meet an institution's specifications. While custom bond issues have less liquidity, they provide slightly higher yields compared to an issuer's publicly traded bonds.

LOS 51.h: Describe structured financial instruments.

CFA® Program Curriculum: Volume 5, page 381

Structured financial instruments are securities designed to change the risk profile of an underlying debt security, often by combining a debt security with a derivative. Sometimes structured financial instruments redistribute risk. Examples of this type of structured instruments are asset-backed securities and collateralized debt obligations. Both of these types of structured securities are discussed in some detail in our review of asset-backed securities.

Study Session 16
Cross-Reference to CFA Institute Assigned Reading #51 – Fixed-Income Markets: Issuance, Trading, and Funding

Study Session 16

Here, we describe several other types of structured instruments with which candidates should be familiar.

1. **Yield enhancement instruments**

   A **credit-linked note** (CLN) has regular coupon payments, but its redemption value depends on whether a specific credit event occurs. If the credit event (e.g., a credit rating downgrade or default of a reference asset) does not occur, the CLN will be redeemed at its par value. If the credit event occurs, the CLN will make a lower redemption payment. Thus, the realized yield on a CLN will be lower if the credit event occurs. Purchasing a CLN can be viewed as buying a note and simultaneously selling a credit default swap (CDS), a derivative security. The buyer of a CDS makes periodic payments to the seller, who will make a payment to the buyer if a specified credit event occurs. The yield on a CLN is higher than it would be on the note alone, without the credit link. This extra yield compensates the buyer of the note (seller of the CDS) for taking on the credit risk of the reference asset, which is why we classify CLNs as a yield enhancement instrument.

2. **Capital protected instruments**

   A capital protected instrument offers a guarantee of a minimum value at maturity as well as some potential upside gain. An example is a security that promises to pay $1,000 at maturity plus a percentage of any gains on a specified stock index over the life of the security. Such a security could be created by combining a zero-coupon bond selling for $950 that matures at $1,000 in 1 year, with a 1-year call option on the reference stock index with a cost of $50. The total cost of the security is $1,000, and the minimum payoff at maturity (if the call option expires with a value of zero) is $1,000. If the call option has a positive value at maturity, the total payment at maturity is greater than $1,000. A structured financial instrument that promises the $1,000 payment at maturity under this structure is called a **guarantee certificate**, because the guaranteed payoff is equal to the initial cost of the structured security. Capital protected instruments that promise a payment at maturity less than the initial cost of the instrument offer less-than-full protection, but greater potential for upside gains because more calls can be purchased.

3. **Participation instruments**

   A participation instrument has payments that are based on the value of an underlying instrument, often a reference interest rate or equity index. Participation instruments do not offer capital protection. One example of a participation instrument is a floating-rate note. With a floating-rate note, the coupon payments are based on the value of a short-term interest rate, such as 90-day LIBOR (the reference rate). When the reference rate increases, the coupon payment increases. Because the coupon payments move with the reference rates on floating-rate securities, their market values remain relatively stable, even when interest rates change.

   Participation is often based on the performance of an equity price, an equity index value, or the price of another asset. Fixed-income portfolio managers who are only permitted to invest in "debt" securities can use participation instruments to gain exposure to returns on an equity index or asset price.

4. **Leveraged instruments**

An **inverse floater** is an example of a leveraged instrument. An inverse floater has coupon payments that increase when a reference rate decreases and decrease when a reference rate increases, the opposite of coupon payments on a floating-rate note. A simple structure might promise to pay a coupon rate, C, equal to a specific rate minus a reference rate, for example, C = 6% – 180-day LIBOR. When 180-day LIBOR increases, the coupon rate on the inverse floater decreases.

Inverse floaters can also be structured with leverage so that the change in the coupon rate is some multiple of the change in the reference rate. As an example, consider a note with C = 6% – (1.2 × 90-day LIBOR) so that the coupon payment rate changes by 1.2 times the change in the reference rate. Such a floater is termed a **leveraged inverse floater**. When the multiplier on the reference rate is less than one, such as 7% – (0.5 × 180-day LIBOR), the instrument is termed a **deleveraged inverse floater**. In either case, a minimum or floor rate for the coupon rate, often 0%, is specified for the inverse floater.

LOS 51.i: Describe short-term funding alternatives available to banks.

CFA® Program Curriculum: Volume 5, page 384

Customer deposits (retail deposits) are a short-term funding source for banks. Checking accounts provide transactions services and immediate availability of funds but typically pay no interest. Money market mutual funds and savings accounts provide less liquidity or less transactions services, or both, and pay periodic interest.

In addition to funds from retail accounts, banks offer interest-bearing **certificates of deposit** (CDs) that mature on specific dates and are offered in a range of short-term maturities. Nonnegotiable CDs cannot be sold and withdrawal of funds often incurs a significant penalty.

Negotiable certificates of deposit can be sold. At the wholesale level, large denomination (typically more than $1 million) negotiable CDs are an important funding source for banks. They typically have maturities of one year or less and are traded in domestic bond markets as well as in the Eurobond market.

Another source of short-term funding for banks is to borrow excess reserves from other banks in the **central bank funds market**. Banks in most countries must maintain a portion of their funds as reserves on deposit with the central bank. At any point in time, some banks may have more than the required amount of reserves on deposit, while others require more reserve deposits. In the market for central bank funds, banks with excess reserves lend them to other banks for periods of one day (overnight funds) and for longer periods up to a year (term funds). **Central bank funds rates** refer to rates for these transactions, which are strongly influenced by the effect of the central bank's open market operations on the money supply and availability of short-term funds.

In the United States, the central bank funds rate is called the Fed funds rate and this rate influences the interest rates of many short-term debt securities.

Other than reserves on deposit with the central bank, funds that are loaned by one bank to another are referred to as **interbank funds**. Interbank funds are loaned between banks for periods of one day to a year. These loans are unsecured and, as with many debt markets, liquidity may decrease severely during times of systemic financial distress.

LOS 51.j: Describe repurchase agreements (repos) and the risks associated with them.

CFA® Program Curriculum: Volume 5, page 386

A **repurchase (repo) agreement** is an arrangement by which one party sells a security to a counterparty with a commitment to buy it back at a later date at a specified (higher) price. The *repurchase price* is greater than the selling price and accounts for the interest charged by the buyer, who is, in effect, lending funds to the seller with the security as collateral. The interest rate implied by the two prices is called the *repo rate*, which is the annualized percentage difference between the two prices. A repurchase agreement for one day is called an *overnight repo* and an agreement covering a longer period is called a *term repo*. The interest cost of a repo is customarily less than the rate on bank loans or other short-term borrowing.

As an example, consider a firm that enters into a repo agreement to sell a 4%, 12-year bond with a par value of $1 million and a market value of $970,000 for $940,000 and to repurchase it 90 days later (the **repo date**) for $947,050.

The implicit interest rate for the 90-day loan period is 947,050 / 940,000 − 1 = 0.75% and the *repo rate* would be expressed as the equivalent annual rate.

The percentage difference between the market value and the amount loaned is called the **repo margin** or the **haircut**. In our example, it is 940,000 / 970,000 − 1 = −3.1%. This margin protects the lender in the event that the value of the security decreases over the term of the repo agreement.

The repo rate is:
- Higher, the longer the repo term.
- Lower, the higher the credit quality of the collateral security.
- Lower when the collateral security is delivered to the lender.
- Higher when the interest rates for alternative sources of funds are higher.

The repo margin is influenced by similar factors. The repo margin is:
- Higher, the longer the repo term.
- Lower, the higher the credit quality of the collateral security.
- Lower, the higher the credit quality of the borrower.
- Lower when the collateral security is in high demand or low supply.

The reason the supply and demand conditions for the collateral security affects pricing is that some lenders want to own a specific bond or type of bond as collateral. For a bond that is high demand, lenders must compete for bonds by offering lower repo lending rates.

Viewed from the standpoint of a bond dealer, a **reverse repo agreement** refers to taking the opposite side of a repurchase transaction, lending funds by buying the collateral security rather than selling the collateral security to borrow funds.

MODULE QUIZ 51.2

To best evaluate your performance, enter your quiz answers online.

1. With which of the following features of a corporate bond issue does an investor *most likely* face the risk of redemption prior to maturity?
    A. Serial bonds.
    B. Sinking fund.
    C. Term maturity structure.

2. A financial instrument is structured such that cash flows to the security holder increase if a specified reference rate increases. This structured financial instrument is *best* described as:
    A. a participation instrument.
    B. a capital protected instrument.
    C. a yield enhancement instrument.

3. Smith Bank lends Johnson Bank excess reserves on deposit with the central bank for a period of three months. Is this transaction said to occur in the interbank market?
    A. Yes.
    B. No, because the interbank market refers to loans for more than one year.
    C. No, because the interbank market does not include reserves at the central bank.

4. In a repurchase agreement, the percentage difference between the repurchase price and the amount borrowed is *most accurately* described as:
    A. the haircut.
    B. the repo rate.
    C. the repo margin.

Study Session 16
Cross-Reference to CFA Institute Assigned Reading #51 – Fixed-Income Markets: Issuance, Trading, and Funding

Study Session 16

KEY CONCEPTS

LOS 51.a

Global bond markets can be classified by the following:

- **Type of issuer**: Government (and government-related), corporate (financial and nonfinancial), securitized.
- **Credit quality**: Investment grade, noninvestment grade.
- **Original maturity**: Money market (one year or less), capital market (more than one year).
- **Coupon**: Fixed rate, floating rate.
- **Currency and geography**: Domestic, foreign, global, eurobond markets; developed, emerging markets.
- **Other classifications**: Indexing, taxable status.

LOS 51.b

Interbank lending rates, such as London Interbank Offered Rate (LIBOR), are frequently used as reference rates for floating-rate debt. An appropriate reference rate is one that matches a floating-rate note's currency and frequency of rate resets, such as 6-month U.S. dollar LIBOR for a semiannual floating-rate note issued in U.S. dollars.

LOS 51.c

Bonds may be issued in the primary market through a public offering or a private placement.

A public offering using an investment bank may be underwritten, with the investment bank or syndicate purchasing the entire issue and selling the bonds to dealers; or on a best-efforts basis, in which the investment bank sells the bonds on commission. Public offerings may also take place through auctions, which is the method commonly used to issue government debt.

A private placement is the sale of an entire issue to a qualified investor or group of investors, which are typically large institutions.

LOS 51.d

Bonds that have been issued previously trade in secondary markets. While some bonds trade on exchanges, most are traded in dealer markets. Spreads between bid and ask prices are narrower for liquid issues and wider for less liquid issues.

Trade settlement is typically T + 2 or T + 3 for corporate bonds and either cash settlement or T + 1 for government bonds.

LOS 51.e

Sovereign bonds are issued by national governments and backed by their taxing power. Sovereign bonds may be denominated in the local currency or a foreign currency.

LOS 51.f

Non-sovereign government bonds are issued by governments below the national level, such as provinces or cities, and may be backed by taxing authority or revenues from a specific project.

Agency or quasi-government bonds are issued by government sponsored entities and may be explicitly or implicitly backed by the government.

Supranational bonds are issued by multilateral agencies that operate across national borders.

LOS 51.g

Debt issued by corporations includes bank debt, commercial paper, corporate bonds, and medium-term notes.

Bank debt includes bilateral loans from a single bank and syndicated loans from multiple banks.

Commercial paper is a money market instrument issued by corporations of high credit quality.

Corporate bonds may have a term maturity structure (all bonds in an issue mature at the same time) or a serial maturity structure (bonds in an issue mature on a predetermined schedule) and may have a sinking fund provision.

Medium-term notes are corporate issues that can be structured to meet the requirements of investors.

LOS 51.h

Structured financial instruments include asset-backed securities and collateralized debt securities as well as the following types:

- Yield enhancement instruments include credit linked notes, which are redeemed at an amount less than par value if a specified credit event occurs on a reference asset, or at par if it does not occur. The buyer receives a higher yield for bearing the credit risk of the reference asset.

- Capital protected instruments offer a guaranteed payment, which may be equal to the purchase price of the instrument, along with participation in any increase in the value of an equity, an index, or other asset.

- Participation instruments are debt securities with payments that depend on the returns on an asset or index, or depend on a reference interest rate. One example is a floating rate bond, which makes coupon payments that change with a short-term reference rate, such as LIBOR. Other participation instruments make coupon payments based on the returns on an index of equity securities or on some other asset.

- An inverse floater is a leveraged instrument that has a coupon rate that varies inversely with a specified reference interest rate, for example, $6\% - (L \times 180\text{-day}$ LIBOR). L is the leverage of the inverse floater. An inverse floater with $L > 1$, so that the coupon rate changes by more than the reference rate, is termed a leveraged inverse floater. An inverse floater with $L < 1$ is a deleveraged floater.

Study Session 16
Cross-Reference to CFA Institute Assigned Reading #51 – Fixed-Income Markets: Issuance, Trading, and Funding

Study Session 16

LOS 51.i

Short-term funding alternatives available to banks include:

- **Customer deposits**, including checking accounts, savings accounts, and money market mutual funds.

- **Negotiable CDs**, which may be sold in the wholesale market.

- **Central bank funds market.** Banks may buy or sell excess reserves deposited with their central bank.

- **Interbank funds.** Banks make unsecured loans to one another for periods up to a year.

LOS 51.j

A repurchase agreement is a form of short-term collateralized borrowing in which one party sells a security to another party and agrees to buy it back at a predetermined future date and price. The repo rate is the implicit interest rate of a repurchase agreement. The repo margin, or haircut, is the difference between the amount borrowed and the value of the security.

Repurchase agreements are an important source of short-term financing for bond dealers. If a bond dealer is lending funds instead of borrowing, the agreement is known as a reverse repo.

ANSWER KEY FOR MODULE QUIZZES

Module Quiz 51.1

1. **B** Fixed-income sector classifications by type of issuer include government, corporate, and structured finance instruments. (LOS 51.a)

2. **C** LIBOR rates are determined in the market for interbank lending. (LOS 51.b)

3. **B** In a best-efforts offering, the investment bank or banks do not underwrite (i.e., purchase all of) a bond issue, but rather sell the bonds on a commission basis. Bonds sold by auction are offered directly to buyers by the issuer (typically a government). (LOS 51.c)

4. **A** The secondary market for bonds is primarily a dealer market in which dealers post bid and ask prices. (LOS 51.d)

5. **A** Sovereign bonds are described as *on-the-run* or *benchmark* when they represent the most recent issue in a specific maturity. (LOS 51.e)

6. **C** Bonds issued by the World Bank, which is a multilateral agency operating globally, are termed *supranational bonds*. (LOS 51.f)

Module Quiz 51.2

1. **B** With a sinking fund, the issuer must redeem part of the issue prior to maturity, but the specific bonds to be redeemed are not known. Serial bonds are issued with a schedule of maturities and each bond has a known maturity date. In an issue with a term maturity structure, all the bonds are scheduled to mature on the same date. (LOS 51.g)

2. **A** Floating-rate notes are an example of a participation instrument. (LOS 51.h)

3. **C** The interbank market refers to short-term borrowing and lending among banks of funds other than those on deposit at a central bank. Loans of reserves on deposit with a central bank are said to occur in the central bank funds market. (LOS 51.i)

4. **B** The repo rate is the percentage difference between the repurchase price and the amount borrowed. The repo margin or haircut is the percentage difference between the amount borrowed and the value of the collateral. (LOS 51.j)

READING 52

Introduction to Fixed-Income Valuation

Study Session 16

EXAM FOCUS

The concepts introduced here are very important for understanding the factors that determine the value of debt securities and various yield measures. The relationships between yield to maturity, spot rates, and forward rates are core material and come up in many contexts throughout the CFA curriculum. Yield spread measures also have many applications. Note that while several of the required learning outcomes have the command word "calculate" in them, a good understanding of the underlying concepts is just as important for exam success on this material.

MODULE 52.1: BOND VALUATION AND YIELD TO MATURITY

Video covering this content is available online.

LOS 52.a: Calculate a bond's price given a market discount rate.

CFA® Program Curriculum: Volume 5, page 402

Calculating the Value of an Annual Coupon Bond

The value of a coupon bond can be calculated by summing the present values of all of the bond's promised cash flows. The market discount rate appropriate for discounting a bond's cash flows is called the bond's **yield-to-maturity** (YTM) or **redemption yield**. If we know a bond's yield-to-maturity, we can calculate its value, and if we know its value (market price), we can calculate its yield-to-maturity.

Consider a newly issued 10-year, $1,000 par value, 10% coupon, annual-pay bond. The coupon payments will be $100 at the end of each year the $1,000 par value will be paid at the end of year 10. First, let's value this bond assuming the appropriate discount rate is 10%. The present value of the bond's cash flows discounted at 10% is:

$$\frac{100}{1.1} + \frac{100}{1.1^2} + \frac{100}{1.1^3} + \ldots\ldots + \frac{100}{1.1^9} + \frac{1,100}{1.1^{10}} = 1,000$$

The calculator solution is:

N = 10; PMT = 100; FV = 1,000; I/Y = 10; CPT → PV= –1,000

where:
N   = number of years
PMT = the *annual* coupon payment
I/Y = the *annual* discount rate
FV   = the par value or selling price at the end of an assumed holding period

 PROFESSOR'S NOTE

Take note of a couple of points here. The discount rate is entered as a whole number in percent, 10, not 0.10. The 10 coupon payments of $100 each are taken care of in the N = 10 and PMT = 100 entries. The principal repayment is in the FV = 1,000 entry. Lastly, note that the PV is negative; it will be the opposite sign to the sign of PMT and FV. The calculator is just "thinking" that to receive the payments and future value (to own the bond), you must pay the present value of the bond today (you must buy the bond). That's why the PV amount is negative; it is a cash outflow to a bond buyer.

Now let's value that same bond with a discount rate of 8%:

$$\frac{100}{1.08} + \frac{100}{1.08^2} + \frac{100}{1.08^3} + \ldots\ldots + \frac{100}{1.08^9} + \frac{1,100}{1.08^{10}} = 1,134.20$$

The calculator solution is:

N = 10; PMT = 100; FV = 1,000; I/Y = **8**; CPT → PV= –1,134.20

If the market discount rate for this bond were 8%, it would sell at a premium of $134.20 above its par value. *When bond yields decrease, the present value of a bond's payments, its market value, increases.*

If we discount the bond's cash flows at 12%, the present value of the bond is:

$$\frac{100}{1.12} + \frac{100}{1.12^2} + \frac{100}{1.12^3} + \ldots\ldots + \frac{100}{1.12^9} + \frac{1,100}{1.12^{10}} = 887.00$$

The calculator solution is:

N = 10; PMT = 100; FV = 1,000; I/Y = **12**; CPT → PV= –887

If the market discount rate for this bond were 12%, it would sell at a discount of $113 to its par value. *When bond yields increase, the present value of a bond's payments, its market value, decreases.*

PROFESSOR'S NOTE

It's worth noting here that a 2% decrease in yield-to-maturity increases the bond's value by more than a 2% increase in yield decreases the bond's value. This illustrates that the bond's price-yield relationship is convex, as we will explain in more detail in a later topic review.

Calculating the value of a bond with semiannual coupon payments. Let's calculate the value of the same bond with semiannual payments.

Rather than $100 per year, the security will pay $50 every six months. With an annual YTM of 8%, we need to discount the coupon payments at 4% per period which results in a present value of:

$$\frac{50}{1.04} + \frac{50}{1.04^2} + \frac{50}{1.04^3} + \text{........} + \frac{50}{1.04^{19}} + \frac{1,050}{1.04^{20}} = 1,135.90$$

The calculator solution is:

N = 20; PMT = 50; FV = 1,000; I/Y = 4; CPT → PV = –1,135.90

The value of a zero-coupon bond is simply the present value of the maturity payment. With a discount rate of 3% per period, a 5-period zero-coupon bond with a par value of $1,000 has a value of:

$$\frac{1,000}{1.03^5} = \$862.61$$

LOS 52.b: Identify the relationships among a bond's price, coupon rate, maturity, and market discount rate (yield-to-maturity).

CFA® Program Curriculum: Volume 5, page 407

So far we have used a bond's cash flows and an assumed discount rate to calculate the value of the bond. We can also calculate the market discount rate given a bond's price in the market, because there is an inverse relationship between price and yield. For a 3-year, 8% annual coupon bond that is priced at 90.393, the market discount rate is:

N = 3; PMT = 8; FV = 100; PV = –90.393; CPT → I/Y = 12%

We can summarize the relationships between price and yield as follows:

1. At a point in time, a decrease (increase) in a bond's YTM will increase (decrease) its price.

2. If a bond's coupon rate is greater than its YTM, its price will be at a premium to par value. If a bond's coupon rate is less than its YTM, its price will be at a discount to par value.

3. The percentage decrease in value when the YTM increases by a given amount is smaller than the increase in value when the YTM decreases by the same amount (the price-yield relationship is convex).

4. Other things equal, the price of a bond with a lower coupon rate is more sensitive to a change in yield than is the price of a bond with a higher coupon rate.

5. Other things equal, the price of a bond with a longer maturity is more sensitive to a change in yield than is the price of a bond with a shorter maturity.

Figure 52.1 illustrates the convex relationship between a bond's price and its yield-to-maturity:

Figure 52.1: Market Yield vs. Bond Value for an 8% Coupon Bond

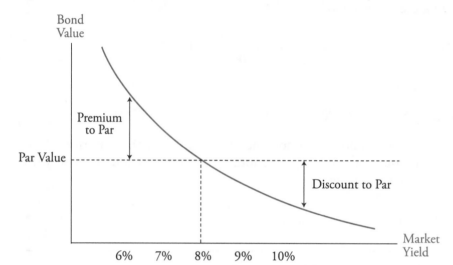

Relationship Between Price and Maturity

Prior to maturity, a bond can be selling at a significant discount or premium to par value. However, regardless of its required yield, the price will converge to par value as maturity approaches. Consider a bond with $1,000 par value and a 3-year life paying 6% semiannual coupons. The bond values corresponding to required yields of 3%, 6%, and 12% as the bond approaches maturity are presented in Figure 52.2.

Figure 52.2: Bond Values and the Passage of Time

Time to Maturity (in years)	YTM = 3%	YTM = 6%	YTM = 12%
3.0	$1,085.46	$1,000.00	$852.48
2.5	1,071.74	1,000.00	873.63
2.0	1,057.82	1,000.00	896.05
1.5	1,043.68	1,000.00	919.81
1.0	1,029.34	1,000.00	945.00
0.5	1,014.78	1,000.00	971.69
0.0	1,000.00	1,000.00	1,000.00

The change in value associated with the passage of time for the three bonds represented in Figure 52.2 is presented graphically in Figure 52.3. This convergence to par value at maturity is known as the **constant-yield price trajectory** because it shows how the bond's price would change as time passes if its yield-to-maturity remained constant.

Figure 52.3: Premium, Par, and Discount Bonds

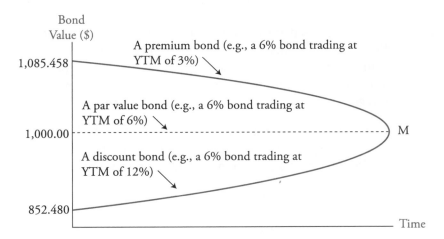

MODULE QUIZ 52.1

To best evaluate your performance, enter your quiz answers online.

1. A 20-year, 10% annual-pay bond has a par value of $1,000. What is the price of the bond if it has a yield-to-maturity of 15%?
    A. $685.14.
    B. $687.03.
    C. $828.39.

2. An analyst observes a 5-year, 10% semiannual-pay bond. The face amount is £1,000. The analyst believes that the yield-to-maturity on a semiannual bond basis should be 15%. Based on this yield estimate, the price of this bond would be:
    A. £828.40.
    B. £1,189.53.
    C. £1,193.04.

3. An analyst observes a 20-year, 8% option-free bond with semiannual coupons. The required yield-to-maturity on a semiannual bond basis was 8%, but suddenly it decreased to 7.25%. As a result, the price of this bond:
    A. increased.
    B. decreased.
    C. stayed the same.

4. A $1,000, 5%, 20-year annual-pay bond has a YTM of 6.5%. If the YTM remains unchanged, how much will the bond value increase over the next three years?
    A. $13.62.
    B. $13.78.
    C. $13.96.

MODULE 52.2: SPOT RATES AND ACCRUED INTEREST

LOS 52.c: Define spot rates and calculate the price of a bond using spot rates.

CFA® Program Curriculum: Volume 5, page 411

The yield-to-maturity is calculated as if the discount rate for every bond cash flow is the same. In reality, discount rates depend on the time period in which the bond payment will be made. **Spot rates** are the market discount rates for a single payment to be received in the future. The discount rates for zero-coupon bonds are spot rates and we sometimes refer to spot rates as *zero-coupon rates* or simply *zero rates*.

In order to price a bond with spot rates, we sum the present values of the bond's payments, each discounted at the spot rate for the number of periods before it will be paid. The general equation for calculating a bond's value using spot rates (S_i) is:

$$\frac{CPN_1}{1+S_1} + \frac{CPN_2}{\left(1+S_2\right)^2} + \ldots\ldots + \frac{CPN_N+FV_N}{\left(1+S_N\right)^N} = PV$$

> **EXAMPLE: Valuing a bond using spot rates**
>
> Given the following spot rates, calculate the value of a 3-year, 5% annual-coupon bond.
>
> Spot rates
>
> 1-year: 3%
>
> 2-year: 4%
>
> 3-year: 5%
>
> **Answer:**
>
> $$\frac{50}{1.03} + \frac{50}{(1.04)^2} + \frac{1,050}{(1.05)^3} = 48.54 + 46.23 + 907.03 = \$1,001.80$$

This price, calculated using spot rates, is sometimes called the *no-arbitrage price* of a bond because if a bond is priced differently there will be a profit opportunity from arbitrage among bonds.

Because the bond value is slightly greater than its par value, we know its YTM is slightly less than its coupon rate of 5%. Using the price of 1,001.80, we can calculate the YTM for this bond as:

N = 3; PMT = 50; FV = 1,000; PV = –1,001.80; CPT → I/Y =4.93%

LOS 52.d: Describe and calculate the flat price, accrued interest, and the full price of a bond.

CFA® Program Curriculum: Volume 5, page 413

The coupon bond values we have calculated so far are calculated on the date a coupon is paid, as the present value of the remaining coupons. For most bond trades, the settlement date, which is when cash is exchanged for the bond, will fall between coupon payment dates. As time passes (and future coupon payment dates get closer), the value of the bond will increase.

The value of a bond between coupon dates can be calculated, using its current YTM, as the value of the bond on its last coupon date (PV) times (1 + YTM / # of coupon periods per year)$^{t/T}$, where t is the number of days since the last coupon payment, and *T* is the number of days in the coupon period. For a given settlement date, this value is referred to as the **full price** of the bond.

Let's work an example for a specific bond:

> **EXAMPLE: Calculating the full price of a bond**
>
> A 5% bond makes coupon payments on June 15 and December 15 and is trading with a YTM of 4%. The bond is purchased and will settle on August 21 when there will be four coupons remaining until maturity. Calculate the full price of the bond using actual days.
>
> *Step 1:* Calculate the value of the bond on the last coupon date (coupons are semiannual, so we use 4 / 2 = 2% for the periodic discount rate):
>
> > N = 4; PMT= 25; FV= 1,000; I/Y =2; CPT → PV= –1,019.04
>
> *Step 2:* Adjust for the number of days since the last coupon payment:
>
> > Days between June 15 and December 15 = 183 days.
> >
> > Days between June 15 and settlement on August 21 = 67 days.
> >
> > Full price = 1,019.04 × (1.02)$^{67/183}$ = 1,026.46.

The accrued interest since the last payment date can be calculated as the coupon payment times the portion of the coupon period that has passed between the last coupon payment date and the settlement date of the transaction. For the bond in the previous example, the accrued interest on the settlement date of August 21 is:

$25 (67 / 183) = $9.15

The full price (invoice price) minus the accrued interest is referred to as the **flat price** of the bond.

> flat price = full price − accrued interest

So for the bond in our example, the flat price = 1,026.46 − 9.15 = 1,017.31.

The flat price of the bond is also referred to as the bond's **clean price**, and the full price is also referred to as the **dirty price**.

Note that the flat price is not the present value of the bond on its last coupon payment date, 1,017.31 < 1,019.04.

So far, in calculating accrued interest, we used the actual number of days between coupon payments and the actual number of days between the last coupon date and the settlement date. This actual/actual method is used most often with government bonds. The 30/360 method is most often used for corporate bonds. This method assumes that there are 30 days in each month and 360 days in a year.

EXAMPLE: Accrued interest

An investor buys a $1,000 par value, 4% annual-pay bond that pays its coupons on May 15. The investor's buy order settles on August 10. Calculate the accrued interest that is owed to the bond seller, using the 30/360 method and the actual/actual method.

Answer:

The annual coupon payment is 4% × $1,000 = $40.

Using the 30/360 method, interest is accrued for 30 − 15 = 15 days in May; 30 days each in June and July; and 10 days in August, or 15 + 30 + 30 + 10 = 85 days.

$$\text{accrued interest (30/360 method)} = \frac{85}{360} \times \$40 = \$9.44$$

Using the actual/actual method, interest is accrued for 31 − 15 = 16 days in May; 30 days in June; 31 days in July; and 10 days in August, or 16 + 30 + 31 + 10 = 87 days.

$$\text{accrued interest (actual/actual method)} = \frac{87}{365} \times \$40 = \$9.53$$

LOS 52.e: Describe matrix pricing.

CFA® Program Curriculum: Volume 5, page 417

Matrix pricing is a method of estimating the required yield-to-maturity (or price) of bonds that are currently not traded or infrequently traded. The procedure is to use the YTMs of traded bonds that have credit quality very close to that of a nontraded or infrequently traded bond and are similar in maturity and coupon, to estimate the required YTM.

EXAMPLE: Pricing an illiquid bond

Rob Phelps, CFA, is estimating the value of a nontraded 4% annual-pay, A+ rated bond that has three years remaining until maturity. He has obtained the following yields-to-maturity on similar corporate bonds:

- A+ rated, 2-year annual-pay, YTM = 4.3%
- A+ rated, 5-year annual-pay, YTM = 5.1%
- A+ rated, 5-year annual-pay, YTM = 5.3%

Estimate the value of the nontraded bond.

Answer:

Step 1: Take the average YTM of the 5-year bonds: (5.1 + 5.3) / 2 = 5.2%.

Step 2: Interpolate the 3-year YTM based on the 2-year and average 5-year YTMs:

   4.3% + (5.2% – 4.3%) × [(3 years – 2 years) / (5 years – 2 years)]
   = 4.6%

Step 3: Price the nontraded bond with a YTM of 4.6%:

   N = 3; PMT = 40; FV = 1,000; I/Y = 4.6; CPT → PV = –983.54

   The estimated value is $983.54 per $1,000 par value.

In using the averages in the preceding example, we have used simple *linear interpolation*. Because the maturity of the nontraded bond is three years, we estimate the YTM on the 3-year bond as the yield on the 2-year bond, plus one-third of the difference between the YTM of the 2-year bond and the average YTM of the 5-year bonds. Note that the difference in maturity between the 2-year bond and the 3-year bond is one year and the difference between the maturities of the 2-year and 5-year bonds is three years.

A variation of matrix pricing used for pricing new bond issues focuses on the spreads between bond yields and the yields of a benchmark bond of similar maturity that is essentially default risk free. Often the yields on Treasury bonds are used as benchmark yields for U.S. dollar-denominated corporate bonds. When estimating the YTM for the new issue bond, the appropriate spread to the yield of a Treasury bond of the same maturity is estimated and added to the yield of the benchmark issue.

EXAMPLE: Estimating the spread for a new 6-year, A rated bond issue

Consider the following market yields:

   5-year, U.S. Treasury bond, YTM 1.48%
   5-year, A rated corporate bond, YTM 2.64%

   7-year, U.S. Treasury bond, YTM 2.15%
   7-year, A rated corporate bond, YTM 3.55%

   6-year U.S. Treasury bond, YTM 1.74%

Estimate the required yield on a newly issued 6-year, A rated corporate bond.

Answer:

1. Calculate the spreads to the benchmark (Treasury) yields.

   Spread on the 5-year corporate bond is 2.64 – 1.48 = 1.16%.

   Spread on the 7-year corporate bond is 3.55 – 2.15 = 1.40%.

2. Calculate the average spread because the 6-year bond is the midpoint of five and seven years.

   Average spread = (1.16 + 1.40) / 2 = 1.28%.

> 3. Add the average spread to the YTM of the 6-year Treasury (benchmark) bond.
>
> 1.74 + 1.28 = 3.02%, which is our estimate of the YTM on the newly issued 6-year, A rated bond.

MODULE QUIZ 52.2

To best evaluate your performance, enter your quiz answers online.

1. If spot rates are 3.2% for one year, 3.4% for two years, and 3.5% for three years, the price of a $100,000 face value, 3-year, annual-pay bond with a coupon rate of 4% is *closest* to:
   A. $101,420.
   B. $101,790.
   C. $108,230.

2. An investor paid a full price of $1,059.04 each for 100 bonds. The purchase was between coupon dates, and accrued interest was $23.54 per bond. What is each bond's flat price?
   A. $1,000.00.
   B. $1,035.50.
   C. $1,082.58.

3. Cathy Moran, CFA, is estimating a value for an infrequently traded bond with six years to maturity, an annual coupon of 7%, and a single-B credit rating. Moran obtains yields-to-maturity for more liquid bonds with the same credit rating:

   ■ 5% coupon, eight years to maturity, yielding 7.20%.

   ■ 6.5% coupon, five years to maturity, yielding 6.40%.

   The infrequently traded bond is *most likely* trading at:
   A. par value.
   B. a discount to par value.
   C. a premium to par value.

Video covering this content is available online.

MODULE 52.3: YIELD MEASURES

LOS 52.f: Calculate and interpret yield measures for fixed-rate bonds, floating-rate notes, and money market instruments.

CFA® Program Curriculum: Volume 5, page 420

Given a bond's price in the market, we can say that the YTM is the discount rate that makes the present value of a bond's cash flows equal to its price. For a 5-year, annual pay 7% bond that is priced in the market at $1,020.78, the YTM will satisfy the following equation:

$$\frac{70}{1+YTM} + \frac{70}{(1+YTM)^2} + \frac{70}{(1+YTM)^3} + \frac{70}{(1+YTM)^4} + \frac{1,070}{(1+YYM)^5}$$

$$= 1,020.78$$

We can calculate the YTM (discount rate) that satisfies this equality as:

N = 5; PMT= 70; FV= 1,000; PV= –1,020.78; CPT → I/Y = 6.5%

By convention, the YTM on a semiannual coupon bond is expressed as two times the semiannual discount rate. For a 5-year, semiannual pay 7% coupon bond, we can calculate the semiannual discount rate as YTM/2 and then double it to get the YTM expressed as an annual yield:

$$\frac{35}{1 + \text{YTM}/\!\!2} + \frac{35}{(1 + \text{YTM}/\!\!2)^2} + \frac{35}{(1 + \text{YTM}/\!\!2)^3} + \cdots + \frac{35}{(1 + \text{YTM}/\!\!2)^9} + \frac{1,035}{(1 + \text{YTM}/\!\!2)^{10}}$$

= 1,020.78

N = 10; PMT = 35; FV = 1,000; PV = –1,020.78; CPT → I/Y = 3.253%

The YTM is 3.253 × 2 = 6.506%.

Yield Measures for Fixed-Rate Bonds

The **effective yield** for a bond depends on how many coupon payments are made each year and is simply the compound return. How frequently coupon payments are made is referred to as the **periodicity** of the annual rate.

An annual-pay bond with an 8% YTM has an effective yield of 8%.

A semiannual-pay bond (periodicity of two) with an 8% YTM has a yield of 4% every six months and an effective yield of $1.04^2 - 1 = 8.16\%$.

A quarterly-pay bond (periodicity of four) with an 8% yield-to-maturity has a yield of 2% every three months and an effective yield of $1.02^4 - 1 = 8.24\%$.

PROFESSOR'S NOTE

This follows the method described in Quantitative Methods for calculating the effective annual yield given a stated annual rate and the number of compounding periods per year.

Most bonds in the United States make semiannual coupon payments (periodicity of two), and yields (YTMs) are quoted on a **semiannual bond basis**, which is simply two times the semiannual discount rate. It may be necessary to adjust the quoted yield on a bond to make it comparable with the yield on a bond with a different periodicity. This is illustrated in the following example.

EXAMPLE: Adjusting yields for periodicity

An Atlas Corporation bond is quoted with a YTM of 4% on a semiannual bond basis. What yields should be used to compare it with a quarterly-pay bond and an annual-pay bond?

Answer:

The first thing to note is that 4% on a semiannual bond basis is an effective yield of 2% per 6-month period.

To compare this with the yield on an annual-pay bond, which is an effective annual yield, we need to calculate the effective annual yield on the semiannual coupon bond, which is $1.02^2 - 1 = 4.04\%$.

For the annual YTM on the quarterly-pay bond, we need to calculate the effective quarterly yield and multiply by four. The quarterly yield (yield per quarter) that is equivalent to a yield of 2% per six months is $1.02^{1/2} - 1 = 0.995\%$. The quoted annual rate for the equivalent yield on a quarterly bond basis is $4 \times 0.995 = 3.98\%$.

Note that we have shown that the effective annual yields are the same for:

- An annual coupon bond with a yield of 4.04% on an annual basis (periodicity of one).

- A semiannual coupon bond with a yield of 4.0% on a semiannual basis (periodicity of two).

- A quarterly coupon bond with a yield of 3.98% on quarterly basis (periodicity of four).

Bond yields calculated using the stated coupon payment dates are referred to as following the **street convention**. Because some coupon dates will fall on weekends and holidays, coupon payments will actually be made the next business day. The yield calculated using these actual coupon payment dates is referred to as the **true yield**. Some coupon payments will be made later when holidays and weekends are taken into account, so true yields will be slightly lower than street convention yields, if only by a few basis points.

When calculating spreads between government bond yields and the yield on a corporate bond, the corporate bond yield is often restated to its yield on actual/actual basis to match the day count convention used on government bonds (rather than the 30/360 day count convention used for calculating corporate bond yields).

Current yield is simple to calculate, but offers limited information. This measure looks at just one source of return: *a bond's annual interest income*—it does not consider capital gains/losses or reinvestment income. The formula for the current yield is:

$$\text{current yield} = \frac{\text{annual cash coupon payment}}{\text{bond price}}$$

EXAMPLE: Computing current yield

Consider a 20-year, $1,000 par value, 6% *semiannual-pay* bond that is currently trading at a flat price of $802.07. Calculate the current yield.

Answer:

The *annual* cash coupon payments total:

$$\text{annual cash coupon payment} = \text{par value} \times \text{stated coupon rate}$$
$$= \$1,000 \times 0.06 = \$60$$

Because the bond is trading at \$802.07, the current yield is:

$$\text{current yield} = \frac{60}{802.07} = 0.0748, \text{ or } 7.48\%.$$

Note that current yield is based on *annual* coupon interest so that it is the same for a semiannual-pay and annual-pay bond with the same coupon rate and price.

The current yield does not account for gains or losses as the bond's price moves toward its par value over time. A bond's **simple yield** takes a discount or premium into account by assuming that any discount or premium declines evenly over the remaining years to maturity. The sum of the annual coupon payment plus (minus) the straight-line amortization of a discount (premium) is divided by the flat price to get the simple yield.

> **EXAMPLE: Computing simple yield**
>
> A 3-year, 8% coupon, semiannual-pay bond is priced at 90.165. Calculate the simple yield.
>
> **Answer:**
>
> The discount from par value is 100 – 90.165 = 9.835. Annual straight-line amortization of the discount is 9.835 / 3 = 3.278.
>
> $$\text{simple yield} = \frac{8 + 3.278}{90.165} = 12.51\%$$

For a callable bond, an investor's yield will depend on whether and when the bond is called. The **yield-to-call** can be calculated for each possible call date and price. The lowest of yield-to-maturity and the various yields-to-call is termed the **yield-to-worst**. The following example illustrates these calculations.

> **EXAMPLE: Yield-to-call and yield-to-worst**
>
> Consider a 10-year, semiannual-pay 6% bond trading at 102 on January 1, 2014. The bond is callable according to the following schedule:
>
>   Callable at 102 on or after January 1, 2019.
>   Callable at 100 on or after January 1, 2022.
>
> Calculate the bond's YTM, yield-to-first call, yield-to-first par call, and yield-to-worst.
>
> **Answer:**
>
> The *yield-to-maturity* on the bond is calculated as:
>
>   N = 20; PMT = 30; FV = 1,000; PV = –1,020; CPT → I/Y = 2.867%
>
>   2 × 2.867 = 5.734% = YTM
>
> To calculate the *yield-to-first call*, we calculate the yield-to-maturity using the number of semiannual periods until the first call date (10) for *N* and the call price (1,020) for *FV*:
>
>   N = 10; PMT = 30; FV = 1,020; PV = –1,020; CPT → I/Y = 2.941%
>
>   2 × 2.941 = 5.882% = yield-to-first call

> To calculate the *yield-to-first par call* (second call date), we calculate the yield-to-maturity using the number of semiannual periods until the first par call date (16) for *N* and the call price (1,000) for *FV*:
>
> N = 16; PMT = 30; FV = 1,000; PV = –1,020; CPT → I/Y = 2.843%
>
> 2 × 2.843 = 5.686% = yield-to-first par call
>
> The lowest yield, 5.686%, is realized if the bond is called at par on January 1, 2022, so the *yield-to-worst* is 5.686%.

The **option-adjusted yield** is calculated by adding the value of the call option to the bond's current flat price. The value of a callable bond is equal to the value of the bond if it did not have the call option, minus the value of the call option (because the issuer *owns* the call option).

The option-adjusted yield will be less than the yield-to-maturity for a callable bond because callable bonds have higher yields to compensate bondholders for the issuer's call option. The option-adjusted yield can be used to compare the yields of bonds with various embedded options to each other and to similar option-free bonds.

Floating-Rate Note Yields

The values of floating rate notes (FRNs) are more stable than those of fixed-rate debt of similar maturity because the coupon interest rates are reset periodically based on a reference rate. Recall that the coupon rate on a floating-rate note is the reference rate plus or minus a margin based on the credit risk of the bond relative to the credit risk of the reference rate instrument. The coupon rate for the next period is set using the current reference rate for the reset period, and the payment at the end of the period is based on this rate. For this reason, we say that interest is paid *in arrears*.

If an FRN is issued by a company that has more (less) credit risk than the banks quoting LIBOR, a margin is added to (subtracted from) LIBOR, the reference rate. The liquidity of an FRN and its tax treatment can also affect the margin.

We call the margin used to calculate the bond coupon payments the **quoted margin** and we call the margin required to return the FRN to its par value the **required margin** (also called the **discount margin**). When the credit quality of an FRN is unchanged, the quoted margin is equal to the required margin and the FRN returns to its par value at each reset date when the next coupon payment is reset to the current market rate (plus or minus the appropriate margin).

If the credit quality of the issuer decreases, the quoted margin will be less than the required margin and the FRN will sell at a discount to its par value. If credit quality has improved, the quoted margin will be greater than the required margin and the FRN will sell at a premium to its par value.

A somewhat simplified way of calculating the value of an FRN on a reset date is to use the current reference rate plus the quoted margin to estimate the future cash flows for the FRN and to discount these future cash flows at the reference rate plus the required (discount) margin. More complex models produce better estimates of value.

Yields for Money Market Instruments

Recall that yields on money market securities can be stated as a discount from face value or as add-on yields, and can be based on a 360-day or 365-day basis. U.S. Treasury bills are quoted as annualized discounts from face value based on a 360-day year. LIBOR and bank CD rates are quoted as add-on yields. We need to be able to:

■ Calculate the actual payment on a money market security given its yield and knowledge of how the yield was calculated.

■ Compare the yields on two securities that are quoted on different yield bases.

Both discount basis and add-on yields in the money market are quoted as simple annual interest. The following example illustrates the required calculations and quote conventions.

EXAMPLE: Money market yields

1. A $1,000 90-day T-bill is priced with an annualized discount of 1.2%. Calculate its market price and its annualized add-on yield based on a 365-day year.

2. A $1 million negotiable CD with 120 days to maturity is quoted with an add-on yield of 1.4% based on a 365-day year. Calculate the payment at maturity for this CD and its bond equivalent yield.

3. A bank deposit for 100 days is quoted with an add-on yield of 1.5% based on a 360-day year. Calculate the bond equivalent yield and the yield on a semiannual bond basis

Answer:

1. The discount from face value is 1.2% × 90 / 360 × 1,000 = $3 so the current price is 1,000 − 3 = $997.

   The equivalent add-on yield for 90 days is 3 / 997 = 0.3009%. The annualized add-on yield based on a 365-day year is 365 / 90 × 0.3009 = 1.2203%. This add-on yield based on a 365-day year is referred to as the **bond equivalent yield** for a money market security.

2. The add-on interest for the 120-day period is 120 / 365 × 1.4% = 0.4603%.

   At maturity, the CD will pay $1 million × (1 + 0.004603) = $1,004,603.

   The quoted yield on the CD is the bond equivalent yield because it is an add-on yield annualized based on a 365-day year.

3. Because the yield of 1.5% is an annualized effective yield calculated based on a 360-day year, the bond equivalent yield, which is based on a 365-day year, is:

   (365 / 360) × 1.5% = 1.5208%

   We may want to compare the yield on a money market security to the YTM of a semiannual-pay bond. The method is to convert the money market security's holding period return to an effective semiannual yield, and then double it.

   Because the yield of 1.5% is calculated as the add-on yield for 100 days times 100 / 360, the 100-day holding period return is 1.5% × 100 / 360 = 0.4167%. The effective annual yield is $1.004167^{365/100} - 1 = 1.5294\%$, the equivalent semiannual yield is $1.015294^{1/2} - 1 = 0.7618\%$, and the annual yield on a semiannual bond basis is 2 × 0.7618% = 1.5236%.

> Because the periodicity of the money market security, 365 / 100, is greater than the periodicity of 2 for a semiannual-pay bond, the simple annual rate for the money market security, 1.5%, is less than the yield on a semiannual bond basis, which has a periodicity of 2.

MODULE QUIZ 52.3

To best evaluate your performance, enter your quiz answers online.

1. A market rate of discount for a single payment to be made in the future is:
   A. a spot rate.
   B. a simple yield.
   C. a forward rate.

2. Based on semiannual compounding, what would the YTM be on a 15-year, zero-coupon, $1,000 par value bond that's currently trading at $331.40?
   A. 3.750%.
   B. 5.151%.
   C. 7.500%.

3. An analyst observes a Widget & Co. 7.125%, 4-year, semiannual-pay bond trading at 102.347% of par (where par is $1,000). The bond is callable at 101 in two years. What is the bond's yield-to-call?
   A. 3.167%.
   B. 5.664%.
   C. 6.334%.

4. A floating-rate note has a quoted margin of +50 basis points and a required margin of +75 basis points. On its next reset date, the price of the note will be:
   A. equal to par value.
   B. less than par value.
   C. greater than par value.

5. Which of the following money market yields is a bond-equivalent yield?
   A. Add-on yield based on a 365-day year.
   B. Discount yield based on a 360-day year.
   C. Discount yield based on a 365-day year.

MODULE 52.4: YIELD CURVES

Video covering this content is available online.

LOS 52.g: Define and compare the spot curve, yield curve on coupon bonds, par curve, and forward curve.

CFA® Program Curriculum: Volume 5, page 433

A **yield curve** shows yields by maturity. Yield curves are constructed for yields of various types and it's very important to understand exactly which yield is being shown. The **term structure** of interest rates refers to the yields at different maturities (terms) for like securities or interest rates. The yields on U.S. Treasury coupon bonds by maturity can be found at Treasury.gov, and several yield curves are available at Bloomberg.com.

The **spot rate yield curve** (spot curve) for U.S. Treasury bonds is also referred to as the *zero curve* (for zero-coupon) or *strip curve* (because zero-coupon U.S. Treasury bonds are also called *stripped Treasuries*). Recall that spot rates are the appropriate yields, and therefore appropriate discount rates, for single payments to be made in the future. Yields on zero-coupon government bonds are spot rates. Earlier in this topic review, we calculated the value of a bond by discounting each separate payment by the spot rate corresponding to the time until the payment will be received. Spot rates are usually quoted on a semiannual bond basis, so they are directly comparable to YTMs quoted for coupon government bonds.

A **yield curve for coupon bonds** shows the YTMs for coupon bonds at various maturities. Yields are calculated for several maturities and yields for bonds with maturities between these are estimated by linear interpolation. Figure 52.4 shows a yield curve for coupon Treasury bonds constructed from yields on 1-month, 3-month, 6-month, 1-year, 2-year, 3-year, 5-year, 7-year, 10-year, 20 year, and 30-year maturities. Yields are expressed on a semiannual bond basis.

Figure 52.4: U.S. Treasury Yield Curve as of August 1, 2013

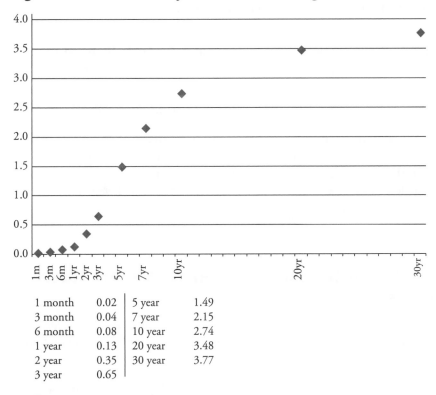

1 month	0.02	5 year	1.49
3 month	0.04	7 year	2.15
6 month	0.08	10 year	2.74
1 year	0.13	20 year	3.48
2 year	0.35	30 year	3.77
3 year	0.65		

Source: www.treasury.gov/resource-center

A **par bond yield curve**, or *par curve*, is not calculated from yields on actual bonds but is constructed from the spot curve. The yields reflect the coupon rate that a hypothetical bond at each maturity would need to have to be priced at par. Alternatively, they can be viewed as the YTM of a par bond at each maturity.

Consider a 3-year annual-pay bond and spot rates for one, two, and three years of S_1, S_2, and S_3. The following equation can be used to calculate the coupon rate necessary for the bond to be trading at par.

$$\frac{PMT}{1 + S_1} + \frac{PMT}{\left(1 + S_2\right)^2} + \frac{PMT + 100}{\left(1 + S_3\right)^3} = 100$$

With spot rates of 1%, 2%, and 3%, a 3-year annual par bond will have a payment that will satisfy:

$$\frac{PMT}{1.01} + \frac{PMT}{(1.02)^2} + \frac{PMT + 100}{(1.03)^3} = 100,$$

so the payment is 2.96 and the par bond coupon rate is 2.96%.

Forward rates are yields for future periods. The rate of interest on a 1-year loan that would be made two years from now is a forward rate. A **forward yield curve** shows the future rates for bonds or money market securities for the same maturities for annual periods in the future. Typically, the forward curve would show the yields of 1-year securities for each future year, quoted on a semiannual bond basis.

LOS 52.h: Define forward rates and calculate spot rates from forward rates, forward rates from spot rates, and the price of a bond using forward rates.

CFA® Program Curriculum: Volume 5, page 437

A forward rate is a borrowing/lending rate for a loan to be made at some future date. The notation used must identify both the length of the lending/borrowing period and when in the future the money will be loaned/borrowed. Thus, 1y1y is the rate for a 1-year loan one year from now; 2y1y is the rate for a 1-year loan to be made two years from now; 3y2y is the 2-year forward rate three years from now; and so on.

The Relationship Between Short-Term Forward Rates and Spot Rates

The idea here is that *borrowing for three years at the 3-year spot rate, or borrowing for one-year periods in three successive years, should have the same cost.* The S_i are the current spot rates for *i* periods.

This relation is illustrated as $(1 + S_3)^3 = (1 + S_1)(1 + 1y1y)(1 + 2y1y)$. Thus, $S_3 = [(1 + S_1)(1 + 1y1y)(1 + 2y1y)]^{1/3} - 1$, which is the geometric mean return we covered in Quantitative Methods.

> **EXAMPLE: Computing spot rates from forward rates**
>
> If the current 1-year spot rate is 2%, the 1-year forward rate one year from today (*1y1y*) is 3%, and the 1-year forward rate two years from today (*2y1y*) is 4%, what is the 3-year spot rate?

Answer:

$$S_3 = [(1.02)(1.03)(1.04)]^{1/3} - 1 = 2.997\%$$

This can be interpreted to mean that a dollar compounded at 2.997% for three years would produce the same ending value as a dollar that earns compound interest of 2% the first year, 3% the next year, and 4% for the third year.

PROFESSOR'S NOTE

You can get a very good approximation of the 3-year spot rate with the simple average of the forward rates. In the previous example, we calculated 2.997% and the simple average of the three annual rates is:

$$\frac{2 + 3 + 4}{3} = 3\%.$$

Forward Rates Given Spot Rates

We can use the same relationships we use to calculate spot rates from forward rates to calculate forward rates from spot rates.

Our basic relation between forward rates and spot rates (for two periods) is:

$$(1 + S_2)^2 = (1 + S_1)(1 + 1y1y)$$

This again tells us that an investment has the same expected yield (borrowing has the same expected cost) whether we invest (borrow) for two periods at the 2-period spot rate, S_2, or for one period at the current 1-year rate, S_1, and for the next period at the forward rate, 1y1y. Given two of these rates, we can solve for the other.

EXAMPLE: Computing a forward rate from spot rates

The 2-period spot rate, S_2, is 8%, and the 1-period spot rate, S_1, is 4%. Calculate the forward rate for one period, one period from now, *1y1y*.

Answer:

The following figure illustrates the problem.

Finding a Forward Rate

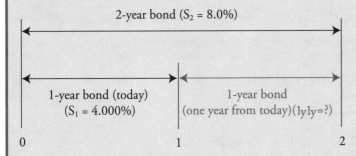

From our original equality, $(1 + S_2)^2 = (1 + S_1)(1 + 1y1y)$, we can get

$$\frac{(1 + S_2)^2}{(1 + S_1)} = (1 + 1y1y)$$

Or, because we know that both choices have the same payoff in two years:

$$(1.08)^2 = (1.04)(1 + 1y1y)$$

$$(1 + 1y1y) = \frac{(1.08)^2}{(1.04)}$$

$$1y1y = \frac{(1.08)^2}{(1.04)} - 1 = \frac{1.1664}{1.04} - 1 = 12.154\%$$

In other words, investors are willing to accept 4.0% on the 1-year bond today (when they could get 8.0% on the 2-year bond today) only because they can get 12.154% on a 1-year bond one year from today. This future rate that can be locked in today is a forward rate.

Similarly, we can back other forward rates out of the spot rates. We know that:

$$(1 + S_3)^3 = (1 + S_1)(1 + 1y1y)(1 + 2y1y)$$

And that:

$$(1 + S_2)^2 = (1 + S_1)(1 + 1y1y), \text{ so we can write } (1 + S_3)^3 = (1 + S_2)^2(1 + 2y1y)$$

This last equation says that investing for three years at the 3-year spot rate should produce the same ending value as investing for two years at the 2-year spot rate, and then for a third year at *2y1y*, the 1-year forward rate, two years from now.

Solving for the forward rate, *2y1y*, we get:

$$\frac{\left(1 + S_3\right)^3}{\left(1 + S_2\right)^2} - 1 = 2y1y$$

EXAMPLE: Forward rates from spot rates

Let's extend the previous example to three periods. The current 1-year spot rate is 4.0%, the current 2-year spot rate is 8.0%, and the current 3-year spot rate is 12.0%. Calculate the 1-year forward rates one and two years from now.

Answer:

We know the following relation must hold:

$$(1 + S_2)^2 = (1 + S_1)(1 + 1y1y)$$

We can use it to solve for the 1-year forward rate one year from now:

$$(1.08)^2 = (1.04)(1 + 1y1y), \text{ so } 1y1y = \frac{(1.08)^2}{(1.04)} - 1 = 12.154\%$$

We also know that the relations:

$$(1 + S_3)^3 = (1 + S_1)(1 + 1y1y)(1 + 2y1y)$$

and, equivalently $(1 + S_3)^3 = (1 + S_2)^2(1 + 2y1y)$ must hold.

Substituting values for S_3 and S_2, we have:

$$(1.12)^3 = (1.08)^2 \times (1 + 2y1y)$$

so that the 1-year forward rate two years from now is:

$$2y1y = \frac{(1.12)^3}{(1.08)^2} - 1 = 20.45\%$$

We can check our results by calculating:

$$S_3 = [(1.04)(1.12154)(1.2045)]^{1/3} - 1 = 12.00\%$$

This may all seem a bit complicated, but the basic relation, that borrowing for successive periods at 1-period rates should have the same cost as borrowing at multiperiod spot rates, can be summed up as:

$(1 + S_2)^2 = (1 + S_1)(1 + 1y1y)$ for two periods, and
$(1 + S_3)^3 = (1 + S_2)^2(1 + 2y1y)$ for three periods.

PROFESSOR'S NOTE

Simple averages also give decent approximations for calculating forward rates from spot rates. In the preceding example, we had spot rates of 4% for one year and 8% for two years. Two years at 8% is 16%, so if the first-year rate is 4%, the second-year rate is close to 16 – 4 = 12% (actual is 12.154). Given a 2-year spot rate of 8% and a 3-year spot rate of 12%, we could approximate the 1-year forward rate from time two to time three as (3 × 12) – (2 × 8) = 20. That may be close enough (actual is 20.45) to answer a multiple-choice question and, in any case, serves as a good check to make sure the exact rate you calculate is reasonable.

We can also calculate implied forward rates for loans for more than one period. Given spot rates of: 1-year = 5%, 2-year = 6%, 3-year = 7%, and 4-year = 8%, we can calculate *2y2y*.

The implied forward rate on a 2-year loan two years from now, *2y2y*, is:

$$\left[\frac{(1 + S_4)^4}{(1 + S_2)^2}\right]^{1/2} - 1 = \left(\frac{1.08^4}{1.06^2}\right)^{1/2} - 1 = 10.04\%.$$

PROFESSOR'S NOTE

The approximation works for multi-period forward rates as well.

The difference between four years at 8% (= 32%) and two years at 6% (= 12%) is 20%. Because that difference is for two years, we divide by two to get an annual rate of 10%, $\frac{(4 \times 8 - 6 \times 2)}{2} = 10$, which is very close to the exact solution of 10.04%.

Valuing a Bond Using Forward Rates

EXAMPLE: Computing a bond value using forward rates

The current 1-year rate, S_1, is 4%, the 1-year forward rate for lending from time = 1 to time = 2 is 1y1y = 5%, and the 1-year forward rate for lending from time = 2 to time = 3 is 2y1y = 6%. Value a 3-year annual-pay bond with a 5% coupon and a par value of $1,000.

Answer:

$$\text{bond value} = \frac{50}{1+S_1} + \frac{50}{(1+S_1)(1+1y1y)} + \frac{1,050}{(1+S_1)(1+1y1y)(1+2y1y)}$$

$$= \frac{50}{1.04} + \frac{50}{(1.04)(1.05)} + \frac{1,050}{(1.04)(1.05)(1.06)} = \$1,000.98$$

> **PROFESSOR'S NOTE**
>
> If you think this looks a little like valuing a bond using spot rates, as we did for arbitrage-free valuation, you are correct. The discount factors are equivalent to spot rate discount factors.
>
> If we have a semiannual coupon bond, the calculation methods are the same, but we would use the semiannual discount rate rather than the annualized rate and the number of periods would be the number of semiannual periods.

Video covering this content is available online.

MODULE 52.5: YIELD SPREADS

LOS 52.i: Compare, calculate, and interpret yield spread measures.

CFA® Program Curriculum: Volume 5, page 441

A **yield spread** is the difference between the yields of two different bonds. Yield spreads are typically quoted in basis points.

A yield spread relative to a benchmark bond is known as a **benchmark spread**. For example, if a 5-year corporate bond has a yield of 6.25% and its benchmark, the 5-year Treasury note, has a yield of 3.50%, the corporate bond has a benchmark spread of 625 − 350 = 275 basis points.

For fixed-coupon bonds, on-the-run government bond yields for the same or nearest maturity are frequently used as benchmarks. The benchmark may change during a bond's life. For a 5-year corporate bond, when issued, the benchmark spread is stated relative to a 5-year government bond yield, but two years later (when it has three years remaining to maturity) its benchmark spread will be stated relative to a 3-year government bond yield. A yield spread over a government bond is also known as a *G*-spread.

An alternative to using government bond yields as benchmarks is to use rates for interest rate swaps in the same currency and with the same tenor as a bond. Yield spreads relative to swap rates are known as **interpolated spreads** or *I*-spreads. *I*-spreads are frequently stated for bonds denominated in euros.

> **PROFESSOR'S NOTE**
>
> For bonds with tenors that do not match an on-the run government bond, yield spreads may be quoted relative to an "interpolated government bond yield." These are still *G*-spreads.

As we noted in an earlier topic review, floating-rate securities typically use LIBOR as a benchmark rate.

Yield spreads are useful for analyzing the factors that affect a bond's yield. If a corporate bond's yield increases from 6.25% to 6.50%, this may have been caused by factors that affect all bond yields (macroeconomic factors) or by firm-specific or industry-specific (microeconomic) factors. If a bond's yield increases but its yield spread remains the same, the yield on its benchmark must have also increased, which suggests macroeconomic factors caused bond yields in general to increase. However, if the yield spread increases, this suggests the increase in the bond's yield was caused by microeconomic factors such as credit risk or the issue's liquidity.

PROFESSOR'S NOTE

Recall from our discussion of the Fisher effect in Economics that an interest rate is composed of the real risk-free rate, the expected inflation rate, and a risk premium. We can think of macroeconomic factors as those that affect the real risk-free rate and expected inflation, and microeconomic factors as those that affect the credit and liquidity risk premium.

Zero-Volatility and Option-Adjusted Spreads

A disadvantage of *G*-spreads and *I*-spreads is that they are theoretically correct only if the spot yield curve is flat so that yields are approximately the same across maturities. Normally, however, the spot yield curve is upward-sloping (i.e., longer-term yields are higher than shorter-term yields).

A method for deriving a bond's yield spread to a benchmark spot yield curve that accounts for the shape of the yield curve is to add an equal amount to each benchmark spot rate and value the bond with those rates. When we find an amount which, when added to the benchmark spot rates, produces a value equal to the market price of the bond, we have the appropriate yield curve spread. A yield spread calculated this way is known as a **zero-volatility spread** or *Z*-spread.

> **EXAMPLE: Zero-volatility spread**
>
> The 1-, 2-, and 3-year spot rates on Treasuries are 4%, 8.167%, and 12.377%, respectively. Consider a 3-year, 9% annual coupon corporate bond trading at 89.464. The YTM is 13.50%, and the YTM of a 3-year Treasury is 12%. Compute the *G*-spread and the *Z*-spread of the corporate bond.
>
> **Answer:**
>
> The *G*-spread is:
>
> $$\text{G-spread} = \text{YTM}_{\text{Bond}} - \text{YTM}_{\text{Treasury}} = 13.50 - 12.00 = 1.50\%.$$
>
> To compute the *Z*-spread, set the present value of the bond's cash flows equal to today's market price. Discount each cash flow at the appropriate zero-coupon bond spot rate *plus* a fixed spread ZS. Solve for ZS in the following equation and you have the *Z*-spread:
>
> $$89.464 = \frac{9}{(1.04 + \text{ZS})^1} + \frac{9}{(1.08167 + \text{ZS})^2} + \frac{109}{(1.12377 + \text{ZS})^3}$$
>
> $\Rightarrow \text{ZS} = 1.67\%$ or 167 basis points

Note that this spread is found by trial-and-error. In other words, pick a number "ZS," plug it into the right-hand side of the equation, and see if the result equals 89.464. If the right-hand side equals the left, then you have found the Z-spread. If not, adjust "ZS" in the appropriate direction and recalculate.

An **option-adjusted spread** (OAS) is used for bonds with embedded options. Loosely speaking, the option-adjusted spread takes the option yield component out of the Z-spread measure; the OAS is the spread to the government spot rate curve that the bond would have if it were option-free.

If we calculate an OAS for a callable bond, it will be less than the bond's Z-spread. The difference is the extra yield required to compensate bondholders for the call option. That extra yield is the option value. Thus, we can write:

option value = Z-spread − OAS

OAS = Z-spread − option value

For example, if a callable bond has a Z-spread of 180 bp and the value of the call option is 60 bp, the bond's OAS is 180 − 60 = 120 bp.

MODULE QUIZ 52.4, 52.5
To best evaluate your performance, enter your quiz answers online.

1. Which of the following yield curves is *least likely* to consist of observed yields in the market?
    A. Forward yield curve.
    B. Par bond yield curve.
    C. Coupon bond yield curve.

2. The 4-year spot rate is 9.45%, and the 3-year spot rate is 9.85%. What is the 1-year forward rate three years from today?
    A. 8.258%.
    B. 9.850%.
    C. 11.059%.

3. Given the following spot and forward rates:
    ■ Current 1-year spot rate is 5.5%.
    ■ One-year forward rate one year from today is 7.63%.
    ■ One-year forward rate two years from today is 12.18%.
    ■ One-year forward rate three years from today is 15.5%.

    The value of a 4-year, 10% annual-pay, $1,000 par value bond is *closest* to:
    A. $996.
    B. $1,009.
    C. $1,086.

4. A corporate bond is quoted at a spread of +235 basis points over an interpolated 12-year U.S. Treasury bond yield. This spread is:
    A. a *G*-spread.
    B. an *I*-spread.
    C. a *Z*-spread.

KEY CONCEPTS

LOS 52.a

The price of a bond is the present value of its future cash flows, discounted at the bond's yield-to-maturity.

For an annual-coupon bond with N years to maturity:

$$\text{price} = \frac{\text{coupon}}{(1 + \text{YTM})} + \frac{\text{coupon}}{(1 + \text{YTM})^2} + \dots + \frac{\text{coupon} + \text{principal}}{(1 + \text{YTM})^N}$$

For a semiannual-coupon bond with N years to maturity:

$$\text{price} = \frac{\text{coupon}}{\left(1 + \frac{\text{YTM}}{2}\right)} + \frac{\text{coupon}}{\left(1 + \frac{\text{YTM}}{2}\right)^2} + \dots + \frac{\text{coupon} + \text{principal}}{\left(1 + \frac{\text{YTM}}{2}\right)^{N \times 2}}$$

LOS 52.b

A bond's price and YTM are inversely related. An increase in YTM decreases the price and a decrease in YTM increases the price.

A bond will be priced at a discount to par value if its coupon rate is less than its YTM, and at a premium to par value if its coupon rate is greater than its YTM.

Prices are more sensitive to changes in YTM for bonds with lower coupon rates and longer maturities, and less sensitive to changes in YTM for bonds with higher coupon rates and shorter maturities.

A bond's price moves toward par value as time passes and maturity approaches.

LOS 52.c

Spot rates are market discount rates for single payments to be made in the future.

The no-arbitrage price of a bond is calculated using (no-arbitrage) spot rates as follows:

$$\text{no-arbitrage price} = \frac{\text{coupon}}{\left(1 + S_1\right)} + \frac{\text{coupon}}{\left(1 + S_2\right)^2} + \dots + \frac{\text{coupon} + \text{principal}}{\left(1 + S_N\right)^N}$$

LOS 52.d

The full price of a bond includes interest accrued between coupon dates. The flat price of a bond is the full price minus accrued interest.

Accrued interest for a bond transaction is calculated as the coupon payment times the portion of the coupon period from the previous payment date to the settlement date.

Methods for determining the period of accrued interest include actual days (typically used for government bonds) or 30-day months and 360-day years (typically used for corporate bonds).

LOS 52.e

Matrix pricing is a method used to estimate the yield-to-maturity for bonds that are not traded or infrequently traded. The yield is estimated based on the yields of traded bonds with the same credit quality. If these traded bonds have different maturities than the bond being valued, linear interpolation is used to estimate the subject bond's yield.

LOS 52.f

The effective yield of a bond depends on its periodicity, or annual frequency of coupon payments. For an annual-pay bond the effective yield is equal to the yield-to-maturity. For bonds with greater periodicity, the effective yield is greater than the yield-to-maturity.

A YTM quoted on a semiannual bond basis is two times the semiannual discount rate.

Bond yields that follow street convention use the stated coupon payment dates. A true yield accounts for coupon payments that are delayed by weekends or holidays and may be slightly lower than a street convention yield.

Current yield is the ratio of a bond's annual coupon payments to its price. Simple yield adjusts current yield by using straight-line amortization of any discount or premium.

For a callable bond, a yield-to-call may be calculated using each of its call dates and prices. The lowest of these yields and YTM is a callable bond's yield-to-worst.

Floating rate notes have a *quoted margin* relative to a reference rate, typically LIBOR. The quoted margin is positive for issuers with more credit risk than the banks that quote LIBOR and may be negative for issuers that have less credit risk than loans to these banks. The *required margin* on a floating rate note may be greater than the quoted margin if credit quality has decreased, or less than the quoted margin if credit quality has increased.

For money market instruments, yields may be quoted on a discount basis or an add-on basis, and may use 360-day or 365-day years. A bond-equivalent yield is an add-on yield based on a 365-day year.

LOS 52.g

A yield curve shows the term structure of interest rates by displaying yields across different maturities.

The spot curve is a yield curve for single payments in the future, such as zero-coupon bonds or stripped Treasury bonds.

The par curve shows the coupon rates for bonds of various maturities that would result in bond prices equal to their par values.

A forward curve is a yield curve composed of forward rates, such as 1-year rates available at each year over a future period.

LOS 52.h

Forward rates are current lending/borrowing rates for short-term loans to be made in future periods.

A spot rate for a maturity of N periods is the geometric mean of forward rates over the N periods. The same relation can be used to solve for a forward rate given spot rates for two different periods.

To value a bond using forward rates, discount the cash flows at times 1 through N by the product of one plus each forward rate for periods 1 to N, and sum them.

For a 3-year annual-pay bond:

$$\text{price} = \frac{\text{coupon}}{(1 + S_1)} + \frac{\text{coupon}}{(1 + S_1)(1 + 1y1y)} + \frac{\text{coupon} + \text{principal}}{(1 + S_1)(1 + 1y1y)(1 + 2y1y)}$$

LOS 52.i

A yield spread is the difference between a bond's yield and a benchmark yield or yield curve. If the benchmark is a government bond yield, the spread is known as a government spread or *G*-spread. If the benchmark is a swap rate, the spread is known as an interpolated spread or *I*-spread.

A zero-volatility spread or *Z*-spread is the percent spread that must be added to each spot rate on the benchmark yield curve to make the present value of a bond equal to its price.

An option-adjusted spread or OAS is used for bonds with embedded options. For a callable bond, the OAS is equal to the *Z*-spread minus the call option value in basis points.

ANSWER KEY FOR MODULE QUIZZES

Module Quiz 52.1

1. **B** N = 20; I/Y = 15; FV = 1,000; PMT = 100; CPT → PV = –$687.03. (LOS 52.a)

2. **A** N = 10; I/Y = 7.5; FV = 1,000; PMT = 50; CPT → PV = –$828.40. (LOS 52.a)

3. **A** The price-yield relationship is inverse. If the required yield decreases, the bond's price will increase, and vice versa. (LOS 52.b)

4. **A** With 20 years to maturity, the value of the bond with an annual-pay yield of 6.5% is N = 20, PMT = 50, FV = 1,000, I/Y = 6.5, CPT → PV = –834.72. With N = 17, CPT → PV = –848.34, so the value will increase $13.62. (LOS 52.a, 52.b)

Module Quiz 52.2

1. **A** bond value $= \dfrac{4,000}{1.032} + \dfrac{4,000}{(1.034)^2} + \dfrac{104,000}{(1.035)^3} = \$101,419.28$ (LOS 52.c)

2. **B** The full price includes accrued interest, while the flat price does not. Therefore, the flat (or clean) price is 1,059.04 – 23.54 = $1,035.50. (LOS 52.d)

3. **C** Using linear interpolation, the yield on a bond with six years to maturity should be 6.40% + (1 / 3)(7.20% – 6.40%) = 6.67%. A bond with a 7% coupon and a yield of 6.67% is at a premium to par value. (LOS 52.e)

Module Quiz 52.3

1. **A** A spot rate is a discount rate for a single future payment. Simple yield is a measure of a bond's yield that accounts for coupon interest and assumes straight-line amortization of a discount or premium. A forward rate is an interest rate for a future period, such as a 3-month rate six months from today. (LOS 52.f)

2. **C** N = 30; FV = 1,000; PMT = 0; PV = –331.40; CPT → I/Y = 3.750 × 2 = 7.500%.

   Alternatively, $\left[\left(\dfrac{1,000}{331.4} \right)^{\frac{1}{30}} - 1 \right] \times 2 = 7.5\%$ (LOS 52.f)

3. **C** N = 4; FV = 1,010; PMT = 35.625; PV = –1,023.47; CPT → I/Y = 3.167 × 2 = 6.334%. (LOS 52.f)

4. **B** If the required margin is greater than the quoted margin, the credit quality of the issue has decreased and the price on the reset date will be less than par value. (LOS 52.f)

5. **A** An add-on yield based on a 365-day year is a bond-equivalent yield. (LOS 52.f)

Module Quiz 52.4, 52.5

1. **B** Par bond yield curves are based on the theoretical yields that would cause bonds at each maturity to be priced at par. Coupon bond yields and forward interest rates can be observed directly from market transactions. (Module 52.4, LOS 52.g)

2. **A** $(1.0945)^4 = (1.0985)^3 \times (1 + 3y1y)$

$$3y1y = \frac{(1.0945)^4}{(1.0985)^3} - 1 = 8.258\%$$

Approximate forward rate = $4(9.45\%) - 3(9.85\%) = 8.25\%$. (Module 52.4, LOS 52.h)

3. **B** Bond value $= \dfrac{100}{1.055} + \dfrac{100}{(1.055)(1.0763)} + \dfrac{100}{(1.055)(1.0763)(1.1218)}$

$+ \dfrac{1,000}{(1.055)(1.0763)(1.1218)(1.155)} = 1,009.03$ (Module 52.4, LOS 52.h)

4. **A** *G*-spreads are quoted relative to an actual or interpolated government bond yield. *I*-spreads are quoted relative to swap rates. *Z*-spreads are calculated based on the shape of the benchmark yield curve. (Module 52.5, LOS 52.i)

READING 53

Introduction to Asset-Backed Securities

EXAM FOCUS

In this topic review we introduce asset-backed securities, describing their benefits, legal structure, and characteristics. Our primary focus is residential mortgage-backed securities (RMBS). Candidates should understand the characteristics of mortgage pass-through securities and how and why collateralized mortgage obligations are created from them. Be prepared to compare and contrast agency RMBS, nonagency RMBS, and commercial MBS. Finally, candidates should know why collateralized debt obligations are created and how they differ from the other securitized debt securities covered.

MODULE 53.1: STRUCTURE OF MORTGAGE-BACKED SECURITIES

Video covering this content is available online.

LOS 53.a: Explain benefits of securitization for economies and financial markets.

CFA® Program Curriculum: Volume 5, page 474

Securitization refers to a process by which financial assets (e.g., mortgages, accounts receivable, or automobile loans) are purchased by an entity that then issues securities supported by the cash flows from those financial assets. The primary benefits of the securitization of financial assets are (1) a reduction in funding costs for firms selling the financial assets to the securitizing entity and (2) an increase in the liquidity of the underlying financial assets.

Consider a bank that makes mortgage loans to home buyers and retains and services these loans (i.e., collects the mortgage payments and performs the necessary recordkeeping functions). To gain exposure to a bank's mortgage loans, investors traditionally could only choose among investing in bank deposits, bank debt securities, or the common equity of banks.

Compared to this traditional structure, with the bank serving the function of financial intermediary between borrowers and lenders, securitization can provide the following benefits:

■ Securitization reduces intermediation costs, which results in lower funding costs for borrowers and higher risk-adjusted returns for lenders (investors).

■ With securitization, the investors' legal claim to the mortgages or other loans is stronger than it is with only a general claim against the bank's overall assets.

■ When a bank securitizes its loans, the securities are actively traded, which increases the liquidity of the bank's assets compared to holding the loans.

■ By securitizing loans, banks are able to lend more than if they could only fund loans with bank assets. When a loan portfolio is securitized, the bank receives the proceeds, which can then be used to make more loans.

■ Securitization has led to financial innovation that allows investors to invest in securities that better match their preferred risk, maturity, and return characteristics. As an example, an investor with a long investment horizon can invest in a portfolio of long-term mortgage loans rather than in only bank bonds, deposits, or equities. The investor can gain exposure to long-term mortgages without having the specialized resources and expertise necessary to provide loan origination and loan servicing functions.

■ Securitization provides diversification and risk reduction compared to purchasing individual loans (whole loans).

LOS 53.b: Describe securitization, including the parties involved in the process and the roles they play.

CFA® Program Curriculum: Volume 5, page 476

We can illustrate the basic structure of a *securitization transaction* with this simplified, fictitious example of Fred Motor Company.

Fred Motor Company sells most of its cars on retail sales installment contracts (i.e., auto loans). The customers buy the automobiles, and Fred loans the customers the money for the purchase (i.e., Fred *originates* the loans) with the autos as collateral and receives principal and interest payments on the loans until they mature. The loans have maturities of 48 to 60 months at various interest rates. Fred is also the *servicer* of the loans (i.e., it collects principal and interest payments, sends out delinquency notices, and repossesses and disposes of the autos if the customers do not make timely payments).

Fred has 50,000 auto loans totaling $1 billion that it would like to remove from its balance sheet and use the proceeds to make more auto loans. It accomplishes this by selling the loan portfolio to a **special purpose entity** (SPE) called Auto Loan Trust for $1 billion (Fred is called the *seller*). The SPE, which is set up for the specific purpose of buying these auto loans and selling asset-backed securities (ABS), is referred to as the *trust* or the *issuer*. The SPE then sells ABS to investors. The loan portfolio is the collateral supporting the ABS because the cash flows from the loans are the source of the funds to make the promised payments to investors. An SPE is sometimes also called a special purpose vehicle (SPV). The SPE is a separate legal entity from Fred.

Let's review the parties to this transaction and their functions:

- The seller (Fred) originates the auto loans and sells the portfolio of loans to Auto Loan Trust, the SPE.

- The issuer/trust (Auto Loan Trust) is the SPE that buys the loans from the seller and issues ABS to investors.

- The servicer (Fred) services the loans.

- In this case, the seller and the servicer are the same entity (Fred Motor Company), but that is not always the case.

The structure of this securitization transaction is illustrated in Figure 53.1.

Figure 53.1: Structure of Fred Motor Company Asset Securitization

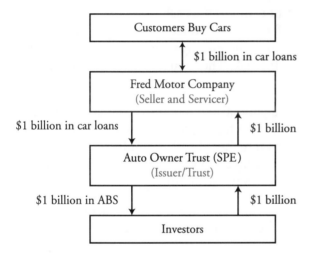

Subsequent to the initial transaction, the principal and interest payments on the original loans are allocated to pay servicing fees to the servicer and principal and interest payments to the owners of the ABS. Often there are several classes of ABS issued by the trust, each with different priority claims to the cash flows from the underlying loans and different specifications of the payments to be received if the cash flows from the loans are not sufficient to pay all the promised ABS cash flows. This flow of funds structure is called a **waterfall structure** because each class of ABS (**tranche**) is paid sequentially, to the extent possible, from the cash flows from the underlying loan portfolio.

ABS are most commonly backed by automobile loans, credit card receivables, home equity loans, manufactured housing loans, student loans, Small Business Administration (SBA) loans, corporate loans, corporate bonds, emerging market bonds, and structured financial products. When the loans owned by the trust (SPE) are mortgages, we refer to the securities issued by the trust as **mortgage-backed securities** (MBS).

Note that the SPE is a separate legal entity from Fred and the buyers of the ABS have no claim on other assets of Fred, only on the loans sold to the SPE. If

Fred had issued corporate bonds to raise the funds to make more auto loans, the bondholders would be subject to the financial risks of Fred. With the ABS structure, a decline in the financial position of Fred, its ability to make cash payments, or its bond rating do not affect the value of the claims of ABS owners to the cash flows from the trust collateral (loan portfolio) because it has been sold by Fred, which is now simply the servicer (not the owner) of the loans. The credit rating of the ABS securities may be higher than the credit rating of bonds issued by Fred, in which case the cost to fund the loans using the ABS structure is lower than if Fred funded additional loans by issuing corporate bonds.

LOS 53.c: Describe typical structures of securitizations, including credit tranching and time tranching.

CFA® Program Curriculum: Volume 5, page 481

Securitizations may involve a single class of ABS so the cash flows to the securities are the same for all security holders. They can also be structured with multiple classes of securities, each with a different claim to the cash flows of the underlying assets. The different classes are often referred to as **tranches**. With this structure, a particular risk of the ABS securities is redistributed across the tranches. Some bear more of the risk and others bear less of the risk. The total risk is unchanged, simply reapportioned.

With **credit tranching**, the ABS tranches will have different exposures to the risk of default of the assets underlying the ABS. With this structure, also called a **senior/subordinated structure**, the subordinated tranches absorb credit losses as they occur (up to their principal values). The level of protection for the senior tranche increases with the proportion of subordinated bonds in the structure.

Let's look at an example to illustrate how a senior/subordinated structure redistributes the credit risk compared to a single-class structure. Consider an ABS with the following bond classes:

Senior Tranche	$300,000,000
Subordinated Tranche A	$80,000,000
Subordinated Tranche B	$30,000,000
Total	$410,000,000

Tranche B is first to absorb any losses (and is termed the *first-loss tranche*) until they exceed $30 million in principal. Any losses from default of the underlying assets greater than $30 million, and up to $110 million, will be absorbed by Subordinated Tranche A. The Senior Tranche is protected from any credit losses of $110 million or less and therefore will have the highest credit rating and offer the lowest yield of the three bond classes. This structure is also called a **waterfall** structure because in liquidation, each subordinated tranche would receive only the "overflow" from the more senior tranche(s) if they are repaid their principal value in full.

With **time tranching**, the first (sequential) tranche receives all principal repayments from the underlying assets up to the principal value of the tranche. The second tranche would then receive all principal repayments from the underlying assets until the principal value of this tranche is paid off. There may be other tranches with sequential claims to remaining principal repayments. Both credit tranching and time tranching are often included in the same structure. More detail about time tranching and the related planned amortization/support tranche structure is included later in this review when we discuss the structures of mortgage-backed securities.

LOS 53.d: Describe types and characteristics of residential mortgage loans that are typically securitized.

CFA® Program Curriculum: Volume 5, page 485

A **residential mortgage loan** is a loan for which the collateral that underlies the loan is residential real estate. If the borrower defaults on the loan, the lender has a legal claim to the collateral property. One key characteristic of a mortgage loan is its **loan-to-value ratio** (LTV), the percentage of the value of the collateral real estate that is loaned to the borrower. The lower the LTV, the higher the borrower's equity in the property.

For a lender, loans with lower LTVs are less risky because the borrower has more to lose in the event of default (so is less likely to default). Also, if the property value is high compared to the loan amount, the lender is more likely to recover the amount loaned if the borrower defaults and the lender repossesses and sells the property. In the United States, mortgages with higher LTV ratios, made to borrowers with good credit, are termed *prime loans*. Mortgages to borrowers of lower credit quality, or that have a lower-priority claim to the collateral in event of default, are termed *subprime loans*.

Typical mortgage terms and structures differ across regions and countries. The key characteristics of mortgage loans include their maturity, the determination of interest charges, how the loan principal is amortized, the terms under which prepayments of loan principal are allowed, and the rights of the lender in the event of default by the borrower. We address each of the characteristics is more detail.

Maturity

The term of a mortgage loan is the time until the final loan payment is made. In the United States, mortgage loans typically have terms from 15 to 30 years. Terms are longer, 20 to 40 years, in many European countries and as long as 50 years in others. In Japan, mortgage loans may have terms of 100 years.

Interest Rate

A **fixed-rate mortgage** has an interest rate that is unchanged over the life of the mortgage.

An **adjustable-rate mortgage** (ARM), also called a **variable-rate mortgage**, has an interest rate that can change over the life of the mortgage. An **index-referenced mortgage** has an interest rate that changes based on a market determined reference rate such as LIBOR or the one-year U.S. Treasury bill rate, although several other reference rates are used.

A mortgage loan may have an interest rate that is fixed for some initial period, but adjusted after that. If the loan becomes an adjustable-rate mortgage after the initial fixed-rate period it is called a *hybrid mortgage*. If the interest rate changes to a different fixed rate after the initial fixed-rate period it is called a *rollover* or *renegotiable mortgage*.

A **convertible mortgage** is one for which the initial interest rate terms, fixed or adjustable, can be changed at the option of the borrower, to adjustable or fixed, for the remaining loan period.

Amortization of Principal

With a **fully amortizing** loan, each payment includes both an interest payment and a repayment of some of the loan principal so there is no loan principal remaining after the last regular mortgage payment. When payments are fixed for the life of the loan, payments in the beginning of the loan term have a large interest component and a small principal repayment component, and payments at the end of the loan terms have a small interest component and large principal repayment component.

A loan is said to be **partially amortizing** when loan payments include some repayment of principal, but there is a lump sum of principal that remains to be paid at the end of the loan period which is called a *balloon payment*. With an **interest-only mortgage**, there is no principal repayment for either an initial period or the life of the loan. If no principal is paid for the life of the loan it is an *interest-only lifetime* mortgage and the balloon payment is the original loan principal amount. Other interest-only mortgages specify that payments are interest-only over some initial period, with partial or full amortization of principal after that.

Prepayment Provisions

A partial or full repayment of principal in excess of the scheduled principal repayments required by the mortgage is referred to as a **prepayment**. If a homeowner sells her home during the mortgage term (a common occurrence), repaying the remaining principal is required and is one type of prepayment. A homeowner who *refinances* her mortgage prepays the remaining principal amount using the proceeds of a new, lower interest rate loan. Some homeowners prepay by paying more than their scheduled payments in order to reduce the principal outstanding, reduce their interest charges, and eventually pay off their loans prior to maturity.

Some loans have no penalty for prepayment of principal while others have a **prepayment penalty**. A prepayment penalty is an additional payment that must be made if principal is prepaid during an initial period after loan origination or, for some mortgages, prepaid anytime during the life of the mortgage. A prepayment penalty benefits the lender by providing compensation when the loan is paid off early because market interest rates have decreased since the mortgage loan was made (i.e., loans are refinanced at a lower interest rate).

Foreclosure

Some mortgage loans are **nonrecourse loans**, which means the lender has no claim against the assets of the borrower except for the collateral property itself. When this is the case, if home values fall so the outstanding loan principal is greater than the home value, borrowers sometimes voluntarily return the property to the lender in what is called a *strategic default*.

Other mortgage loans are **recourse loans** under which the lender has a claim against the borrower for the amount by which the sale of a repossessed collateral property falls short of the principal outstanding on the loan. Understandably, borrowers are more likely to default on nonrecourse loans than on recourse loans. In Europe, most residential mortgages are recourse loans. In the United States, they are recourse loans in some states and nonrecourse in others.

LOS 53.e: Describe types and characteristics of residential mortgage-backed securities, including mortgage pass-through securities and collateralized mortgage obligations, and explain the cash flows and risks for each type.

LOS 53.f: Define prepayment risk and describe the prepayment risk of mortgage-backed securities.

CFA® Program Curriculum: Volume 5, page 490

Residential mortgage-backed securities (RMBS) in the United States are termed **agency RMBS** or **nonagency RMBS**, depending on the issuer of the securities. Agency RMBS are issued by the Government National Mortgage Association (GNMA or Ginnie Mae), the Federal National Mortgage Association (Fannie Mae), and the Federal Home Loan Mortgage Corporation (Freddie Mac). Ginnie Mae securities are guaranteed by the GNMA and are considered to be backed by the full faith and credit of the U.S. government. Fannie Mae and Freddie Mac also guarantee the MBS they issue but are *government-sponsored enterprises* (GSE). While they are not considered to be backed by the full faith and credit of the U.S. government, these securities are considered to have very high credit quality.

Agency RMBS are **mortgage pass-through securities**. Each mortgage pass-through security represents a claim on the cash flows from a pool of mortgages. Any number of mortgages may be used to form the pool, and any mortgage included in the pool is referred to as a **securitized mortgage**. The mortgages in the pool typically have different maturities and different mortgage rates. The **weighted average maturity** (WAM) of the pool is equal to the weighted average of the final maturities of all the mortgages in the pool, weighted by each mortgage's outstanding principal balance as a proportion of the total outstanding principal value of all the mortgages in the pool. The **weighted average coupon** (WAC) of the pool is the weighted average of the interest rates of all the mortgages in the pool. The investment characteristics of mortgage pass-through securities are a function of their cash flow features and the strength of the guarantee provided.

In order to be included in agency MBS pools, loans must meet certain criteria, including a minimum percentage down payment, a maximum LTV ratio, maximum size, minimum documentation required, and insurance purchased by the borrower.

Loans that meet the standards for inclusion in agency MBS are called *conforming loans*. Loans that do not meet the standards are called *nonconforming* loans. Nonconforming mortgages can be securitized by private companies for *nonagency RMBS*.

Investors in mortgage pass-through securities receive the monthly cash flows generated by the underlying pool of mortgages, less any servicing and guarantee/insurance fees. The fees account for the fact that **pass-through rates** (i.e., the coupon rate on the MBS, also called its *net interest* or *net coupon*) are less than the mortgage rate of the underlying mortgages in the pool.

Figure 53.2: Mortgage Pass-Through Cash Flow

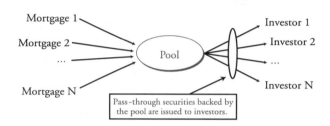

The timing of the cash flows to pass-through security holders does not exactly coincide with the cash flows generated by the pool. This is due to the delay between the time the mortgage service provider receives the mortgage payments and the time the cash flows are *passed through* to the security holders.

 MODULE QUIZ 53.1

To best evaluate your performance, enter your quiz answers online.

1. Economic benefits of securitization *least likely* include:
   A. reducing excessive lending by banks.
   B. reducing funding costs for firms that securitize assets.
   C. increasing the liquidity of the underlying financial assets.

2. In a securitization, the issuer of asset-backed securities is *best* described as:
   A. the SPE.
   B. the seller.
   C. the servicer.

3. A mortgage-backed security with a senior/subordinated structure is said to feature:
   A. time tranching.
   B. credit tranching.
   C. a pass-through structure.

4. A mortgage that has a balloon payment equal to the original loan principal is:
   A. a convertible mortgage.
   B. a fully amortizing mortgage.
   C. an interest-only lifetime mortgage.

5. Residential mortgages that may be included in agency RMBS are *least likely* required to have:
    A. a minimum loan-to-value ratio.
    B. insurance on the mortgaged property.
    C. a minimum percentage down payment.

6. The primary motivation for issuing collateralized mortgage obligations (CMOs) is to reduce:
    A. extension risk.
    B. funding costs.
    C. contraction risk.

MODULE 53.2: PREPAYMENT RISK AND NON-MORTGAGE-BACKED ABS

Video covering this content is available online.

Prepayment Risk

An important characteristic of pass-through securities is their **prepayment risk.** Because the mortgage loans used as collateral for agency MBS have no prepayment penalty, the MBS themselves have significant prepayment risk. Recall that prepayments are principal repayments in excess of the scheduled principal repayments for amortizing loans. The risk that prepayments will be slower than expected is called *extension risk* and the risk that prepayments will be more rapid than expected is called *contraction risk.*

Prepayments cause the timing and amount of cash flows from mortgage loans and MBS to be uncertain; rapid prepayment reduces the amount of principal outstanding on the loans supporting the MBS so the total interest paid over the life of the MBS is reduced. Because of this, it is necessary to make specific assumptions about prepayment rates in order to value mortgage pass-through securities. The single monthly mortality rate (SMM) is the percentage by which prepayments reduce the month-end principal balance, compared to what it would have been with only scheduled principal payments (with no prepayments). The **conditional prepayment rate** (CPR) is an annualized measure of prepayments. Prepayment rates depend on the weighted average coupon rate of the loan pool, current interest rates, and prior prepayments of principal.

The Public Securities Association (PSA) *prepayment benchmark* assumes that the monthly prepayment rate for a mortgage pool increases as it ages (becomes *seasoned*). The PSA benchmark is expressed as a monthly series of CPRs. If the prepayment rate (CPR) of an MBS is expected to be the same as the PSA standard benchmark CPR, we say the PSA is 100 (100% of the benchmark CPR). A pool of mortgages may have prepayment rates that are faster or slower than PSA 100, depending on the current level of interest rates and the coupon rate of the issue. A PSA of 50 means that prepayments are 50% of the PSA benchmark CPR, and a PSA of 130 means that prepayments are 130% of the PSA benchmark CPR.

Based on an assumption about the prepayment rate for an MBS, we can calculate its weighted average life, or simply average life, which is the expected number of years until all the loan principal is repaid. Because of prepayments, the average life of an MBS will be less than its weighted average maturity. During periods of falling interest rates, the refinancing of mortgage loans will accelerate prepayments and reduce the average life of an MBS. A high PSA, such as 400, will reduce the average life of an MBS to only 4.5 years, compared to an average life of about 11 years for an MBS with a PSA of 100.

Collateralized Mortgage Obligations

Collateralized mortgage obligations (CMO) are securities that are collateralized by RMBS. Each CMO has multiple bond classes (CMO tranches) that have different exposures to prepayment risk. The total prepayment risk of the underlying RMBS is not changed; the prepayment risk is simply reapportioned among the various CMO tranches.

Institutional investors have different tolerances for prepayment risk. Some are primarily concerned with extension risk while others may want to minimize exposure to contraction risk. By partitioning and distributing the cash flows generated by RMBS into different risk packages to better match investor preferences, CMOs increase the potential market for securitized mortgages and perhaps reduce funding costs as a result.

CMOs are securities backed by mortgage pass-through securities (i.e., they are securities secured by other securities). Interest and principal payments from the mortgage pass-through securities are allocated in a specific way to different bond classes called tranches, so that each tranche has a different claim against the cash flows of the mortgage pass-throughs. Each CMO tranche has a different mixture of contraction and extension risk. Hence, CMO securities can be more closely matched to the unique asset/liability needs of institutional investors and investment managers.

The primary CMO structures include sequential-pay tranches, planned amortization class tranches (PACs), support tranches, and floating-rate tranches.

Sequential Pay CMO

One way to reapportion the prepayment risk inherent in the underlying pass-through MBS is to separate the cash flows into tranches that are retired sequentially (i.e., create a **sequential pay CMO**). As an example of this structure, we consider a simple CMO with two tranches. Both tranches receive interest payments at a specified coupon rate, but all principal payments (both scheduled payments and prepayments) are paid to Tranche 1 (the *short tranche*) until its principal is paid off. Principal payments then flow to Tranche 2 until its principal is paid off.

Contraction and extension risk still exist with this structure, but they have been redistributed to some extent between the two tranches. The short tranche, which matures first, offers investors relatively more protection against extension risk. The other tranche provides relatively more protection against contraction risk. Let's expand this example with some specific numbers to illustrate how sequential pay structures work.

Consider the simplified CMO structure presented in Figure 53.3. Payments to the two sequential-pay tranches are made first to Tranche A and then to Tranche B.

Figure 53.3: Sequential Pay CMO Structure

| Tranche | CMO Structure | |
	Outstanding Par Value	Coupon Rate
A	$200,000,000	8.50%
B	50,000,000	8.50%

Payments from the underlying collateral (which has a pass-through coupon rate of 8.5%) for the first five months, as well as months 183 through 187, are shown in Figure 53.4. These payments include scheduled payments plus estimated prepayments based on an assumed prepayment rate. (Note that some totals do not match due to rounding.)

Figure 53.4: CMO Projected Cash Flows

Month	Beginning Principal Balance	Principal Payment	Interest	Total Cash Flow = Principal Plus Interest
1	$250,000,000	$391,128	$1,770,833	$2,161,961
2	249,608,872	454,790	1,768,063	2,222,853
3	249,154,082	518,304	1,764,841	2,283,145
4	248,635,778	581,620	1,761,170	2,342,790
5	248,054,157	644,690	1,757,050	2,401,741
183	$51,491,678	$545,153	$364,733	$909,886
184	50,946,525	540,831	360,871	901,702
185	50,405,694	536,542	357,040	893,582
186	49,869,152	532,287	353,240	885,526
187	49,336,866	528,065	349,469	877,534

PROFESSOR'S NOTE

This example is provided as an illustration of how cash flows are allocated to sequential tranches. The LOS does not require you to do the calculations that underlie the numbers in Figure 53.4. The important point here is how the cash flows are allocated to each tranche.

Planned Amortization Class (PAC) CMO

Another CMO structure has one or more **planned amortization class** (PAC) tranches and **support tranches**. A PAC tranche is structured to make predictable payments, regardless of actual prepayments to the underlying MBS. The PAC tranches have both reduced contraction risk and reduced extension risk compared to the underlying MBS.

Reducing the prepayment risk of the PAC tranches is achieved by increasing the prepayment risk of the CMO's support tranches. If principal repayments are more rapid than expected, the support tranche receives the principal repayments in excess of those specifically allocated to the PAC tranches. Conversely, if the actual principal repayments are slower than expected, principal repayments to the support tranche are curtailed so the scheduled PAC payments can be made. The larger the support tranche(s) relative to the PAC tranches, the smaller the probability that the cash flows to the PAC tranches will differ from their scheduled payments.

For a given CMO structure there are limits to how fast or slow actual prepayment experience can be before the support tranches can no longer either provide or absorb prepayments in the amounts required to keep the PAC payments to their scheduled amounts. The upper and lower bounds on the actual prepayment rates for which the support tranches are sufficient to either provide or absorb actual prepayments in order to keep the PAC principal repayments on schedule are called the **initial PAC collar**.

A PAC may have an initial collar given as 100 – 300 PSA. This means the PAC will make its scheduled payments to investors unless actual prepayment experience is outside these bounds (i.e., above 300 PSA or below 100 PSA). If the prepayment rate is outside of these bounds so payments to a PAC tranche are either sooner or later than promised, the PAC tranche is referred to as a **broken PAC**.

Support tranches have both more contraction risk and more extension risk than the underlying MBS and have a higher promised interest rate than the PAC tranche.

As an example, Figure 53.5 shows the average life for a hypothetical structure that includes a PAC I tranche and a support tranche at various PSA speeds, assuming the PSA speed stays at that level for the entire life of the PAC tranche.

Figure 53.5: Average Life Variability of PAC I Tranche vs. Support Tranche

PSA Speed	PAC I Tranche		Support Tranche
0	13.2		24.0
50	8.8		21.1
100	6.5	↑	17.1
150	6.5		13.3
200	6.5	Initial Collar	10.4
250	6.5	↓	5.2
300	6.5		2.9
350	5.9		2.4
400	5.4		1.8
450	4.6		1.5
500	4.2		1.2

Figure 53.5 illustrates that the PAC I tranche has less prepayment risk than the support tranche because the variability of its average life is significantly lower.

- When prepayment speeds fall and prepayments decrease, the support tranche average life is significantly longer than the average life of the PAC I tranche. Thus, the support tranche has significantly more extension risk.

- When prepayment speeds rise and prepayments increase, the support tranche average life is much shorter than that of the PAC I tranche. Thus, the support tranche also has significantly more contraction risk.

- Within the initial PAC collar of 100 to 300 PSA, the average life of the PAC I tranche is constant at 6.5 years.

Nonagency RMBS

RMBS not issued by GNMA, Fannie Mae, or Freddie Mac are referred to as **nonagency RMBS**. They are not guaranteed by the government, so credit risk is an important consideration. The credit quality of a nonagency MBS depends on the credit quality of the borrowers as well as the characteristics of the loans, such as their LTV ratios. To be investment grade, most nonagency RMBS include some sort of **credit enhancement**. The level of credit enhancement is directly proportional to the credit rating desired by the issuer. Rating agencies determine the exact amount of credit enhancement necessary for an issue to hold a specific rating.

Credit tranching (subordination) is often used to enhance the credit quality of senior RMBS securities. A **shifting interest mechanism** is a method for addressing a decrease in the level of credit protection provided by junior tranches as prepayments or defaults occur in a senior/subordinated structure. If prepayments or credit losses decrease the credit enhancement of the senior securities, the shifting interest mechanism suspends payments to the subordinated securities for a period of time until the credit quality of the senior securities is restored.

LOS 53.g: Describe characteristics and risks of commercial mortgage-backed securities.

CFA® Program Curriculum: Volume 5, page 503

Commercial mortgage-backed securities (CMBS) are backed by income-producing real estate, typically in the form of:

- Apartments (multi-family).
- Warehouses (industrial use property).
- Shopping centers.
- Office buildings.
- Health care facilities.
- Senior housing.
- Hotel/resort properties.

An important difference between residential and commercial MBS is the obligations of the borrowers of the underlying loans. Residential MBS loans are repaid by homeowners; commercial MBS loans are repaid by real estate investors who, in turn, rely on tenants and customers to provide the cash flow to repay the mortgage loan. CMBS mortgages are structured as **nonrecourse loans**, meaning the lender can *only* look to the collateral as a means to repay a delinquent loan if the cash flows from the property are insufficient. In contrast, a residential mortgage lender with recourse can go back to the borrower personally in an attempt to collect any excess of the loan amount above the net proceeds from foreclosing on and selling the property.

For these reasons, the analysis of CMBS securities focuses on the credit risk of the property and not the credit risk of the borrower. The analysis of CMBS structures focuses on two key ratios to assess credit risk.

1. **Debt-to-service-coverage ratio (DSC)** is a basic cash flow coverage ratio of the amount of cash flow from a commercial property available to make debt service payments compared to the required debt service cost.

$$\text{debt-to-service coverage ratio} = \frac{\text{net operating income}}{\text{debt service}}$$

   Net operating income (NOI) is calculated after the deduction for real estate taxes but before any relevant income taxes. This ratio, which is typically between one and two, indicates greater protection to the lender when it is higher. Debt service coverage ratios below one indicate that the borrower is not generating sufficient cash flow to make the debt payments and is likely to default. Remember: *the higher the better* for this ratio from the perspective of the lender and the MBS investor.

2. **Loan-to-value ratio** compares the loan amount on the property to its current fair market or appraisal value.

$$\text{loan-to-value ratio} = \frac{\text{current mortgage amount}}{\text{current appraised value}}$$

   The lower this ratio, the more protection the mortgage lender has in making the loan. Loan-to-value ratios determine the amount of collateral available, above the loan amount, to provide a cushion to the lender should the property be foreclosed on and sold. Remember: *the lower the better* for this ratio from the perspective of the lender and the MBS investor.

The basic **CMBS structure** is created to meet the risk and return needs of the CMBS investor. As with residential MBS securities, rating organizations such as S&P and Moody's assess the credit risk of each CMBS issue and determine the appropriate credit rating. Each CMBS is segregated into tranches. Losses due to default are first absorbed by the tranche with the lowest priority. Sometimes this most-junior tranche is not rated and is then referred to as the equity tranche, residual tranche, or first-loss tranche.

As with any fixed-rate security, call protection is valuable to the bondholder. In the case of MBS, call protection is equivalent to prepayment protection (i.e., restrictions on the early return of principal through prepayments). CMBS provide call protection in two ways: loan-level call protection provided by the terms of the individual mortgages and call protection provided by the CMBS structure.

There are several means of creating **loan-level call protection:**

- *Prepayment lockout.* For a specific period of time (typically two to five years), the borrower is prohibited from prepaying the mortgage loan.

- *Defeasance.* Should the borrower insist on making principal payments on the mortgage loan, the mortgage loan can be defeased. This is accomplished by using the prepaid principal to purchase a portfolio of government securities that is sufficient to make the remaining required payments on the CMBS. Given the high credit quality of government securities, defeased loans increase the credit quality of a CMBS loan pool.

- *Prepayment penalty points.* A penalty fee expressed in points may be charged to borrowers who prepay mortgage principal. Each point is 1% of the principal amount prepaid.

- *Yield maintenance charges.* The borrower is charged the amount of interest lost by the lender should the loan be prepaid. This *make whole* charge is designed to make lenders indifferent to prepayment, as cash flows are equivalent (at current market rates) whether the loan is prepaid or not.

With all loan call protection programs, any prepayment penalties received are distributed to the CMBS investors in a manner determined by the structure of the CMBS issue.

To create **CMBS-level call protection**, CMBS loan pools are segregated into tranches with a specific sequence of repayment. Those tranches with a higher priority will have a higher credit rating than lower priority tranches because loan defaults will first affect the lower tranches. A wide variety of features can be used to provide call protection to the more senior tranches of the CMBS.

Commercial mortgages are typically amortized over a period longer than the loan term; for example, payments for a 20-year commercial mortgage may be determined based on a 30-year amortization schedule. At the end of the loan term, the loan will still have principal outstanding that needs to be paid; this amount is called a **balloon payment**. If the borrower is unable to arrange refinancing to make this payment, the borrower is in default. This possibility is called balloon risk. The lender will be forced to extend the term of the loan during a workout period, during which time the borrower will be charged a higher interest rate. Because balloon risk entails extending the term of the loan, it is also referred to as extension risk for CMBS.

LOS 53.h: Describe types and characteristics of non-mortgage asset-backed securities, including the cash flows and risks of each type.

CFA® Program Curriculum: Volume 5, page 508

In addition to those backed by mortgages, there are ABS that are backed by various types of financial assets including small business loans, accounts receivable, credit card receivables, automobile loans, home equity loans, and manufactured housing loans. Each of these types of ABS has different risk characteristics and their structures vary to some extent as well. Here we explain the characteristics of two types, ABS backed by automobile loans and ABS backed by credit card receivables. These two have an important difference in that automobile loans are fully amortizing while credit card receivables are nonamortizing.

Auto Loan ABS

Auto loan-backed securities are backed by loans for automobiles. Auto loans have maturities from 36 to 72 months. Issuers include the financial subsidiaries of auto manufacturers, commercial banks, credit unions, finance companies, and other small financial institutions.

The cash flow components of auto loan-backed securities include interest payments, scheduled principal payments, and prepayments. Auto loans prepay if the cars are sold, traded in, or repossessed. Prepayments also occur if the car is stolen or wrecked and the loan is paid off from insurance proceeds. Finally, the borrower may simply use excess cash to reduce or pay off the loan balance.

Automobile loan ABS all have some sort of credit enhancement to make them attractive to institutional investors. Many have a senior-subordinated structure, with a junior tranche that absorbs credit risk. One or more internal credit enhancement methods, a reserve account, an excess interest spread, or overcollateralization, is also often present in these structures. Just as with mortgages, prime loans refer to those made to borrowers with higher credit ratings and sub-prime loans refers to those made to borrowers with low credit ratings.

Credit Card ABS

Credit card receivable-backed securities are ABS backed by pools of credit card debt owed to banks, retailers, travel and entertainment companies, and other credit card issuers.

The cash flow to a pool of credit card receivables includes finance charges, annual fees, and principal repayments. Credit cards have periodic payment schedules, but because their balances are revolving (i.e., nonamortizing), the principal amount is maintained for a period of time. Interest on credit card ABS is paid periodically, but no principal is paid to the ABS holders during the **lockout period**, which may last from 18 months to 10 years after the ABS are created.

If the underlying credit card holders make principal payments during the lockout period, these payments are used to purchase additional credit card receivables, keeping the overall value of the receivables pool relatively constant. Once the lockout period ends, principal payments are passed through to security holders. Credit card ABS typically have an early (rapid) amortization provision that provides for earlier amortization of principal when it is necessary to preserve the credit quality of the securities.

Interest rates on credit card ABS are sometimes fixed but often they are floating. Interest payments may be monthly, quarterly, or for longer periods.

LOS 53.i: Describe collateralized debt obligations, including their cash flows and risks.

CFA® Program Curriculum: Volume 5, page 512

A **collateralized debt obligation** (CDO) is a structured security issued by an SPE for which the collateral is a pool of debt obligations. When the collateral securities are corporate and emerging market debt, they are called *collateralized bond obligations* (CBO). *Collateralized loan obligations* (CLO) are supported by a portfolio of leveraged bank loans. Unlike the ABS we have discussed, CDOs do not rely on interest payments from the collateral pool. CDOs have a **collateral manager** who buys and sells securities in the collateral pool in order to generate the cash to make the promised payments to investors.

Structured finance CDOs are those where the collateral is ABS, RMBS, other CDOs, and CMBS.

Synthetic CDOs are those where the collateral is a portfolio of credit default swaps on structured securities.

PROFESSOR'S NOTE

Credit default swaps are derivative securities that decrease (increase) in value as the credit quality of their reference securities increases (decreases).

CDOs issue three classes of bonds (tranches): senior bonds, mezzanine bonds, and subordinated bonds (sometimes called the equity or residual tranche). The subordinated tranche has characteristics more similar to those of equity investments than bond investments. In creating a CDO, the structure must be able to offer an attractive return on the subordinated tranche, after accounting for the required yields on the senior and mezzanine bond classes.

An investment in the equity or residual tranche can be viewed as a leveraged investment where borrowed funds (raised from selling the senior and mezzanine tranches) are used to purchase the debt securities in the CDO's collateral pool. To the extent the collateral manager meets his goal of earning returns in excess of borrowing costs (the promised return to CDO investors), these excess returns are paid to the CDO manager and the equity tranche.

The CDO structure typically is to issue a floating-rate senior tranche that is 70%–80% of the total and a smaller mezzanine tranche that pays a fixed rate of interest. If the securities in the collateral pool pay a fixed rate of interest, the collateral manager may enter into an interest rate swap that pays a floating rate of interest in exchange for a fixed rate of interest in order to make the collateral yield more closely match the funding costs in an environment of changing interest rates. The term *arbitrage CDO* is used for CDOs structured to earn returns from the spread between funding costs and portfolio returns.

The collateral manager may use interest earned on portfolio securities, cash from maturing portfolio securities, and cash from the sale of portfolio securities to cover the promised payments to holders of the CDOs senior and mezzanine bonds.

MODULE QUIZ 53.2

To best evaluate your performance, enter your quiz answers online.

1. The risk that mortgage prepayments will occur more slowly than expected is *best* characterized as:
   A. default risk.
   B. extension risk.
   C. contraction risk.

2. For investors in commercial mortgage-backed securities, balloon risk in commercial mortgages results in:
   A. call risk.
   B. extension risk.
   C. contraction risk.

3. During the lockout period of a credit card ABS:
   A. no new receivables are added to the pool.
   B. investors do not receive interest payments.
   C. investors do not receive principal payments.

4. A debt security that is collateralized by a pool of the sovereign debt of several developing countries is *most likely*:
   A. a CMBS.
   B. a CDO.
   C. a CMO.

KEY CONCEPTS

LOS 53.a

The primary benefits of the securitization of financial assets are:

■ Reduce the funding costs for firms selling the financial assets to the securitizing entity.

■ Increase the liquidity of the underlying financial assets.

LOS 53.b

Parties to a securitization are a seller of financial assets, a special purpose entity (SPE), and a servicer.

■ The seller is the firm that is raising funds through the securitization.

■ An SPE is an entity independent of the seller. The SPE buys financial assets from the seller and issues asset-backed securities (ABS) supported by these financial assets.

■ The servicer carries out collections and other responsibilities related to the financial assets. The servicer may be the same entity as the seller but does not have to be.

The SPE may issue a single class of ABS or multiple classes with different priorities of claims to cash flows from the pool of financial assets.

LOS 53.c

Asset-backed securities (ABS) can be a single class of securities or multiple classes with differing claims to the cash flows from the underlying assets. Time tranching refers to classes that receive the principal payments from underlying securities sequentially as each prior tranche is repaid in full. With credit tranching, any credit losses are first absorbed by the tranche with the lowest priority, and after that by any other subordinated tranches, in order. Some structures have both time tranching and credit tranching.

LOS 53.d

Characteristics of residential mortgage loans include:

■ Maturity.

■ Interest rate: fixed-rate, adjustable-rate, or convertible.

■ Amortization: full, partial, or interest-only.

■ Prepayment penalties.

■ Foreclosure provisions: recourse or nonrecourse.

The loan-to-value (LTV) ratio indicates the percentage of the value of the real estate collateral that is loaned. Lower LTVs indicate less credit risk.

LOS 53.e

Agency residential mortgage-backed securities (RMBS) are guaranteed and issued by GNMA, Fannie Mae, or Freddie Mac. Mortgages that back agency RMBS must be conforming loans that meet certain minimum credit quality standards. Nonagency RMBS are issued by private companies and may be backed by nonconforming mortgages.

Key characteristics of RMBS include:

- Pass-through rate, the coupon rate on the RMBS.

- Weighted average maturity (WAM) and weighted average coupon (WAC) of the underlying pool of mortgages.

- Conditional prepayment rate (CPR), which may be compared to the Public Securities Administration (PSA) benchmark for expected prepayment rates.

Nonagency RMBS typically include credit enhancement. External credit enhancement is a third-party guarantee. Internal credit enhancement includes reserve funds (cash or excess spread), overcollateralization, and senior/subordinated structures.

Collateralized mortgage obligations (CMOs) are collateralized by pools of residential MBS. CMOs are structured with tranches that have different exposures to prepayment risks.

In a sequential-pay CMO, all scheduled principal payments and prepayments are paid to each tranche in sequence until that tranche is paid off. The first tranche to be paid principal has the most contraction risk and the last tranche to be paid principal has the most extension risk.

A planned amortization class (PAC) CMO has PAC tranches that receive predictable cash flows as long as the prepayment rate remains within a predetermined range, and support tranches that have more contraction risk and more extension risk than the PAC tranches.

LOS 53.f

Prepayment risk refers to uncertainty about the timing of the principal cash flows from an ABS. Contraction risk is the risk that loan principal will be repaid more rapidly than expected, typically when interest rates have decreased. Extension risk is the risk that loan principal will be repaid more slowly than expected, typically when interest rates have increased.

LOS 53.g

Commercial mortgage-backed securities (CMBS) are backed by mortgages on income-producing real estate properties. Because commercial mortgages are nonrecourse loans, analysis of CMBS focuses on credit risk of the properties. CMBS are structured in tranches with credit losses absorbed by the lowest priority tranches in sequence.

Call (prepayment) protection in CMBS includes loan-level call protection such as prepayment lockout periods, defeasance, prepayment penalty points, and yield maintenance charges, and CMBS-level call protection provided by the lower-priority tranches.

Study Session 16
Cross-Reference to CFA Institute Assigned Reading #53 – Introduction to Asset-Backed Securities

Study Session 16

LOS 53.h

Asset-backed securities may be backed by financial assets other than mortgages. Two examples are auto loan ABS and credit card ABS.

Auto loan ABS are backed by automobile loans, which are typically fully amortizing but with shorter maturities than residential mortgages. Prepayments result when autos are sold or traded in, stolen or wrecked and paid off from insurance proceeds, refinanced, or paid off from the borrower's excess cash.

Credit card ABS are backed by credit card receivables, which are revolving debt (nonamortizing). Credit card ABS typically have a lockout period during which only interest is paid to investors and principal payments on the receivables are used to purchase additional receivables.

LOS 53.i

Collateralized debt obligations (CDOs) are structured securities backed by a pool of debt obligations that is managed by a collateral manager. CDOs include:

- Collateralized bond obligations (CBOs) backed by corporate and emerging market debt.
- Collateralized loan obligations (CLOs) backed by leveraged bank loans.
- Structured finance CDOs backed by residential or commercial MBS, ABS, or other CLOs.
- Synthetic CDOs backed by credit default swaps on structured securities.

ANSWER KEY FOR MODULE QUIZZES

Module Quiz 53.1

1. **A** Banks that securitize loans they hold as assets receive cash with which they can make additional loans. The primary benefits of securitization to the economy include reducing firms' funding costs and increasing the liquidity of the financial assets that are securitized. (LOS 53.a)

2. **A** ABS are issued by a special purpose entity (SPE), which is an entity created for that specific purpose. In a securitization, the firm that is securitizing financial assets is described as the seller because it sells the assets to the SPE. The servicer is the entity that deals with collections on the securitized assets. (LOS 53.b)

3. **B** Senior and subordinated tranches are characteristics of a mortgage-backed security with credit tranching. (LOS 53.c)

4. **C** An interest-only lifetime mortgage includes no repayment of principal in its monthly payments so the balloon payment at maturity is equal to the original loan principal. A fully amortizing mortgage has no balloon payment at maturity. A convertible mortgage gives the borrower an option to change the loan from fixed-rate to adjustable-rate or from adjustable-rate to fixed-rate. (LOS 53.d)

5. **A** Conforming loans that may be securitized in agency RMBS have a *maximum* loan-to-value ratio, along with other requirements such as minimum percentage down payments and insurance on the mortgaged property. (LOS 53.e)

6. **B** Issuing CMOs may allow the issuer to raise funds at a lower cost by creating tranches that appeal to investors with different preferences for extension risk and contraction risk. CMOs do not reduce these risks compared to their pool of collateral; they only distribute the risks among the various CMO tranches. (LOS 53.e)

Module Quiz 53.2

1. **B** Extension risk is the risk that prepayments will be slower than expected. Contraction risk is the risk that prepayments will be faster than expected. (LOS 53.e, 53.f)

2. **B** Balloon risk is the possibility that a commercial mortgage borrower will not be able to refinance the principal that is due at the maturity date of the mortgage. This results in a default that is typically resolved by extending the term of the loan during a workout period. Thus, balloon risk is a source of extension risk for CMBS investors. (LOS 53.g)

3. **C**   During the lockout period on a credit card receivables-backed ABS, no principal payments are made to investors. (LOS 53.h)

4. **B**   A collateralized debt obligation (CDO) is backed by an underlying pool of debt securities, which may include emerging markets debt. Both collateralized mortgage obligations and commercial mortgage-backed securities are backed by mortgages only. (LOS 53.i)

READING 54

Understanding Fixed-Income Risk and Return

EXAM FOCUS

"Risk" in the title of this topic review refers primarily to risk arising from uncertainty about future interest rates. Measurement of credit risk is addressed in the following topic review. That said, there is a significant amount of testable material covered in this review. Calculations required by the learning outcomes include the sources of bond returns, three duration measures, money duration, the price value of a basis point, and approximate convexity. You must also be able to estimate a bond's price change for a given change in yield based on its duration and convexity. Important concepts include how bond characteristics affect interest rate risk, factors that affect a bond's reinvestment risk, and the interaction among price risk, reinvestment risk, and the investment horizon.

MODULE 54.1: SOURCES OF RETURNS, DURATION

Video covering this content is available online.

LOS 54.a: Calculate and interpret the sources of return from investing in a fixed-rate bond.

CFA® Program Curriculum: Volume 5, page 530

There are **three sources of returns** from investing in a fixed-rate bond:

1. Coupon and principal payments.

2. Interest earned on coupon payments that are reinvested over the investor's holding period for the bond.

3. Any capital gain or loss if the bond is sold prior to maturity.

We will assume that a bond makes all of its promised coupon and principal payments on time (i.e., we are not addressing credit risk). Additionally, we assume that the *interest rate earned on reinvested coupon payments is the same as the YTM on the bond*. There are five results to gain from the analysis presented here.

Given the assumptions just listed:

1. An investor who holds a fixed-rate bond to maturity will earn an annualized rate of return equal to the YTM of the bond when purchased.

2. An investor who sells a bond prior to maturity will earn a rate of return equal to the YTM at purchase if the YTM at sale has not changed since purchase.

3. If the market YTM for the bond, our assumed reinvestment rate, increases (decreases) after the bond is purchased but before the first coupon date, a buy-and-hold investor's realized return will be higher (lower) than the YTM of the bond when purchased.

4. If the market YTM for the bond, our assumed reinvestment rate, *increases* after the bond is purchased but before the first coupon date, a bond investor will earn a rate of return that is lower than the YTM at bond purchase if the bond is held for a *short* period.

5. If the market YTM for the bond, our assumed reinvestment rate, *decreases* after the bond is purchased but before the first coupon date, a bond investor will earn a rate of return that is lower than the YTM at bond purchase if the bond is held for a *long* period.

We will present mathematical examples to demonstrate each of these results as well as some intuition as to why these results must hold.

A bond investor's **annualized holding period rate of return** is calculated as the compound annual return earned from the bond over the investor's holding period. This is the compound rate of return that, based on the purchase price of the bond, would provide an amount at the time of the sale or maturity of the bond equal to the sum of coupon payments, sale or maturity value, and interest earned on reinvested coupons.

We will illustrate this calculation (and the first result listed earlier) with a 6% annual-pay three-year bond purchased at a YTM of 7% and held to maturity.

With an annual YTM of 7%, the bond's purchase price is $973.76.

$$N = 3; I/Y = 7; PMT = 60; FV = 1,000; CPT \rightarrow PV = -973.76$$

At maturity, the investor will have received coupon income and reinvestment income equal to the future value of an annuity of three $60 coupon payments calculated with an interest rate equal to the bond's YTM. This amount is

$$60(1.07)^2 + 60(1.07) + 60 = \$192.89$$

$$N = 3; I/Y = 7; PV = 0; PMT = 60; CPT \rightarrow FV = -192.89$$

We can easily calculate the amount earned from reinvestment of the coupons as

$$192.89 - 3(60) = \$12.89$$

Adding the maturity value of $1,000 to $192.89, we can calculate the investor's

rate of return over the three-year holding period as $\left(\dfrac{1,192.89}{973.76}\right)^{\frac{1}{3}} - 1 = 7\%$ and

demonstrate that $973.76 invested at a compound annual rate of 7% would return $1,192.89 after three years.

We can calculate an investor's rate of return on the same bond purchased at a YTM of 5%.

Price at purchase:

N = 3; I/Y = 5; FV = 1,000; PMT = 60; CPT → PV = –1,027.23

Coupons and reinvestment income:

$60(1.05)^2 + 60(1.05) + 60 = \$189.15$ or

N = 3; I/Y = 5; PV = 0; PMT = 60; CPT → FV = –189.15

Holding period return:

$\left(\dfrac{1,189.15}{1,027.23}\right)^{\frac{1}{3}} - 1 = 5\%$

With these examples, we have demonstrated our first result: that for a fixed-rate bond that does not default and has a reinvestment rate equal to the YTM, an investor who holds the bond until maturity will earn a rate of return equal to the YTM at purchase, regardless of whether the bond is purchased at a discount or a premium.

The intuition is straightforward. If the bond is selling at a discount, the YTM is greater than the coupon rate because together, the amortization of the discount and the higher assumed reinvestment rate on coupon income increase the bond's return. For a bond purchased at a premium, the YTM is less than the coupon rate because both the amortization of the premium and the reduction in interest earned on reinvestment of its cash flows decrease the bond's return.

Now let's examine the second result—that an investor who sells a bond prior to maturity will earn a rate of return equal to the YTM as long as the YTM has not changed since purchase. For such an investor, we call the time the bond will be held the investor's **investment horizon**. The value of a bond that is sold at a discount or premium to par will move to the par value of the bond by the maturity date. At dates between the purchase and the sale, the value of a bond at the same YTM as when it was purchased is its **carrying value** and reflects the amortization of the discount or premium since the bond was purchased.

PROFESSOR'S NOTE

Carrying value is a price along a bond's constant-yield price trajectory. We applied this concept in Financial Reporting and Analysis when we used the effective interest method to calculate the carrying value of a bond liability.

Capital gains or losses at the time a bond is sold are measured relative to this carrying value, as illustrated in the following example.

> **EXAMPLE:** Capital gain or loss on a bond
>
> An investor purchases a 20-year bond with a 5% semiannual coupon and a yield to maturity of 6%. Five years later the investor sells the bond for a price of 91.40. Determine whether the investor realizes a capital gain or loss, and calculate its amount.
>
> **Answer:**
>
> Any capital gain or loss is based on the bond's carrying value at the time of sale, when it has 15 years (30 semiannual periods) to maturity. The carrying value is calculated using the bond's YTM at the time the investor purchased it.
>
> N = 30; I/Y = 3; PMT = 2.5; FV = 100; CPT → PV = –90.20
>
> Because the selling price of 91.40 is greater than the carrying value of 90.20, the investor realizes a capital gain of 91.40 – 90.20 = 1.20 per 100 of face value.

Bonds held to maturity have no capital gain or loss. Bonds sold prior to maturity at the same YTM as at purchase will also have no capital gain or loss. Using the 6% three-year bond from our earlier examples, we can demonstrate this for an investor with a two-year holding period (investment horizon).

When the bond is purchased at a YTM of 7% (for $973.76), we have:

Price at sale: (at end of year 2, YTM = 7%):

1,060 / 1.07 = 990.65 or

N = 1; I/Y = 7; FV = 1,000; PMT = 60; CPT → PV = –990.65

which is the carrying value of the bond.

Coupon interest and reinvestment income for two years:

60(1.07) + 60 = $124.20 or

N = 2; I/Y = 7; PV = 0; PMT = 60; CPT → FV = –124.20

Investor's annual compound rate of return over the two-year holding period is:

$$\left(\frac{124.20 + 990.65}{973.76}\right)^{\frac{1}{2}} - 1 \ = \ 7\%$$

This result can be demonstrated for the case where the bond is purchased at a YTM of 5% ($1,027.23) as well:

Price at sale (at end of year 2, YTM = 5%):

1,060 / 1.05 = 1,009.52 or

N = 1; I/Y = 5; FV = 1,000; PMT = 60; CPT → PV = –1,009.52

which is the carrying value of the bond.

Coupon interest and reinvestment income for two years:

60(1.05) + 60 = 123.00 or

N = 2; I/Y = 5; PV = 0; PMT = 60; CPT → FV = –123.00

Investor's annual compound rate of return over the two-year holding period is:

$$\left(\frac{123.00 + 1{,}009.52}{1{,}027.23}\right)^{\frac{1}{2}} - 1 = 5\%$$

For a bond investor with an investment horizon less than the bond's term to maturity, the annual holding period return will be equal to the YTM at purchase (under our assumptions), if the bond is sold at that YTM. The intuition here is that if a bond will have a rate of return equal to its YTM at maturity, which we showed, if we sell some of the remaining value of the bond discounted at that YTM, we will have earned that YTM up to the date of sale.

Now let's examine our third result: that if rates rise (fall) before the first coupon date, an investor who holds a bond to maturity will earn a rate of return greater (less) than the YTM at purchase.

Based on our previous result that an investor who holds a bond to maturity will earn a rate of return equal to the YTM at purchase if the reinvestment rate is also equal to the YTM at purchase, the intuition of the third result is straightforward. If the YTM, which is also the reinvestment rate for the bond, increases (decreases) after purchase, the return from coupon payments and reinvestment income will increase (decrease) as a result and increase (decrease) the investor's rate of return on the bond above (below) its YTM at purchase. The following calculations demonstrate these results for the three-year 6% bond in our previous examples.

For a three-year 6% bond purchased at par (YTM of 6%), first assume that the YTM and reinvestment rate increases to 7% after purchase but before the first coupon payment date. The bond's annualized holding period return is calculated as:

Coupons and reinvestment interest:

$60(1.07)^2 + 60(1.07) + 60 = \$192.89$

N = 3; I/Y = 7; PV = 0; PMT = 60; CPT → FV = −192.89

Investor's annual compound holding period return:

$$\left(\frac{1{,}192.89}{1{,}000}\right)^{\frac{1}{3}} - 1 = 6.06\%$$

which is greater than the 6% YTM at purchase.

If the YTM decreases to 5% after purchase but before the first coupon date, we have the following.

Coupons and reinvestment interest:

$60(1.05)^2 + 60(1.05) + 60 = \$189.15$

N = 3; I/Y = 5; PV = 0; PMT = 60; CPT → FV = −189.15

Investor's annual compound holding period return:

$$\left(\frac{1{,}189.15}{1{,}000}\right)^{\frac{1}{3}} - 1 = 5.94\%$$

which is less than the 6% YTM at purchase.

Note that in both cases, the investor's rate of return is between the YTM at purchase and the assumed reinvestment rate (the new YTM).

We now turn our attention to the fourth and fifth results concerning the effects of the length of an investor's holding period on the rate of return for a bond that experiences an increase or decrease in its YTM before the first coupon date.

We have already demonstrated that when the YTM increases (decreases) after purchase but before the first coupon date, an investor who holds the bond to maturity will earn a rate of return greater (less) than the YTM at purchase. Now, we examine the rate of return earned by an investor with an investment horizon (expected holding period) less than the term to maturity under the same circumstances.

Consider a three-year 6% bond purchased at par by an investor with a one-year investment horizon. If the YTM increases from 6% to 7% after purchase and the bond is sold after one year, the rate of return can be calculated as follows.

Bond price just after first coupon has been paid with YTM = 7%:

N = 2; I/Y = 7; FV = 1,000; PMT = 60; CPT → PV = –981.92

There is no reinvestment income and only one coupon of $60 received so the holding period rate of return is simply:

$$\left(\frac{981.92 + 60}{1,000}\right) - 1 = 4.19\%$$

which is less than the YTM at purchase.

If the YTM *decreases* to 5% after purchase and the bond is sold at the end of one year, the investor's rate of return can be calculated as follows.

Bond price just after first coupon has been paid with YTM = 5%:

N = 2; I/Y = 5; FV = 1,000; PMT = 60; CPT → PV = –1,018.59

And the holding period rate of return is simply:

$$\left(\frac{1,018.59 + 60}{1,000}\right) - 1 = 7.86\%$$

which is greater than the YTM at purchase.

The intuition of this result is based on the idea of a trade-off between **market price risk** (the uncertainty about price due to uncertainty about market YTM) and **reinvestment risk** (uncertainty about the total of coupon payments and reinvestment income on those payments due to the uncertainty about future reinvestment rates).

Previously, we showed that for a bond held to maturity, the investor's rate of return increased with an increase in the bond's YTM and decreased with a decrease in the bond's YTM. For an investor who intends to hold a bond to maturity, there is no interest rate risk as we have defined it. Assuming no default, the bond's value at maturity is its par value regardless of interest rate changes so that the investor has only reinvestment risk. Her realized return will increase when interest earned on reinvested cash flows increases, and decrease when the reinvestment rate decreases.

For an investor with a short investment horizon, interest rate risk increases and reinvestment risk decreases. For the investor with a one-year investment horizon, there was no reinvestment risk because the bond was sold before any interest on coupon payments was earned. The investor had only market price risk so an increase in yield decreased the rate of return over the one-year holding period because the sale price is lower. Conversely, a decrease in yield increased the one-year holding period return to more than the YTM at purchase because the sale price is higher.

To summarize:

short investment horizon: market price risk > reinvestment risk

long investment horizon: reinvestment risk > market price risk

---

LOS 54.b: Define, calculate, and interpret Macaulay, modified, and effective durations.

CFA® Program Curriculum: Volume 5, page 537

Macaulay Duration

Duration is used as a measure of a bond's interest rate risk or sensitivity of a bond's *full* price to a change in its yield. The measure was first introduced by Frederick Macaulay and his formulation is referred to as **Macaulay duration**.

A bond's (annual) Macaulay duration is calculated as the weighted average of the number of years until each of the bond's promised cash flows is to be paid, where the weights are the present values of each cash flow as a percentage of the bond's full value.

Consider a newly issued three-year 4% annual-pay bond with a yield to maturity of 5%. The present values of each of the bond's promised payments, discounted at 5%, and their weights in the calculation of Macaulay duration, are shown in the following table.

$C_1 = 40$ $PV_1 = 40 / 1.05$ $= 38.10$ $W_1 = 38.10 / 972.77 = 0.0392$

$C_2 = 40$ $PV_2 = 40 / 1.05^2$ $= 36.28$ $W_2 = 36.28 / 972.77 = 0.0373$

$C_3 = 1,040$ $PV_3 = 1,040 / 1.05^3 = \underline{898.39}$ $W_3 = 898.39 / 972.77 = \underline{0.9235}$

                                          972.77   1.0000

Note that the present values of all the promised cash flows sum to 972.77 (the full value of the bond) and the weights sum to 1.

Now that we have the weights, and because we know the time until each promised payment is to be made, we can calculate the Macaulay duration for this bond:

$0.0392(1) + 0.0373(2) + 0.9235(3) = 2.884$ years

The Macaulay duration of a semiannual-pay bond can be calculated in the same way: as a weighted average of the number of *semiannual periods* until the cash flows are to be received. In this case, the result is the number of semiannual periods rather than years.

Because of the improved measures of interest rate risk described next, we say that Macaulay duration is the weighted-average time to the receipt of principal and interest payments, rather than our best estimate of interest rate sensitivity. Between coupon dates, the Macaulay duration of a coupon bond decreases with the passage of time and then goes back up significantly at each coupon payment date.

Modified Duration

Modified duration (ModDur) is calculated as Macaulay duration (MacDur) divided by one plus the bond's yield to maturity. For the bond in our earlier example, we have:

$$\text{ModDur} = 2.884 \, / \, 1.05 = 2.747$$

Modified duration provides an approximate percentage change in a bond's price for a 1% change in yield to maturity. The price change for a given change in yield to maturity can be calculated as:

$$\text{approximate percentage change in bond price} = -\text{ModDur} \times \Delta \text{YTM}$$

Based on a ModDur of 2.747, the price of the bond should fall by approximately $2.747 \times 0.1\% = 0.2747\%$ in response to a 0.1% increase in YTM. The resulting price estimate of $970.098 is very close to the value of the bond calculated directly using a YTM of 5.1%, which is $970.100.

For an annual-pay bond, the general form of modified duration is:

$$\text{ModDur} = \text{MacDur} \, / \, (1 + \text{YTM})$$

For a semiannual-pay bond with a YTM quoted on a semiannual bond basis:

$$\text{ModDur}_{\text{SEMI}} = \text{MacDur}_{\text{SEMI}} \, / \, (1 + \text{YTM} \, / \, 2)$$

This modified duration can be annualized (from semiannual periods to annual periods) by dividing by two, and then used as the approximate change in price for a 1% change in a bond's YTM.

Approximate Modified Duration

We can approximate modified duration directly using bond values for an increase in YTM and for a decrease in YTM of the same size.

In Figure 54.1 we illustrate this method. The calculation of approximate modified duration is based on a given change in YTM. V_- is the price of the bond if YTM is *decreased* by ΔYTM and V_+ is the price of the bond if the YTM is *increased* by ΔYTM. Note that $V_- > V_+$. Because of the convexity of the price-yield relationship, the price increase (to V_-), for a given decrease in yield, is larger than the price decrease (to V_+).

$$\text{approximate modified duration} = \frac{V_- - V_+}{2 \times V_0 \times \Delta YTM}$$

The formula uses the average of the magnitudes of the price increase and the price decrease, which is why $V_- - V_+$ (in the numerator) is divided by 2 (in the denominator).

V_0, the current price of the bond, is in the denominator to convert this average price change to a percentage, and the ΔYTM term is in the denominator to scale the duration measure to a 1% change in yield by convention. Note that the ΔYTM term in the denominator must be entered as a decimal (rather than in a whole percentage) to properly scale the duration estimate.

Figure 54.1: Approximate Modified Duration

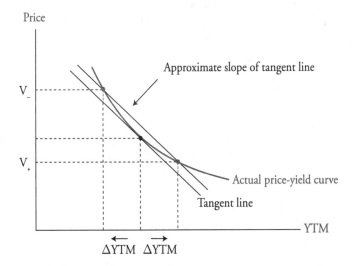

EXAMPLE: Calculating approximate modified duration

A bond is trading at a full price of 980. If its yield to maturity increases by 50 basis points, its price will decrease to 960. If its yield to maturity decreases by 50 basis points, its price will increase to 1,002. Calculate the approximate modified duration.

Answer:

The approximate modified duration is $\dfrac{1,002 - 960}{2 \times 980 \times 0.005} = 4.29$, and the approximate change in price for a 1% change in YTM is 4.29%.

Note that modified duration is a *linear estimate* of the relation between a bond's price and YTM, whereas the actual relation is convex, not linear. This means that the modified duration measure provides good estimates of bond prices for small changes in yield, but increasingly poor estimates for larger changes in yield as the effect of the curvature of the price-yield curve is more pronounced.

Effective Duration

So far, all of our duration measures have been calculated using the YTM and prices of straight (option-free) bonds. This is straightforward because both the future cash flows and their timing are known with certainty. This is not the case with bonds that have embedded options, such as a callable bond or a mortgage-backed bond.

We say mortgage-backed bonds have a *prepayment option*, which is similar to a call option on a corporate bond. The borrowers (people who take out mortgages) typically have the option to pay off the principal value of their loans, in whole or in part, at any time. These prepayments accelerate when interest rates fall significantly because borrowers can refinance their home loans at a lower rate and pay off the remaining principal owed on an existing loan.

Thus, the pricing of bonds with embedded put, call, or prepayment options begins with the benchmark yield curve, not simply the current YTM of the bond. The appropriate measure of interest rate sensitivity for these bonds is **effective duration**.

The calculation of effective duration is the same as the calculation of approximate modified duration with the change in YTM, Δy, replaced by Δcurve, the change in the benchmark yield curve used with a bond pricing model to generate V_- and V_+. The formula for calculating effective duration is:

$$\text{effective duration} = \frac{V_- - V_+}{2 \times V_0 \times \Delta\text{curve}}$$

Another difference between calculating effective duration and the methods we have discussed so far is that the effects of changes in benchmark yields and changes in the yield spread for credit and liquidity risk are separated. Modified duration makes no distinction between changes in the benchmark yield and changes in the spread. Effective duration reflects only the sensitivity of the bond's value to changes in the benchmark yield curve. Changes in the credit spread are sometimes addressed with a separate "credit duration" measure.

Finally, note that unlike modified duration, effective duration does not necessarily provide better estimates of bond prices for smaller changes in yield. It may be the case that larger changes in yield produce more predictable prepayments or calls than small changes.

LOS 54.c: Explain why effective duration is the most appropriate measure of interest rate risk for bonds with embedded options.

CFA® Program Curriculum: Volume 5, page 545

For bonds with embedded options, the future cash flows depend not only on future interest rates but also on the path that interest rates take over time (did they fall to a new level or rise to that level?). We must use effective duration to estimate the interest rate risk of these bonds. The effective duration measure must also be based on bond prices from a pricing model. The fact that bonds with embedded options have uncertain future cash flows means that our present value calculations for bond value based on YTM cannot be used.

MODULE QUIZ 54.1

To best evaluate your performance, enter your quiz answers online.

1. The largest component of returns for a 7-year zero-coupon bond yielding 8% and held to maturity is:
   A. capital gains.
   B. interest income.
   C. reinvestment income.

2. An investor buys a 10-year bond with a 6.5% annual coupon and a YTM of 6%. Before the first coupon payment is made, the YTM for the bond decreases to 5.5%. Assuming coupon payments are reinvested at the YTM, the investor's return when the bond is held to maturity is:
   A. less than 6.0%.
   B. equal to 6.0%.
   C. greater than 6.0%.

3. Assuming coupon interest is reinvested at a bond's YTM, what is the interest portion of an 18-year, $1,000 par, 5% annual coupon bond's return if it is purchased at par and held to maturity?
   A. $576.95
   B. $1,406.62.
   C. $1,476.95.

4. An investor buys a 15-year, £800,000, zero-coupon bond with an annual YTM of 7.3%. If she sells the bond after three years for £346,333 she will have:
   A. a capital gain.
   B. a capital loss.
   C. neither a capital gain nor a capital loss.

5. A 14% annual-pay coupon bond has six years to maturity. The bond is currently trading at par. Using a 25 basis point change in yield, the approximate modified duration of the bond is *closest* to:
   A. 0.392.
   B. 3.888.
   C. 3.970.

6. Which of the following measures is *lowest* for a callable bond?
   A. Macaulay duration.
   B. Effective duration.
   C. Modified duration.

7. Effective duration is more appropriate than modified duration for estimating interest rate risk for bonds with embedded options because these bonds:
   A. tend to have greater credit risk than option-free bonds.
   B. exhibit high convexity that makes modified duration less accurate.
   C. have uncertain cash flows that depend on the path of interest rate changes.

Video covering this
content is available
online.

MODULE 54.2: INTEREST RATE RISK AND MONEY DURATION

LOS 54.d: Define key rate duration and describe the use of key rate durations in measuring the sensitivity of bonds to changes in the shape of the benchmark yield curve.

CFA® Program Curriculum: Volume 5, page 549

Recall that duration is an adequate measure of bond price risk only for parallel shifts in the yield curve. The impact of nonparallel shifts can be measured using a concept known as **key rate duration**. A key rate duration, also known as a **partial duration**, is defined as the sensitivity of the value of a bond or portfolio to changes in the spot rate for a specific maturity, holding other spot rates constant. A bond or portfolio will have a key rate duration for each maturity range on the spot rate curve.

Key rate duration is particularly useful for measuring the effect of a nonparallel shift in the yield curve on a bond portfolio. We can use the key rate duration for each maturity to compute the effect on the portfolio of the interest rate change at that maturity. The effect on the overall portfolio is the sum of these individual effects.

LOS 54.e: Explain how a bond's maturity, coupon, and yield level affect its interest rate risk.

CFA® Program Curriculum: Volume 5, page 549

Other things equal, an *increase in a bond's maturity* will (usually) increase its interest rate risk. The present values of payments made further in the future are more sensitive to changes in the discount rate used to calculate present value than are the present values of payments made sooner.

We must say "usually" because there are instances where an increase in a discount coupon bond's maturity will decrease its Macaulay duration. For a discount bond, duration first increases with longer maturity and then decreases over a range of relatively long maturities until it approaches the duration of a perpetuity, which is (1 + YTM) / YTM.

Other things equal, an *increase in the coupon rate* of a bond will decrease its interest rate risk. For a given maturity and YTM, the duration of a zero coupon bond will be greater than that of a coupon bond. Increasing the coupon rate means more of a bond's value will be from payments received sooner so that the value of the bond will be less sensitive to changes in yield.

Other things equal, an *increase (decrease) in a bond's YTM* will decrease (increase) its interest rate risk. To understand this, we can look to the convexity of the price-yield curve and use its slope as our proxy for interest rate risk. At lower yields, the price-yield curve has a steeper slope indicating that price is more sensitive to a given change in yield.

©2018 Kaplan, Inc.

Adding either a put or a call provision will decrease a straight bond's interest rate risk as measured by effective duration. With a call provision, the value of the call increases as yields fall, so a decrease in yield will have less effect on the price of the bond, which is the price of a straight bond minus the value of the call option held by the issuer. With a put option, the bondholder's option to sell the bond back to the issuer at a set price reduces the negative impact of yield increases on price.

LOS 54.f: Calculate the duration of a portfolio and explain the limitations of portfolio duration.

CFA® Program Curriculum: Volume 5, page 555

There are two approaches to estimating the duration of a portfolio. The first is to calculate the weighted average number of periods until the portfolio's cash flows will be received. The second approach is to take a weighted average of the durations of the individual bonds in the portfolio.

The first approach is theoretically correct but not often used in practice. The yield measure for calculating portfolio duration with this approach is the **cash flow yield**, the IRR of the bond portfolio. This is inconsistent with duration capturing the relationship between YTM and price. This approach will not work for a portfolio that contains bonds with embedded options because the future cash flows are not known with certainty and depend on interest rate movements.

The second approach is typically used in practice. Using the durations of individual portfolio bonds makes it possible to calculate the duration for a portfolio that contains bonds with embedded options by using their effective durations. The weights for the calculation of portfolio duration under this approach are simply the full price of each bond as a proportion of the total portfolio value (using full prices). These proportions of total portfolio value are multiplied by the corresponding bond durations to get portfolio duration.

$$\text{portfolio duration} = W_1 D_1 + W_2 D_2 + \ldots + W_N D_N$$

where:
W_i = full price of bond i divided by the total value of the portfolio
D_i = the duration of bond i
N = the number of bonds in the portfolio

One limitation of this approach is that for portfolio duration to "make sense" the YTM of every bond in the portfolio must change by the same amount. Only with this assumption of a **parallel shift** in the yield curve is portfolio duration calculated with this approach consistent with the idea of the percentage change in portfolio value per 1% change in YTM.

We can think of the second approach as a practical approximation of the theoretically correct duration that the first approach describes. This approximation is less accurate when there is greater variation in yields among portfolio bonds, but is the same as the portfolio duration under the first approach when the yield curve is flat.

LOS 54.g: Calculate and interpret the money duration of a bond and price value of a basis point (PVBP).

CFA® Program Curriculum: Volume 5, page 557

The **money duration** of a bond position (also called *dollar duration*) is expressed in currency units.

money duration = annual modified duration × full price of bond position

Money duration is sometimes expressed as money duration per 100 of bond par value.

money duration per 100 units of par value = annual modified duration × full bond price per 100 of par value

Multiplying the money duration of a bond times a given change in YTM (as a decimal) will provide the change in bond value for that change in YTM.

> **EXAMPLE: Money duration**
>
> 1. Calculate the money duration on a coupon date of a $2 million par value bond that has a modified duration of 7.42 and a full price of 101.32, expressed for the whole bond and per $100 of face value.
>
> 2. What will be the impact on the value of the bond of a 25 basis points increase in its YTM?
>
> **Answer:**
>
> 1. The money duration for the bond is modified duration times the full value of the bond:
>
>   7.42 × $2,000,000 × 101.32 = $15,035,888
>
>   The money duration per $100 of par value is:
>
>   7.42 × 101.32 = $751.79
>
>   Or, $15,035,888 / ($2,000,000 / $100) = $751.79
>
> 2. $15,035,888 × 0.0025 = $37,589.72
>
>   The bond value decreases by $37,589.72.

The **price value of a basis point** (PVBP) is the money change in the full price of a bond when its YTM changes by one basis point, or 0.01%. We can calculate the PVBP directly for a bond by calculating the average of the decrease in the full value of a bond when its YTM increases by one basis point and the increase in the full value of the bond when its YTM decreases by one basis point.

> **EXAMPLE: Calculating the price value of a basis point**
>
> A newly issued, 20-year, 6% annual-pay straight bond is priced at 101.39. Calculate the price value of a basis point for this bond assuming it has a par value of $1 million.
>
> **Answer:**
>
> First we need to find the YTM of the bond:
>
> N = 20; PV = –101.39; PMT = 6; FV = 100; CPT→I/Y = 5.88

Now we need the values for the bond with YTMs of 5.89 and 5.87.

I/Y = 5.89; CPT → PV = –101.273 (V$_+$)

I/Y = 5.87; CPT → PV = –101.507 (V_)

PVBP (per $100 of par value) = (101.507 – 101.273) / 2 = 0.117

For the $1 million par value bond, each 1 basis point change in the yield to maturity will change the bond's price by 0.117 × $1 million × 0.01 = $1,170.

MODULE QUIZ 54.2

To best evaluate your performance, enter your quiz answers online.

1. A bond portfolio manager who wants to estimate the sensitivity of the portfolio's value to changes in the 5-year spot rate should use:
   A. a key rate duration.
   B. a Macaulay duration.
   C. an effective duration.

2. Which of the following three bonds (similar except for yield and maturity) has the *least* Macaulay duration? A bond with:
   A. 5% yield and 10-year maturity.
   B. 5% yield and 20-year maturity.
   C. 6% yield and 10-year maturity.

3. Portfolio duration has limited usefulness as a measure of interest rate risk for a portfolio because it:
   A. assumes yield changes uniformly across all maturities.
   B. cannot be applied if the portfolio includes bonds with embedded options.
   C. is accurate only if the portfolio's internal rate of return is equal to its cash flow yield.

4. The current price of a $1,000, 7-year, 5.5% semiannual coupon bond is $1,029.23. The bond's price value of a basis point is *closest* to:
   A. $0.05.
   B. $0.60.
   C. $5.74.

MODULE 54.3: CONVEXITY AND YIELD VOLATILITY

Video covering this content is available online.

LOS 54.h: Calculate and interpret approximate convexity and distinguish between approximate and effective convexity.

CFA® Program Curriculum: Volume 5, page 559

Earlier we explained that modified duration is a linear approximation of the relationship between yield and price and that, because of the convexity of the true price-yield relation, duration-based estimates of a bond's full price for a given change in YTM will be increasingly different from actual prices. This is illustrated in Figure 54.2. Duration-based price estimates for a decrease and for an increase in YTM are shown as Est._ and Est.$_+$.

Figure 54.2: Price-Yield Curve for an Option-Free, 8%, 20-Year Bond

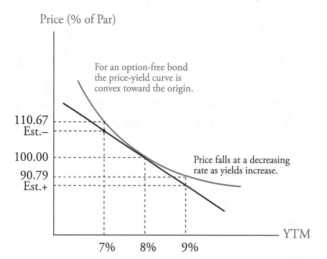

Estimates of the price impact of a change in yield based only on modified duration can be improved by introducing a second term based on the bond's convexity. **Convexity** is a measure of the curvature of the price-yield relation. The more curved it is, the greater the convexity adjustment to a duration-based estimate of the change in price for a given change in YTM.

A bond's convexity can be estimated as:

$$\text{approximate convexity} = \frac{V_- + V_+ - 2V_0}{(\Delta \text{YTM})^2 V_0}$$

where:
the variables are the same as those we used in calculating approximate modified duration

Effective convexity, like effective duration, must be used for bonds with embedded options.

The calculation of effective convexity is the same as the calculation of approximate convexity, except that the change in the yield *curve*, rather than a change in the bond's YTM, is used.

$$\text{approximate effective convexity} = \frac{V_- + V_+ - 2V_0}{(\Delta \text{curve})^2 V_0}$$

A bond's convexity is increased or decreased by the same bond characteristics that affect duration. A longer maturity, a lower coupon rate, or a lower yield to maturity will all increase convexity, and vice versa. For two bonds with equal duration, the one with cash flows that are more dispersed over time will have the greater convexity.

While the convexity of any option-free bond is positive, the convexity of a callable bond can be negative at low yields. This is because at low yields the call option becomes more valuable and the call price puts an effective limit on increases in bond value as shown in Figure 54.3. For a bond with negative convexity, the price increase from a decrease in YTM is *smaller* than the price decrease from an increase in YTM.

Figure 54.3: Price-Yield Function of a Callable vs. an Option-Free Bond

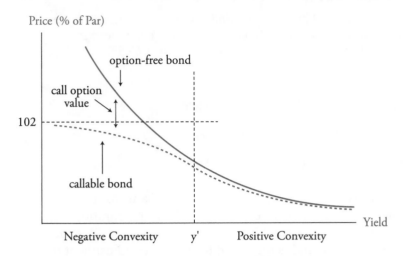

A putable bond has greater convexity than an otherwise identical option-free bond. In Figure 54.4 we illustrate the price-yield relation for a putable bond. At higher yields, the put becomes more valuable so that the value of the putable bond falls less than that of an option-free bond as yield increases.

Figure 54.4: Comparing the Price-Yield Curves for Option-Free and Putable Bonds

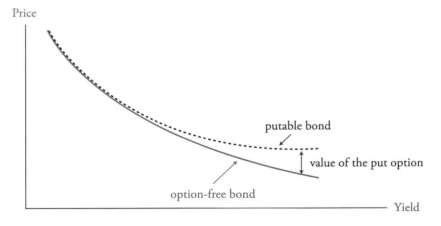

LOS 54.i: Estimate the percentage price change of a bond for a specified change in yield, given the bond's approximate duration and convexity.

CFA® Program Curriculum: Volume 5, page 559

By taking account of both a bond's duration (first-order effects) and convexity (second-order effects), we can improve an estimate of the effects of a change in yield on a bond's value, especially for larger changes in yield.

$$\text{change in full bond price} = -\text{annual modified duration}(\Delta YTM)$$
$$+ \tfrac{1}{2}\ \text{annual convexity}(\Delta YTM)^2$$

> **EXAMPLE:** Estimating price changes with duration and convexity
>
> Consider an 8% bond with a full price of $908 and a YTM of 9%. Estimate the percentage change in the full price of the bond for a 30 basis point increase in YTM assuming the bond's duration is 9.42 and its convexity is 68.33.
>
> **Answer:**
>
> The duration effect is −9.42 × 0.003 = 0.02826 = −2.826%.
>
> The convexity effect is 0.5 × 68.33 × (0.003)^2 = 0.000307 = 0.0307%.
>
> The expected change in bond price is (−0.02826 + 0.000307) = −2.7953%.

Note that the convexity adjustment to the price change is the same for both an increase and a decrease in yield. As illustrated in Figure 54.5, the duration-only based estimate of the increase in price resulting from a decrease in yield is too low for a bond with positive convexity, and is improved by a positive adjustment for convexity. The duration-only based estimate of the decrease in price resulting from an increase in yield is larger than the actual decrease, so it's also improved by a positive adjustment for convexity.

Figure 54.5: Duration-Based Price Estimates vs. Actual Bond Prices

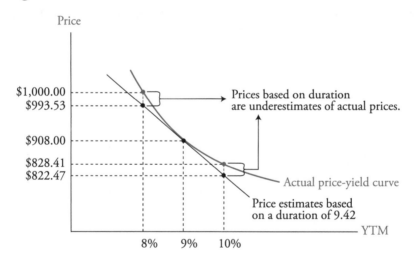

LOS 54.j: Describe how the term structure of yield volatility affects the interest rate risk of a bond.

CFA® Program Curriculum: Volume 5, page 568

The **term structure of yield volatility** refers to the relation between the volatility of bond yields and their times to maturity. We have seen that the sensitivity of a bond's price with respect to a *given* change in yield depends on its duration and convexity. From an investor's point of view, it's the volatility of a bond's price that is of concern. The volatility of a bond's price has two components: the sensitivity of the bond's price to a given change in yield and the volatility of the bond's yield.

In calculating duration and convexity, we implicitly assumed that the yield curve shifted in a parallel manner. In practice, this is often not the case. For example, changes in monetary policy may have more of an effect on short-term interest rates than on longer-term rates.

It could be the case that a shorter-term bond has more price volatility than a longer-term bond with a greater duration because of the greater volatility of the shorter-term yield.

LOS 54.k: Describe the relationships among a bond's holding period return, its duration, and the investment horizon.

CFA® Program Curriculum: Volume 5, page 569

Macaulay duration has an interesting application in matching a bond to an investor's investment horizon. When the investment horizon and the bond's Macaulay duration are matched, a parallel shift in the yield curve prior to the first coupon payment will not (or will minimally) affect the investor's horizon return.

Earlier, we illustrated the effect of a change in yield that occurs prior to the first coupon payment. Our results showed that for an investor with a short investment horizon (anticipated holding period), the market price risk of the bond outweighs its reinvestment risk. Because of this, an increase in yield prior to the first coupon date was shown to reduce the horizon yield for a short investment horizon and increase the horizon yield for a longer-term investment horizon. For a longer investment horizon, the increase in reinvestment income from the yield increase was greater than the decrease in the sale price of the bond.

For a decrease in yield, an investor with a short investment horizon will have a capital gain and only a small decrease in reinvestment income. An investor with a long horizon will be more affected by the decrease in reinvestment income and will have a horizon return that is less than the bond's original yield.

When the investment horizon just matches the Macaulay duration, the effect of a change in YTM on the sale price of a bond and on reinvestment income just offset each other. We can say that for such an investment, market price risk and reinvestment risk offset each other. The following example illustrates this result.

> **EXAMPLE: Investment horizon yields**
>
> Consider an eight-year, 8.5% bond priced at 89.52 to yield 10.5% to maturity. The Macaulay duration of the bond is 6. We can calculate the horizon yield for horizons of 3 years, 6 years, and 8 years, assuming the YTM falls to 9.5% prior to the first coupon date.
>
> **Answer:**
>
> *Sale after 3 years*
>
> Bond price:
>
> N = 5; PMT = 8.5; FV = 100; I/Y = 9.5; CPT → PV = 96.16

Coupons and interest on reinvested coupons:

N = 3; PMT = 8.5; PV = 0; I/Y = 9.5; CPT → FV = 28.00

Horizon return:

$[(96.16 + 28.00) / 89.52]^{1/3} - 1 = 11.520\%$

Sale after 6 years

Bond price:

N = 2; PMT = 8.5; FV = 100; I/Y = 9.5; CPT → PV = 98.25

Coupons and interest on reinvested coupons:

N = 6; PMT = 8.5; PV = 0; I/Y = 9.5; CPT → FV = 64.76

Horizon return:

$[(98.25 + 64.76) / 89.52]^{1/6} - 1 = 10.505\%$

Held to maturity, 8 years

Maturity value = 100

Coupons and interest on reinvested coupons:

N = 8; PMT = 8.5; PV = 0; I/Y = 9.5; CPT → FV = 95.46

Horizon return:

$[(100 + 95.46) / 89.52]^{1/8} - 1 = 10.253\%$

For an investment horizon equal to the bond's Macaulay duration of 6, the horizon return is equal to the original YTM of 10.5%. For a shorter three-year investment horizon, the price increase from a reduction in the YTM to 9.5% dominates the decrease in reinvestment income so the horizon return, 11.520%, is greater than the original YTM. For an investor who holds the bond to maturity, there is no price effect and the decrease in reinvestment income reduces the horizon return to 10.253%, less than the original YTM.

The difference between a bond's Macaulay duration and the bondholder's investment horizon is referred to as a **duration gap**. A positive duration gap (Macaulay duration greater than the investment horizon) exposes the investor to market price risk from increasing interest rates. A negative duration gap (Macaulay duration less than the investment horizon) exposes the investor to reinvestment risk from decreasing interest rates.

LOS 54.l: Explain how changes in credit spread and liquidity affect yield-to-maturity of a bond and how duration and convexity can be used to estimate the price effect of the changes.

CFA® Program Curriculum: Volume 5, page 574

The benchmark yield curve's interest rates have two components; the real rate of return and expected inflation. A bond's spread to the benchmark curve also has two components, a premium for credit risk and a premium for lack of liquidity relative to the benchmark securities.

Because we are treating the yields associated with each component as additive, a given increase or decrease in any of these components of yield will increase or decrease the bond's YTM by the same amount.

With a direct relationship between a bond's yield spread to the benchmark yield curve and its YTM, we can estimate the impact on a bond's value of a change in spread using the formula we introduced earlier for the price effects of a given change in YTM.

$$\%\Delta \text{ bond value} = -\text{duration}(\Delta\text{spread}) + \tfrac{1}{2} \text{ convexity}(\Delta\text{spread})^2$$

EXAMPLE: Price effect of spread changes

Consider a bond that is valued at $180,000 that has a duration of 8 and a convexity of 22. The bond's spread to the benchmark curve increases by 25 basis points due to a credit downgrade. What is the approximate change in the bond's market value?

Answer:

With Δspread = 0.0025 we have:

$(-8 \times 0.0025) + (0.5 \times 22 \times 0.0025^2) = -1.99\%$ and the bond's value will fall by approximately $1.99\% \times 180,000 = \$3,588$.

MODULE QUIZ 54.3

To best evaluate your performance, enter your quiz answers online.

1. A bond has a convexity of 114.6. The convexity effect, if the yield decreases by 110 basis points, is *closest* to:
   A. –1.673%.
   B. +0.693%.
   C. +1.673%.

2. The modified duration of a bond is 7.87. The approximate percentage change in price using duration only for a yield decrease of 110 basis points is *closest* to:
   A. –8.657%.
   B. +7.155%.
   C. +8.657%.

3. Assume a bond has an effective duration of 10.5 and a convexity of 97.3. Using both of these measures, the estimated percentage change in price for this bond, in response to a decline in yield of 200 basis points, is *closest* to:
    A. 19.05%.
    B. 22.95%.
    C. 24.89%.

4. Two bonds are similar in all respects except maturity. Can the shorter-maturity bond have greater interest rate risk than the longer-term bond?
    A. No, because the shorter-maturity bond will have a lower duration.
    B. Yes, because the shorter-maturity bond may have a higher duration.
    C. Yes, because short-term yields can be more volatile than long-term yields.

5. An investor with an investment horizon of six years buys a bond with a modified duration of 6.0. This investment has:
    A. no duration gap.
    B. a positive duration gap.
    C. a negative duration gap.

6. Which of the following *most accurately* describes the relationship between liquidity and yield spreads relative to benchmark government bond rates? All else being equal, bonds with:
    A. less liquidity have lower yield spreads.
    B. greater liquidity have higher yield spreads.
    C. less liquidity have higher yield spreads.

KEY CONCEPTS

LOS 54.a

Sources of return from a bond investment include:

- Coupon and principal payments.
- Reinvestment of coupon payments.
- Capital gain or loss if bond is sold before maturity.

Changes in yield to maturity produce market price risk (uncertainty about a bond's price) and reinvestment risk (uncertainty about income from reinvesting coupon payments). An increase (a decrease) in YTM decreases (increases) a bond's price but increases (decreases) its reinvestment income.

LOS 54.b

Macaulay duration is the weighted average number of coupon periods until a bond's scheduled cash flows.

Modified duration is a linear estimate of the percentage change in a bond's price that would result from a 1% change in its YTM.

$$\text{approximate modified duration} = \frac{V_- - V_+}{2V_0 \Delta \text{YTM}}$$

Effective duration is a linear estimate of the percentage change in a bond's price that would result from a 1% change in the benchmark yield curve.

$$\text{effective duration} = \frac{V_- - V_+}{2V_0 \Delta \text{curve}}$$

LOS 54.c

Effective duration is the appropriate measure of interest rate risk for bonds with embedded options because changes in interest rates may change their future cash flows. Pricing models are used to determine the prices that would result from a given size change in the benchmark yield curve.

LOS 54.d

Key rate duration is a measure of the price sensitivity of a bond or a bond portfolio to a change in the spot rate for a specific maturity. We can use the key rate durations of a bond or portfolio to estimate its price sensitivity to changes in the shape of the yield curve.

LOS 54.e

Holding other factors constant:

- Duration increases when maturity increases.
- Duration decreases when the coupon rate increases.
- Duration decreases when YTM increases.

LOS 54.f

There are two methods for calculating portfolio duration:

- Calculate the weighted average number of periods until cash flows will be received using the portfolio's IRR (its cash flow yield). This method is better theoretically but cannot be used for bonds with options.

- Calculate the weighted average of durations of bonds in the portfolio (the method most often used). Portfolio duration is the percentage change in portfolio value for a 1% change in yield, only for parallel shifts of the yield curve.

LOS 54.g

Money duration is stated in currency units and is sometimes expressed per 100 of bond value.

money duration = annual modified duration × full price of bond position

money duration per 100 units of par value =
annual modified duration × full bond price per 100 of par value

The price value of a basis point is the change in the value of a bond, expressed in currency units, for a change in YTM of one basis point, or 0.01%.

$$PVBP = [(V_- - V_+) / 2] \times \text{par value} \times 0.01$$

LOS 54.h

Convexity refers to the curvature of a bond's price-yield relationship.

$$\text{approximate convexity} = \frac{V_- + V_+ - 2V_0}{(\Delta YTM)^2 V_0}$$

Effective convexity is appropriate for bonds with embedded options:

$$\text{approximate effective convexity} = \frac{V_- + V_+ - 2V_0}{(\Delta curve)^2 V_0}$$

LOS 54.i

Given values for approximate annual modified duration and approximate annual convexity, the percentage change in the full price of a bond can be estimated as:

$$\%\Delta \text{ full bond price} = -\text{annual modified duration}(\Delta YTM)$$
$$+ \frac{1}{2} \text{ annual convexity}(\Delta YTM)^2$$

LOS 54.j

The term structure of yield volatility refers to the relationship between maturity and yield volatility. Short-term yields may be more volatile than long-term yields. As a result, a short-term bond may have more price volatility than a longer-term bond with a higher duration.

LOS 54.k

Over a short investment horizon, a change in YTM affects market price more than it affects reinvestment income.

Over a long investment horizon, a change in YTM affects reinvestment income more than it affects market price.

Macaulay duration may be interpreted as the investment horizon for which a bond's market price risk and reinvestment risk just offset each other.

$$\text{duration gap} = \text{Macaulay duration} - \text{investment horizon}$$

LOS 54.l

A bond's yield spread to the benchmark curve includes a premium for credit risk and a premium for illiquidity.

Given values for duration and convexity, the effect on the value of a bond from a given change in its yield spread (Δspread) can be estimated as:

$$-\text{duration}(\Delta\text{spread}) + \frac{1}{2}\text{convexity}(\Delta\text{spread})^2$$

ANSWER KEY FOR MODULE QUIZZES

Module Quiz 54.1

1. **B** The increase in value of a zero-coupon bond over its life is interest income. A zero-coupon bond has no reinvestment risk over its life. A bond held to maturity has no capital gain or loss. (LOS 54.a)

2. **A** The decrease in the YTM to 5.5% will decrease the reinvestment income over the life of the bond so that the investor will earn less than 6%, the YTM at purchase. (LOS 54.a)

3. **B** The interest portion of a bond's return is the sum of the coupon payments and interest earned from reinvesting coupon payments over the holding period.

   N = 18; PMT = 50 ; PV = 0; I/Y = 5%; CPT → FV = –1,406.62

   (LOS 54.a)

4. **A** The price of the bond after three years that will generate neither a capital gain nor a capital loss is the price if the YTM remains at 7.3%. After three years, the present value of the bond is $800,000 / 1.073^{12} = 343,473.57$, so she will have a capital gain relative to the bond's carrying value. (LOS 54.a)

5. **B** $V_- = 100.979$

   N = 6; PMT = 14.00; FV = 100; I/Y = 13.75; CPT → PV = –100.979

   $V_+ = 99.035$

   I/Y = 14.25; CPT → PV = –99.035V_0 = 100.000

   $\Delta y = 0.0025$

   Approximate modified duration $= \dfrac{V_- - V_+}{2V_0 \Delta YTM} = \dfrac{100.979 - 99.035}{2(100)(0.0025)} = 3.888$

   (LOS 54.b)

6. **B** The interest rate sensitivity of a bond with an embedded call option will be less than that of an option-free bond. Effective duration takes the effect of the call option into account and will, therefore, be less than Macaulay or modified duration. (LOS 54.b)

7. **C** Because bonds with embedded options have cash flows that are uncertain and depend on future interest rates, effective duration must be used. (LOS 54.c)

Module Quiz 54.2

1. **A** Key rate duration refers to the sensitivity of a bond or portfolio value to a change in one specific spot rate. (LOS 54.d)

2. **C** Other things equal, Macaulay duration is less when yield is higher and when maturity is shorter. The bond with the highest yield and shortest maturity must have the lowest Macaulay duration. (LOS 54.e)

3. **A** Portfolio duration is limited as a measure of interest rate risk because it assumes parallel shifts in the yield curve; that is, the discount rate at each maturity changes by the same amount. Portfolio duration can be calculated using effective durations of bonds with embedded options. By definition, a portfolio's internal rate of return is equal to its cash flow yield. (LOS 54.f)

4. **B** PVBP = initial price − price if yield is changed by 1 basis point.

   First, we need to calculate the yield so we can calculate the price of the bond with a 1 basis point change in yield. Using a financial calculator: PV = −1,029.23; FV = 1,000; PMT = 27.5 = (0.055 × 1,000) / 2; N = 14 = 2 × 7 years; CPT → I/Y = 2.49998, multiplied by 2 = 4.99995, or 5.00%.

   Next, compute the price of the bond at a yield of 5.00% + 0.01%, or 5.01%. Using the calculator: FV = 1,000; PMT = 27.5; N = 14; I/Y = 2.505 (5.01 / 2); CPT → PV = $1,028.63.

   Finally, PVBP = $1,029.23 − $1,028.63 = $0.60. (LOS 54.g)

Module Quiz 54.3

1. **B** Convexity effect = ½ × convexity × $(\Delta YTM)^2$ = (0.5)(114.6)(0.011)^2 = 0.00693 = 0.693% (LOS 54.h)

2. **C** −7.87 × (−1.10%) = 8.657% (LOS 54.i)

3. **B** Total estimated price change = (duration effect + convexity effect) {[−10.5 × (−0.02)] + [½ × 97.3 × (−0.02)^2]} × 100 = 21.0% + 1.95% = 22.95% (LOS 54.i)

4. **C** In addition to its sensitivity to changes in yield (i.e., duration), a bond's interest rate risk includes the volatility of yields. A shorter-maturity bond may have more interest rate risk than an otherwise similar longer-maturity bond if short-term yields are more volatile than long-term yields. (LOS 54.j)

5. **B** Duration gap is Macaulay duration minus the investment horizon. Because modified duration equals Macaulay duration / (1 + YTM), Macaulay duration is greater than modified duration for any YTM greater than zero. Therefore, this bond has a Macaulay duration greater than six years and the investment has a positive duration gap. (LOS 54.k)

6. **C** The less liquidity a bond has, the higher its yield spread relative to its benchmark. This is because investors require a higher yield to compensate them for giving up liquidity. (LOS 54.l)

READING 55

Fundamentals of Credit Analysis

EXAM FOCUS

This topic review introduces credit analysis, primarily for corporate bonds, but considerations for credit analysis of high yield, sovereign, and non-sovereign government bonds are also covered. Focus on credit ratings, credit spreads, and the impact on return when ratings and spreads change.

MODULE 55.1: CREDIT RISK AND BOND RATINGS

Video covering this content is available online.

LOS 55.a: Describe credit risk and credit-related risks affecting corporate bonds.

LOS 55.b: Describe default probability and loss severity as components of credit risk.

CFA® Program Curriculum: Volume 5, page 592

Credit risk is the risk associated with losses stemming from the failure of a borrower to make timely and full payments of interest or principal. Credit risk has two components: *default risk* and *loss severity*.

■ **Default risk** is the probability that a borrower (bond issuer) fails to pay interest or repay principal when due.

■ **Loss severity**, or *loss given default*, refers to the value a bond investor will lose if the issuer defaults. Loss severity can be stated as a monetary amount or as a percentage of a bond's value (principal and unpaid interest).

The **expected loss** is equal to the default risk multiplied by the loss severity. Expected loss can likewise be stated as a monetary value or as a percentage of a bond's value.

The **recovery rate** is the percentage of a bond's value an investor will receive if the issuer defaults. Loss severity as a percentage is equal to one minus the recovery rate.

Bonds with credit risk trade at higher yields than bonds thought to be free of credit risk. The difference in yield between a credit-risky bond and a credit-risk-free bond of similar maturity is called its **yield spread**. For example, if a 5-year corporate bond is trading at a spread of +250 basis points to Treasuries and the yield on 5-year Treasury notes is 4.0%, the yield on the corporate bond is 4.0% + 2.5% = 6.5%.

Bond prices are inversely related to spreads; a wider spread implies a lower bond price and a narrower spread implies a higher price. The size of the spread reflects the creditworthiness of the issuer and the liquidity of the market for its bonds. **Spread risk** is the possibility that a bond's spread will widen due to one or both of these factors.

- **Credit migration risk** or **downgrade risk** is the possibility that spreads will increase because the issuer has become less creditworthy. As we will see later in this topic review, credit rating agencies assign ratings to bonds and issuers, and may upgrade or downgrade these ratings over time.

- **Market liquidity risk** is the risk of receiving less than market value when selling a bond and is reflected in the size of the bid-ask spreads. Market liquidity risk is greater for the bonds of less creditworthy issuers and for the bonds of smaller issuers with relatively little publicly traded debt.

LOS 55.c: Describe seniority rankings of corporate debt and explain the potential violation of the priority of claims in a bankruptcy proceeding.

CFA® Program Curriculum: Volume 5, page 595

Each category of debt from the same issuer is ranked according to a **priority of claims** in the event of a default. A bond's priority of claims to the issuer's assets and cash flows is referred to as its **seniority ranking**.

Debt can be either **secured debt** or **unsecured debt**. Secured debt is backed by collateral, while unsecured debt or *debentures* represent a general claim to the issuer's assets and cash flows. Secured debt has higher priority of claims than unsecured debt.

Secured debt can be further distinguished as *first lien* or *first mortgage* (where a specific asset is pledged), *senior secured*, or *junior secured* debt. Unsecured debt is further divided into *senior*, *junior*, and *subordinated* gradations. The highest rank of unsecured debt is senior unsecured. Subordinated debt ranks below other unsecured debt.

The general seniority rankings for debt repayment priority are the following:

- First lien or first mortgage.
- Senior secured debt.
- Junior secured debt.
- Senior unsecured debt.

■ Senior subordinated debt.

■ Subordinated debt.

■ Junior subordinated debt.

All debt within the same category is said to rank **pari passu**, or have same priority of claims. All senior secured debt holders, for example, are treated alike in a corporate bankruptcy.

Recovery rates are highest for debt with the highest priority of claims and decrease with each lower rank of seniority. The lower the seniority ranking of a bond, the higher its credit risk. Investors require a higher yield to accept a lower seniority ranking.

In the event of a default or reorganization, senior lenders have claims on the assets before junior lenders and equity holders. A strict priority of claims, however, is not always applied in practice. Although in theory the priority of claims is absolute, in many cases lower-priority debt holders (and even equity investors) may get paid even if senior debt holders are not paid in full.

Bankruptcies can be costly and take a long time to settle. During bankruptcy proceedings, the value of a company's assets could deteriorate due to loss of customers and key employees, while legal expenses mount. A bankruptcy reorganization plan is confirmed by a vote among all classes of investors with less than 100% recovery rate. To avoid unnecessary delays, negotiation and compromise among various claimholders may result in a reorganization plan that does not strictly conform to the original priority of claims. By such a vote or by order of the bankruptcy court, the final plan may differ from absolute priority.

LOS 55.d: Distinguish between corporate issuer credit ratings and issue credit ratings and describe the rating agency practice of "notching."

CFA® Program Curriculum: Volume 5, page 603

Credit rating agencies assign ratings to categories of bonds with similar credit risk. Rating agencies rate both the issuer (i.e., the company issuing the bonds) and the debt issues, or the bonds themselves. Issuer credit ratings are called **corporate family ratings** (CFR), while issue-specific ratings are called **corporate credit ratings** (CCR). Issuer ratings are based on the overall creditworthiness of the company. The issuers are rated on their senior unsecured debt.

Figure 55.1 shows ratings scales used by Standard & Poor's, Moody's, and Fitch, three of the major credit rating agencies.

Figure 55.1: Credit Rating Categories

(a) Investment grade ratings		(b) Noninvestment grade ratings	
Moody's	Standard & Poor's, Fitch	Moody's	Standard & Poor's, Fitch
Aaa	AAA	Ba1	BB+
Aa1	AA+	Ba2	BB
Aa2	AA	Ba3	BB–
Aa3	AA–	B1	B+
A1	A+	B2	B
A2	A	B3	B–
A3	A–	Caa1	CCC+
Baa1	BBB+	Caa2	CCC
Baa2	BBB	Caa3	CCC–
Baa3	BBB–	Ca	CC
		C	C
		C	D

Triple A (AAA or Aaa) is the highest rating. Bonds with ratings of Baa3/BBB– or higher are considered **investment grade**. Bonds rated Ba1/BB+ or lower are considered **noninvestment grade** and are often called *high yield bonds* or *junk bonds*.

Bonds in default are rated D by Standard & Poor's and Fitch and are included in Moody's lowest rating category, C. When a company defaults on one of its several outstanding bonds, provisions in bond indentures may trigger default on the remaining issues as well. Such a provision is called a *cross default provision*.

A borrower can have multiple debt issues that vary not only by maturities and coupons but also by credit rating. Issue credit ratings depend on the seniority of a bond issue and its covenants. **Notching** is the practice by rating agencies of assigning different ratings to bonds of the same issuer. Notching is based on several factors, including seniority of the bonds and its impact on potential loss severity.

An example of a factor that rating agencies consider when notching an issue credit rating is **structural subordination**. In a holding company structure, both the parent company and the subsidiaries may have outstanding debt. A subsidiary's debt covenants may restrict the transfer of cash or assets "upstream" to the parent company before the subsidiary's debt is serviced. In such a case, even though the parent company's bonds are not junior to the subsidiary's bonds, the subsidiary's bonds have a priority claim to the subsidiary's cash flows. Thus the parent company's bonds are effectively subordinated to the subsidiary's bonds.

Notching is less common for highly rated issuers than for lower-rated issuers. For lower-rated issuers, higher default risk leads to significant differences between recovery rates of debt with different seniority, leading to more notching.

LOS 55.e: Explain risks in relying on ratings from credit rating agencies.

CFA® Program Curriculum: Volume 5, page 605

Relying on ratings from credit rating agencies has some risks. Four specific risks are:

1. **Credit ratings are dynamic.** Credit ratings change over time. Rating agencies may update their default risk assessments during the life of a bond. Higher credit ratings tend to be more stable than lower credit ratings.

2. **Rating agencies are not perfect.** Ratings mistakes occur from time to time. For example, subprime mortgage securities were assigned much higher ratings than they deserved.

3. **Event risk is difficult to assess.** Risks that are specific to a company or industry are difficult to predict and incorporate into credit ratings. Litigation risk to tobacco companies is one example. Events that are difficult to anticipate, such as natural disasters, acquisitions, and equity buybacks using debt, are not easily captured in credit ratings.

4. **Credit ratings lag market pricing.** Market prices and credit spreads change much faster than credit ratings. Additionally, two bonds with same rating can trade at different yields. Market prices reflect expected losses, while credit ratings only assess default risk.

LOS 55.f: Explain the four Cs (Capacity, Collateral, Covenants, and Character) of traditional credit analysis.

CFA® Program Curriculum: Volume 5, page 611

A common way to categorize the key components of credit analysis is by the **four Cs of credit analysis**: capacity, collateral, covenants, and character.

Capacity

Capacity refers to a corporate borrower's ability repay its debt obligations on time. Analysis of capacity is similar to the process used in equity analysis. Capacity analysis entails three levels of assessment: (1) industry structure, (2) industry fundamentals, and (3) company fundamentals.

Industry Structure

The first level of a credit analyst's assessment is industry structure. Industry structure can be described by Porter's five forces: threat of entry, power of suppliers, power of buyers, threat of substitution, and rivalry among existing competitors.

PROFESSOR'S NOTE

We describe industry analysis based on Porter's five forces in the Study Session on equity valuation.

Industry Fundamentals

The next level of a credit analyst's assessment is industry fundamentals, including the influence of macroeconomic factors on an industry's growth prospects and profitability. Industry fundamentals evaluation focuses on:

■ **Industry cyclicality.** Cyclical industries are sensitive to economic performance. Cyclical industries tend to have more volatile earnings, revenues, and cash flows, which make them more risky than noncyclical industries.

■ **Industry growth prospects.** Creditworthiness is most questionable for the weaker companies in a slow-growing or declining industry.

■ **Industry published statistics.** Industry statistics provided by rating agencies, investment banks, industry periodicals, and government agencies can be a source for industry performance and fundamentals.

Company Fundamentals

The last level of credit analysts' assessment is company fundamentals. A corporate borrower should be assessed on:

■ **Competitive position.** Market share changes over time and cost structure relative to peers are some of the factors to analyze.

■ **Operating history.** The performance of the company over different phases of business cycle, trends in margins and revenues, and current management's tenure.

■ **Management's strategy and execution.** This includes the soundness of the strategy, the ability to execute the strategy, and the effects of management's decisions on bondholders.

■ **Ratios and ratio analysis.** As we will discuss later in this topic review, leverage and coverage ratios are important tools for credit analysis.

Collateral

Collateral analysis is more important for less creditworthy companies. The market value of a company's assets can be difficult to observe directly. Issues to consider when assessing collateral values include:

■ **Intangible assets.** Patents are considered high-quality intangible assets because they can be more easily sold to generate cash flows than other intangibles. Goodwill is not considered a high-quality intangible asset and is usually written down when company performance is poor.

■ **Depreciation.** High depreciation expense relative to capital expenditures may signal that management is not investing sufficiently in the company. The quality of the company's assets may be poor, which may lead to reduced operating cash flow and potentially high loss severity.

■ **Equity market capitalization.** A stock that trades below book value may indicate that company assets are of low quality.

■ **Human and intellectual capital.** These are difficult to value, but a company may have intellectual property that can function as collateral.

Covenants

Covenants are the terms and conditions the borrowers and lenders have agreed to as part of a bond issue. Covenants protect lenders while leaving some operating flexibility to the borrowers to run the company. There are two types of covenants: (1) *affirmative covenants* and (2) *negative covenants*.

Affirmative covenants require the borrower to take certain actions, such as paying interest, principal, and taxes; carrying insurance on pledged assets; and maintaining certain financial ratios within prescribed limits.

Negative covenants restrict the borrower from taking certain actions, such as incurring additional debt or directing cash flows to shareholders in the form of dividends and stock repurchases.

Covenants that are overly restrictive of an issuer's operating activities may reduce the issuer's ability to repay. On the other hand, covenants create a legally binding contractual framework for repayment of the debt obligation, which reduces uncertainty for the debt holders. A careful credit analysis should include an assessment of whether the covenants protect the interests of the bondholders without unduly constraining the borrower's operating activities.

Character

Character refers to management's integrity and its commitment to repay the loan. Factors such as management's business qualifications and operating record are important for evaluating character. Character analysis includes an assessment of:

- **Soundness of strategy.** Management's ability to develop a sound strategy.

- **Track record.** Management's past performance in executing its strategy and operating the company without bankruptcies, restructurings, or other distress situations that led to additional borrowing.

- **Accounting policies and tax strategies.** Use of accounting policies and tax strategies that may be hiding problems, such as revenue recognition issues, frequent restatements, and frequently changing auditors.

- **Fraud and malfeasance record.** Any record of fraud or other legal and regulatory problems.

- **Prior treatment of bondholders.** Benefits to equity holders at the expense of debt holders, through actions such as debt-financed acquisitions and special dividends, especially if they led to credit rating downgrades.

 MODULE QUIZ 55.1

To best evaluate your performance, enter your quiz answers online.

1. The two components of credit risk are:
   A. default risk and yield spread.
   B. default risk and loss severity.
   C. loss severity and yield spread.

2. Expected loss can decrease with an increase in a bond's:
   A. default risk.
   B. loss severity.
   C. recovery rate.

3. Absolute priority of claims in a bankruptcy might be violated because:
   A. of the pari passu principle.
   B. creditors negotiate a different outcome.
   C. available funds must be distributed equally among creditors.

4. "Notching" is *best* described as a difference between:
   A. an issuer credit rating and an issue credit rating.
   B. a company credit rating and an industry average credit rating.
   C. an investment grade credit rating and a noninvestment grade credit rating.

5. Which of the following statements is *least likely* a limitation of relying on ratings from credit rating agencies?
   A. Credit ratings are dynamic.
   B. Firm-specific risks are difficult to rate.
   C. Credit ratings adjust quickly to changes in bond prices.

6. Ratio analysis is *most likely* used to assess a borrower's:
   A. capacity.
   B. character.
   C. collateral.

Video covering this content is available online.

MODULE 55.2: EVALUATING CREDIT QUALITY

LOS 55.g: Calculate and interpret financial ratios used in credit analysis.

LOS 55.h: Evaluate the credit quality of a corporate bond issuer and a bond of that issuer, given key financial ratios of the issuer and the industry.

CFA® Program Curriculum: Volume 5, page 615

Ratio analysis is part of capacity analysis. Two primary categories of ratios for credit analysis are *leverage ratios* and *coverage ratios*. Credit analysts calculate company ratios to assess the viability of a company, to find trends over time, and to compare companies to industry averages and peers.

Profits and Cash Flows

Profits and cash flows are needed to service debt. Here we examine four profit and cash flow metrics commonly used in ratio analysis by credit analysts.

1. **Earnings before interest, taxes, depreciation, and amortization (EBITDA).**
   EBITDA is a commonly used measure that is calculated as operating income plus depreciation and amortization. A drawback to using this measure for credit analysis is that it does not adjust for capital expenditures and changes in working capital, which are necessary uses of funds for a going concern. Cash needed for these uses is not available to debt holders.

2. **Funds from operations (FFO).** Funds from operations are net income from continuing operations plus depreciation, amortization, deferred taxes, and noncash items. FFO is similar to cash flow from operations (CFO) except that FFO excludes changes in working capital.

3. **Free cash flow before dividends.** Free cash flow before dividends is net income plus depreciation and amortization minus capital expenditures minus increase in working capital. Free cash flow before dividends excludes nonrecurring items.

4. **Free cash flow after dividends.** This is free cash flow before dividends minus the dividends. If free cash flow after dividends is greater than zero, it represents cash that could pay down debt or accumulate on the balance sheet. Either outcome is a form of deleveraging, a positive indicator for creditworthiness.

Leverage Ratios

Analysts should adjust debt reported on the financial statements by including the firm's obligations such as underfunded pension plans (net pension liabilities) and off-balance-sheet liabilities such as operating leases.

The most common measures of leverage used by credit analysts are the debt-to-capital ratio, the debt-to-EBITDA ratio, the FFO-to-debt ratio, and the ratio of FCF after dividends to debt.

1. **Debt/capital.** Capital is the sum of total debt and shareholders' equity. The debt-to-capital ratio is the percentage of the capital structure financed by debt. A lower ratio indicates less credit risk. If the financial statements list high values for intangible assets such as goodwill, an analyst should calculate a second debt-to-capital ratio adjusted for a writedown of these assets' after-tax value.

2. **Debt/EBITDA.** A higher ratio indicates higher leverage and higher credit risk. This ratio is more volatile for firms in cyclical industries or with high operating leverage because of their high variability of EBITDA.

3. **FFO/debt.** Because this ratio divides a cash flow measure by the value of debt, a higher ratio indicates lower credit risk.

4. **FCF after dividends/debt.** Greater values indicate a greater ability to service existing debt.

Coverage Ratios

Coverage ratios measure the borrower's ability to generate cash flows to meet interest payments. The two most commonly used are EBITDA-to-interest and EBIT-to-interest.

1. **EBITDA/interest expense.** A higher ratio indicates lower credit risk. This ratio is used more often than the EBIT-to-interest expense ratio. Because depreciation and amortization are still included as part of the cash flow measure, this ratio will be higher than the EBIT version.

2. **EBIT/interest expense.** A higher ratio indicates lower credit risk. This ratio is the more conservative measure because depreciation and amortization are subtracted from earnings.

Ratings agencies publish benchmark values for financial ratios that are associated with each ratings classification. Credit analysts can evaluate the potential for upgrades and downgrades based on subject company ratios relative to these benchmarks.

EXAMPLE: Credit analysis based on ratios

An analyst is assessing the credit quality of York, Inc. and Zale, Inc., relative to each other and their industry average. Selected financial information appears in the following table.

	York, Inc.	Zale, Inc.	Industry Average
Earnings before interest and taxes	$550,000	$2,250,000	$1,400,000
Funds from operations	$300,000	$850,000	$600,000
Interest expense	$40,000	$160,000	$100,000
Total debt	$1,000,000	$2,500,000	$2,400,000
Total capital	$4,000,000	$6,500,000	$6,000,000

Footnotes to the two companies' financial statements disclose that York, Inc. has goodwill of $500,000 and operating lease obligations with a present value of $900,000, while Zale, Inc. has a net pension liability of $200,000 and no operating lease obligations. The analyst determines that the appropriate industry averages are goodwill of $200,000, operating leases with a present value of $200,000, and no net pension asset or liability.

Explain how the analyst should adjust York's and Zale's financial statements, calculate adjusted financial ratios, and evaluate the relative creditworthiness of York and Zale.

Answer:

The recommended analyst adjustments are to add operating lease obligations and net pension liabilities to total debt before calculating leverage ratios. An analyst should also consider total capital both including and excluding goodwill.

The following table shows the results of these analyst adjustments.

	York, Inc.	Zale, Inc.	Industry Average
Earnings before interest and taxes	$550,000	$2,250,000	$1,400,000
Funds from operations	$300,000	$850,000	$600,000
Interest expense	$40,000	$160,000	$100,000
Total debt	**$1,900,000**	**$2,700,000**	**$2,600,000**
Total capital, including goodwill	$4,000,000	$6,500,000	$6,000,000
Total capital, excluding goodwill	**$3,500,000**	$6,500,000	**$5,800,000**

Leverage and coverage ratios based on these adjusted data are as follows:

EBIT / interest:

York: $550,000 / $40,000 = 13.8×

Zale: $2,250,000 / $160,000 = 14.1×

Industry average: $1,400,000 / $100,000 = 14.0×

Both York and Zale have interest coverage in line with their industry average.

FFO / total debt:

York: $300,000 / $1,900,000 = 15.8%

Zale: $850,000 / $2,700,000 = 31.5%

Industry average: $600,000 / $2,600,000 = 23.1%

Zale's funds from operations relative to its debt level are greater than the industry average, while York is generating less FFO relative to its debt level.

Total debt / total capital (including goodwill):

York: $1,900,000 / $4,000,000 = 47.5%

Zale: $2,700,000 / $6,500,000 = 41.5%

Industry average: $2,600,000 / $6,000,000 = 43.3%

Total debt / total capital (excluding goodwill):

York: $1,900,000 / $3,500,000 = 54.3%

Zale: $2,700,000 / $6,500,000 = 41.5%

Industry average: $2,600,000 / $5,800,000 = 44.8%

York is more leveraged than Zale and the industry average, especially after adjusting for goodwill.

Based on these data, Zale, Inc. appears to be more creditworthy than York, Inc.

LOS 55.i: Describe factors that influence the level and volatility of yield spreads.

CFA® Program Curriculum: Volume 5, page 628

We can think of the yield on an option-free corporate bond as the sum of the real risk-free interest rate, the expected inflation rate, a maturity premium, a liquidity premium, and a credit spread. All bond prices and yields are affected by changes in the first three of these components. The last two components are the yield spread:

yield spread = liquidity premium + credit spread

Yield spreads on corporate bonds are affected primarily by five interrelated factors:

1. **Credit cycle.** The market's perception of overall credit risk is cyclical. At the top of the credit cycle, the bond market perceives low credit risk and is generally

bullish. Credit spreads narrow as the credit cycle improves. Credit spreads widen as the credit cycle deteriorates.

2. **Economic conditions.** Credit spreads narrow as the economy strengthens and investors expect firms' credit metrics to improve. Conversely, credit spreads widen as the economy weakens.

3. **Financial market performance.** Credit spreads narrow in strong-performing markets overall, including the equity market. Credit spreads widen in weak-performing markets. In steady-performing markets with low volatility of returns, credit spreads also tend to narrow as investors reach for yield.

4. **Broker-dealer capital.** Because most bonds trade over the counter, investors need broker-dealers to provide market-making capital for bond markets to function. Yield spreads are narrower when broker-dealers provide sufficient capital but can widen when market-making capital becomes scarce.

5. **General market demand and supply.** Credit spreads narrow in times of high demand for bonds. Credit spreads widen in times of low demand for bonds. Excess supply conditions, such as large issuance in a short period of time, can lead to widening spreads.

Yield spreads on lower-quality issues tend to be more volatile than spreads on higher-quality issues.

LOS 55.j: Explain special considerations when evaluating the credit of high yield, sovereign, and non-sovereign government debt issuers and issues.

CFA® Program Curriculum: Volume 5, page 638

High Yield Debt

High yield or *noninvestment grade* corporate bonds are rated below Baa3/BBB by credit rating agencies. These bonds are also called *junk bonds* because of their higher perceived credit risk.

Reasons for noninvestment grade ratings may include:

- High leverage.
- Unproven operating history.
- Low or negative free cash flow.
- High sensitivity to business cycles.
- Low confidence in management.
- Unclear competitive advantages.
- Large off-balance-sheet liabilities.
- Industry in decline.

Because high yield bonds have higher default risk than investment grade bonds, credit analysts must pay more attention to loss severity. Special considerations for high yield bonds include their liquidity, financial projections, debt structure, corporate structure, and covenants.

Liquidity. Liquidity or availability of cash is critical for high yield issuers. High yield issuers have limited access to additional borrowings, and available funds tend to be more expensive for high yield issuers. Bad company-specific news and difficult financial market conditions can quickly dry up the liquidity of debt markets. Many high yield issuers are privately owned and cannot access public equity markets for needed funds.

Analysts focus on six sources of liquidity (in order of reliability):

1. Balance sheet cash.

2. Working capital.

3. Operating cash flow (CFO).

4. Bank credit.

5. Equity issued.

6. Sales of assets.

For a high yield issuer with few or unreliable sources of liquidity, significant amounts of debt coming due within a short time frame may indicate potential default. Running out of cash with no access to external financing to refinance or service existing debt is the primary reason why high yield issuers default. For high yield financial firms that are highly levered and depend on funding long-term assets with short-term liabilities, liquidity is critical.

Financial projections. Projecting future earnings and cash flows, including stress scenarios and accounting for changes in capital expenditures and working capital, are important for revealing potential vulnerabilities to the inability to meet debt payments.

Debt structure. High yield issuers' capital structures often include different types of debt with several levels of seniority and hence varying levels of potential loss severity. Capital structures typically include secured bank debt, second lien debt, senior unsecured debt, subordinated debt, and preferred stock. Some of these, especially subordinated debt, may be convertible to common shares.

A credit analyst will need to calculate leverage for each level of the debt structure when an issuer has multiple layers of debt with a variety of expected recovery rates.

High yield companies for which secured bank debt is a high proportion of the capital structure are said to be *top heavy* and have less capacity to borrow from banks in financially stressful periods. Companies that have top-heavy capital structures are more likely to default and have lower recovery rates for unsecured debt issues.

Corporate structure. Many high-yield companies use a holding company structure. A parent company receives dividends from the earnings of subsidiaries as its primary source of operating income. Because of structural subordination, subsidiaries' dividends paid upstream to a parent company are subordinate to interest payments. These dividends can be insufficient to pay the debt obligations of the parent, thus reducing the recovery rate for debt holders of the parent company.

Despite structural subordination, a parent company's credit rating may be superior to subsidiaries' ratings because the parent can benefit from having access to multiple cash flows from diverse subsidiaries.

Some complex corporate structures have intermediate holding companies that carry their own debt and do not own 100% of their subsidiaries' stock. These companies are typically a result of mergers, acquisitions, or leveraged buyouts.

Default of one subsidiary may not necessarily result in cross default. Analysts need to scrutinize bonds' indentures and other legal documents to fully understand the impact of complex corporate structures. To analyze these companies, analysts should calculate leverage ratios at each level of debt issuance and on a consolidated basis.

Covenants. Important covenants for high yield debt include:

- **Change of control put.** This covenant gives debt holders the right to require the issuer to buy back debt (typically for par value or a value slightly above par) in the event of an acquisition. For investment grade bonds, a change of control put typically applies only if an acquisition of the borrower results in a rating downgrade to below investment grade.

- **Restricted payments.** The covenant protects lenders by limiting the amount of cash that may be paid to equity holders.

- **Limitations on liens.** The covenant limits the amount of secured debt that a borrower can carry. Unsecured debt holders prefer the issuer to have less secured debt, which increases the recovery amount available to them in the event of default.

- **Restricted versus unrestricted subsidiaries.** Issuers can classify subsidiaries as restricted or unrestricted. Restricted subsidiaries' cash flows and assets can be used to service the debt of the parent holding company. This benefits creditors of holding companies because their debt is pari passu with the debt of restricted subsidiaries, rather than structurally subordinated. Restricted subsidiaries are typically the holding company's larger subsidiaries that have significant assets. Tax and regulatory issues can factor into the classification of subsidiary's restriction status. A subsidiary's restriction status is found in the bond indenture.

Bank covenants are often more restrictive than bond covenants, and when covenants are violated, banks can block additional loans until the violation is corrected. If a violation is not remedied, banks can trigger a default by accelerating the full repayment of a loan.

In terms of the factors that affect their return, high yield bonds may be viewed as a hybrid of investment grade bonds and equity. Compared to investment grade bonds, high yield bonds show greater price and spread volatility and are more highly correlated with the equity market.

High yield analysis can include some of the same techniques as equity market analysis, such as enterprise value. **Enterprise value** (EV) is equity market capitalization plus total debt minus excess cash. For high yield companies that are not publicly traded, comparable public company equity data can be used to estimate EV. Enterprise value analysis can indicate a firm's potential for additional leverage, or the potential credit damage that might result from a leveraged buyout. An analyst can compare firms based on the differences between their EV/EBITDA and debt/EBITDA ratios. Firms with a wider difference between these ratios have greater equity relative to their debt and therefore have less credit risk.

Sovereign Debt

Sovereign debt is issued by national governments. Sovereign credit analysis must assess both the government's ability to service debt and its willingness to do so. The assessment of willingness is important because bondholders usually have no legal recourse if a national government refuses to pay its debts.

A basic framework for evaluating and assigning a credit rating to sovereign debt includes five key areas:

1. **Institutional effectiveness** includes successful policymaking, absence of corruption, and commitment to honor debts.

2. **Economic prospects** include growth trends, demographics, income per capita, and size of government relative to the private economy.

3. **International investment position** includes the country's foreign reserves, its external debt, and the status of its currency in international markets.

4. **Fiscal flexibility** includes the government's willingness and ability to increase revenue or cut expenditures to ensure debt service, as well as trends in debt as a percentage of GDP.

5. **Monetary flexibility** includes the ability to use monetary policy for domestic economic objectives (this might be lacking with exchange rate targeting or membership in a monetary union) and the credibility and effectiveness of monetary policy.

Credit rating agencies assign each national government two ratings: (1) a local currency debt rating and (2) a foreign currency debt rating. The ratings are assigned separately because defaults on foreign currency denominated debt have historically exceeded those on local currency debt. Foreign currency debt typically has a higher default rate and a lower credit rating because the government must purchase foreign currency in the open market to make interest and principal payments, which exposes it to the risk of significant local currency depreciation. In contrast, local currency debt can be repaid by raising taxes, controlling domestic spending, or simply printing more money. Ratings can differ as much as two notches for local and foreign currency bonds.

Sovereign defaults can be caused by events such as war, political instability, severe devaluation of the currency, or large declines in the prices of the country's export commodities. Access to debt markets can be difficult for sovereigns in bad economic times.

Non-Sovereign Government Bonds

Non-sovereign government debt is issued by local governments (cities, states, and counties) and quasi-governmental entities. **Municipal bonds** are a significant part of the overall U.S. bond market. Interest payments from municipal bonds are most often exempt from national income taxes. Default rates for municipal bonds are very low relative to general corporate bonds.

Most municipal bonds can be classified as *general obligation bonds* or *revenue bonds*. **General obligation** (GO) bonds are unsecured bonds backed by the full faith credit of the issuing governmental entity, which is to say they are supported by its taxing power. **Revenue bonds** are issued to finance specific projects, such as airports, toll bridges, hospitals, and power generation facilities.

Unlike sovereigns, municipalities cannot use monetary policy to service their debt and usually must balance their operating budgets. Municipal governments' ability to service their general obligation debt depends ultimately on the local economy (i.e., the tax base). Economic factors to assess in evaluating the creditworthiness of GO bonds include employment, trends in per capita income and per capita debt, tax base dimensions (depth, breadth, and stability), demographics, and ability to attract new jobs (location, infrastructure). Credit analysts must also observe revenue variability through economic cycles. Relying on highly variable taxes that are subject to economic cycles, such as capital gains and sales taxes, can signal higher credit risk. Municipalities may have long-term obligations such as underfunded pensions and post-retirement benefits. Inconsistent reporting requirements for municipalities are also an issue.

Revenue bonds often have higher credit risk than GO bonds because the project is the sole source of funds to service the debt. Analysis of revenue bonds combines analysis of the project, using techniques similar to those for analyzing corporate bonds, with analysis of the financing of the project.

MODULE QUIZ 55.2

To best evaluate your performance, enter your quiz answers online.

1. Higher credit risk is indicated by a higher:
    A. FFO/debt ratio.
    B. debt/EBITDA ratio.
    C. EBITDA/interest expense ratio.

2. Compared to other firms in the same industry, an issuer with a credit rating of AAA should have a lower:
    A. FFO/debt ratio.
    B. operating margin.
    C. debt/capital ratio.

3. Credit spreads tend to widen as:
    A. the credit cycle improves.
    B. economic conditions worsen.
    C. broker-dealers become more willing to provide capital.

4. Compared to shorter duration bonds, longer duration bonds:
    A. have smaller bid-ask spreads.
    B. are less sensitive to credit spreads.
    C. have less certainty regarding future creditworthiness.

5. One key difference between sovereign bonds and municipal bonds is that sovereign issuers:
    A. can print money.
    B. have governmental taxing power.
    C. are affected by economic conditions.

KEY CONCEPTS

LOS 55.a

Credit risk refers to the possibility that a borrower fails to make the scheduled interest payments or return of principal.

Spread risk is the possibility that a bond loses value because its credit spread widens relative to its benchmark. Spread risk includes credit migration or downgrade risk and market liquidity risk.

LOS 55.b

Credit risk is composed of default risk, which is the probability of default, and loss severity, which is the portion of the value of a bond or loan a lender or investor will lose if the borrower defaults. The expected loss is the probability of default multiplied by the loss severity.

LOS 55.c

Corporate debt is ranked by seniority or priority of claims. Secured debt is a direct claim on specific firm assets and has priority over unsecured debt. Secured or unsecured debt may be further ranked as senior or subordinated. Priority of claims may be summarized as follows:

- First mortgage or first lien.
- Second or subsequent lien.
- Senior secured debt.
- Senior unsecured debt.
- Senior subordinated debt.
- Subordinated debt.
- Junior subordinated debt.

LOS 55.d

Issuer credit ratings, or corporate family ratings, reflect a debt issuer's overall creditworthiness and typically apply to a firm's senior unsecured debt.

Issue credit ratings, or corporate credit ratings, reflect the credit risk of a specific debt issue. Notching refers to the practice of adjusting an issue credit rating upward or downward from the issuer credit rating to reflect the seniority and other provisions of a debt issue.

LOS 55.e

Lenders and bond investors should not rely exclusively on credit ratings from rating agencies for the following reasons:

- Credit ratings can change during the life of a debt issue.
- Rating agencies cannot always judge credit risk accurately.
- Firms are subject to risk of unforeseen events that credit ratings do not reflect.
- Market prices of bonds often adjust more rapidly than credit ratings.

LOS 55.f

Components of traditional credit analysis are known as the four Cs:

- Capacity: The borrower's ability to make timely payments on its debt.

- Collateral: The value of assets pledged against a debt issue or available to creditors if the issuer defaults.

- Covenants: Provisions of a bond issue that protect creditors by requiring or prohibiting actions by an issuer's management.

- Character: Assessment of an issuer's management, strategy, quality of earnings, and past treatment of bondholders.

LOS 55.g

Credit analysts use profitability, cash flow, and leverage and coverage ratios to assess debt issuers' capacity.

- Profitability refers to operating income and operating profit margin, with operating income typically defined as earnings before interest and taxes (EBIT).

- Cash flow may be measured as earnings before interest, taxes, depreciation, and amortization (EBITDA); funds from operations (FFO); free cash flow before dividends; or free cash flow after dividends.

- Leverage ratios include debt-to-capital, debt-to-EBITDA, and FFO-to-debt.

- Coverage ratios include EBIT-to-interest expense and EBITDA-to-interest expense.

LOS 55.h

Lower leverage, higher interest coverage, and greater free cash flow imply lower credit risk and a higher credit rating for a firm. When calculating leverage ratios, analysts should include in a firm's total debt its obligations such as underfunded pensions and off-balance-sheet financing.

For a specific debt issue, secured collateral implies lower credit risk compared to unsecured debt, and higher seniority implies lower credit risk compared to lower seniority.

LOS 55.i

Corporate bond yields comprise the real risk-free rate, expected inflation rate, credit spread, maturity premium, and liquidity premium. An issue's yield spread to its benchmark includes its credit spread and liquidity premium.

The level and volatility of yield spreads are affected by the credit and business cycles, the performance of financial markets as a whole, availability of capital from broker-dealers, and supply and demand for debt issues. Yield spreads tend to narrow when the credit cycle is improving, the economy is expanding, and financial markets and investor demand for new debt issues are strong. Yield spreads tend to widen when the credit cycle, the economy, and financial markets are weakening, and in periods when the supply of new debt issues is heavy or broker-dealer capital is insufficient for market making.

LOS 55.j

High yield bonds are more likely to default than investment grade bonds, which increases the importance of estimating loss severity. Analysis of high yield debt should focus on liquidity, projected financial performance, the issuer's corporate and debt structures, and debt covenants.

Credit risk of sovereign debt includes the issuing country's ability and willingness to pay. Ability to pay is greater for debt issued in the country's own currency than for debt issued in a foreign currency. Willingness refers to the possibility that a country refuses to repay its debts.

Analysis of non-sovereign government debt is similar to analysis of sovereign debt, focusing on the strength of the local economy and its effect on tax revenues. Analysis of municipal revenue bonds is similar to analysis of corporate debt, focusing on the ability of a project to generate sufficient revenue to service the bonds.

ANSWER KEY FOR MODULE QUIZZES

Module Quiz 55.1

1. **B** Credit risk is composed of default risk and loss severity. Yield spreads reflect the credit risk of a borrower. (LOS 55.a)

2. **C** An increase in the recovery rate means that the loss severity has decreased, which decreases expected loss. (LOS 55.b)

3. **B** A negotiated bankruptcy settlement does not always follow the absolute priority of claims. (LOS 55.c)

4. **A** Notching refers to the credit rating agency practice of distinguishing between the credit rating of an issuer (generally for its senior unsecured debt) and the credit rating of particular debt issues from that issuer, which may differ from the issuer rating because of provisions such as seniority. (LOS 55.d)

5. **C** Bond prices and credit spreads change much faster than credit ratings. (LOS 55.e)

6. **A** Ratio analysis is used to assess a corporate borrower's capacity to repay its debt obligations on time. (LOS 55.f)

Module Quiz 55.2

1. **B** A higher debt/EBITDA ratio is sign of higher leverage and higher credit risk. Higher FFO/debt and EBITDA/interest expense ratios indicate lower credit risk. (LOS 55.g, 55.h)

2. **C** A low debt/capital ratio is an indicator of low leverage. An issuer rated AAA is likely to have a high operating margin and a high FFO/debt ratio compared to its industry group. (LOS 55.g, 55.h)

3. **B** Credit spreads widen as economic conditions worsen. Spreads narrow as the credit cycle improves and as broker-dealers provide more capital to bond markets. (LOS 55.i)

4. **C** Longer duration bonds usually have longer maturities and carry more uncertainty of future creditworthiness. (LOS 55.i)

5. **A** Sovereign entities can print money to repay debt, while municipal borrowers cannot. Both sovereign and municipal entities have taxing powers, and both are affected by economic conditions. (LOS 55.j)

TOPIC ASSESSMENT: FIXED INCOME

You have now finished the Fixed Income topic section. The following Topic Assessment provides immediate feedback on how effective your study has been for this material. The number of questions on this test is equal to the number of questions for the topic on one-half of the actual Level I CFA exam. Questions are more exam-like than typical Module Quiz or QBank questions; a score of less than 70% indicates that your study likely needs improvement. These tests are best taken timed; allow 1.5 minutes per question.

After you've completed this Topic Assessment, you may additionally log in to your Schweser.com online account and enter your answers in the Topic Assessments product. Select "Performance Tracker" to view a breakdown of your score. Select "Compare with Others" to display how your score on the Topic Assessment compares to the scores of others who entered their answers.

1. An estimate of the increase in an option-free bond's price, based only on its duration:
    A. will be too small.
    B. will be too large.
    C. may be either too small or too large.

2. Three companies in the same industry have exhibited the following average ratios over a 5-year period:

5-Year Averages	Alden	Barrow	Collison
Operating margin	13.3%	15.0%	20.7%
Debt/EBITDA	4.6×	0.9×	2.8×
EBIT/interest	3.6×	8.9×	5.7×
FFO/debt	12.5%	14.6%	11.5%
Debt/capital	60.8%	23.6%	29.6%

    Based only on the information given, the company that *most likely* has the highest credit rating is:
    A. Alden.
    B. Barrow.
    C. Collison.

3. The difference between a convertible bond and a bond with warrants is that a bondholder who exercises warrants:
    A. does not pay cash for the common stock.
    B. obtains common stock at a lower price per share.
    C. continues to hold the bond after exercising the warrants.

4. Which of the following is *least likely* a common form of external credit enhancement?
    A. Overcollateralization.
    B. A corporate guarantee.
    C. A letter of credit from a bank.

5. Nonconforming mortgage loans may be securitized by:
   A. government-sponsored enterprises, but not by private companies.
   B. private companies, but not by government-sponsored enterprises.
   C. neither private companies nor government-sponsored enterprises.

6. Which of the following bonds would appreciate the *most* if the yield curve shifts down by 50 basis points at all maturities?
   A. 4-year 8%, 8% YTM.
   B. 5-year 8%, 7.5% YTM.
   C. 5-year 8.5%, 8% YTM.

7. Which of the following provisions would *most likely* increase the required yield to maturity on a debt security?
   A. Call option.
   B. Put option.
   C. Floor on a floating-rate security.

8. Other things equal, a corporate bond's yield spread is likely to be *most* volatile if the bond is rated:
   A. AA with 5 years to maturity.
   B. AAA with 3 years to maturity.
   C. BBB with 15 years to maturity.

9. In a repurchase agreement, the repo rate is likely to be higher:
   A. if delivery to the lender is required.
   B. when the quality of the collateral is high.
   C. for longer-dated repos.

10. An investor in longer-term coupon bonds who has a short investment horizon is *most likely*:
    A. more concerned with market price risk than reinvestment risk.
    B. more concerned with reinvestment risk than market price risk.
    C. equally concerned about market price risk and reinvestment risk.

11. A bank loan department is trying to determine the correct rate for a 2-year loan to be made two years from now. If current implied Treasury effective annual spot rates are 1-year = 2%, 2-year = 3%, 3-year = 3.5%, and 4-year = 4.5%, the base (risk-free) forward rate for the loan before adding a risk premium is *closest* to:
    A. 4.5%.
    B. 6.0%.
    C. 9.0%.

12. Coyote Corporation has an issuer credit rating of AA, but its most recently issued bonds have an issue credit rating of AA–. This difference is *most likely* due to the newly issued bonds having:
    A. been issued as senior subordinated debt.
    B. been affected by restricted subsidiary status.
    C. additional covenants that protect the bondholders.

13. An institution is *most likely* to be restricted from investing in which of the following fixed income classifications?
    A. High yield.
    B. Index-linked.
    C. Variable-rate.

14. Annual-pay yields of annual-coupon sovereign bonds are as follows:

Maturity and Coupon	Yield to Maturity
1-year, 5% coupon	2.342%
1-year, 0% coupon	2.350%
2-year, 5% coupon	2.496%
2-year, 0% coupon	2.500%
3-year, 5% coupon	2.711%
3-year, 0% coupon	2.725%

The 3-year, 5% annual coupon bond is *most likely*:
A. overvalued.
B. undervalued.
C. fairly valued.

TOPIC ASSESSMENT ANSWERS: FIXED INCOME

1. **A** Duration is a linear measure, but the relationship between bond price and yield for an option-free bond is convex. For a given decrease in yield, the estimated price increase using duration alone will be smaller than the actual price increase. (Study Session 17, Module 54.1, LOS 54.b)

2. **B** Four of the five credit metrics given indicate that Barrow should have the highest credit rating of these three companies. Barrow has higher interest coverage and lower leverage than either Alden or Collison. (Study Session 17, Module 55.2, LOS 55.h)

3. **C** Warrants give holders the option to buy shares of the issuer's common stock at a predetermined price. A bondholder who exercises warrants pays the exercise price to the issuer and receives common shares but continues to hold the bond. With convertible bonds, a bondholder who exercises the conversion option exchanges the bond for a predetermined number of common shares. Exercise prices of warrants and conversion prices of convertible bonds are not necessarily related. (Study Session 16, Module 50.2, LOS 50.f)

4. **A** External credit enhancements are financial guarantees from third parties that generally support the performance of the bond. Overcollateralization is a form of internal credit enhancement. (Study Session 16, Module 50.1, LOS 50.d)

5. **B** Nonconforming mortgages are those that do not meet the requirements to be included in agency RMBS such as those issued by government-sponsored enterprises. Private companies may securitize nonconforming mortgages. (Study Session 16, Module 53.1, LOS 53.d)

6. **B** The bond with the highest duration will benefit the most from a decrease in rates. The lower the coupon, the lower the yield to maturity, and the longer the time to maturity, then the higher the duration will be. (Study Session 17, Module 54.2, LOS 54.e)

7. **A** Call options favor the issuer and increase the required YTM. A put option or a floor protects the bondholder against falling rates, which reduces a bond's required YTM. (Study Session 16, Module 50.2, LOS 50.f)

8. **C** Spread volatility is typically greatest for lower quality and longer maturities. The BBB rated 15-year corporate bond has the lowest credit quality and longest maturity of the three choices. (Study Session 17, Module 55.2, LOS 55.i)

9. **C** The repo rate tends to be higher for longer-dated repos than for shorter-dated repos. High quality collateral or delivery of the collateral reduces the repo rate. (Study Session 16, Module 51.2, LOS 51.j)

10. **A** Over a short investment horizon, an increase in interest rates is likely to decrease the return on a coupon bond because the decrease in price more than offsets the increase in reinvestment income. Over a long investment horizon, a decrease in interest rates is likely to decrease the return on a coupon bond because the decrease in reinvestment income more than offsets the increase in price. Therefore, an investor with a short horizon is more concerned with market price risk and an investor with a long horizon is more concerned with reinvestment risk. (Study Session 17, Module 54.3, LOS 54.k)

11. **B** The forward rate is $[1.045^4 / 1.03^2]^{1/2} - 1 = 6.02\%$, or use the approximation $[4.5(4) - 3(2)] / 2 = 6$. (Study Session 16, Module 52.4, LOS 52.h)

12. **A** The issuer's corporate family rating (CFR) is AA, while the bond's corporate credit rating (CCR) is lower, AA–. One possible reason for this notching difference is that the bond may have a lower seniority ranking. CFR ratings are based on senior unsecured debt. If the newly issued bond is a senior subordinated debt, it has a lower priority of claims and hence a lower rating. Restricted status would affect both CFR and CCR. Additional covenants that protect bondholders would enhance the issue's CCR. (Study Session 16, Module 55.1, LOS 55.d)

13. **A** High yield bonds are those that are classified as noninvestment grade. Some institutions are restricted from investing in this sector of the fixed income market. (Study Session 16, Module 51.1, LOS 51.a)

14. **C** The price of the 3-year coupon bond (as a percentage of par) is: N = 3; I/Y = 2.711; PMT = 5; FV = 100; CPT → PV = –106.51

The no-arbitrage price of the 3-year coupon bond based on spot (zero-coupon) rates is:

$$\frac{5}{1.02350} + \frac{5}{(1.02500)^2} + \frac{105}{(1.02725)^3} = 106.51$$

Because the 3-year coupon bond's price equals its no-arbitrage value, the bond is fairly valued. (Study Session 16, Modules 52.1, 52.2, LOS 52.a, 52.c)

READING
56

Derivative Markets and Instruments

EXAM FOCUS

This topic review contains introductory material that describes specific types of derivatives. Definitions and terminology are presented along with information about derivatives markets. Upon completion of this review, candidates should be familiar with the basic concepts that underlie derivatives and the general arbitrage framework. The next topic review will build on these concepts to explain how prices of derivatives are determined.

MODULE 56.1: FORWARDS AND FUTURES

LOS 56.a: Define a derivative and distinguish between exchange-traded and over-the-counter derivatives.

Video covering this content is available online.

CFA® Program Curriculum: Volume 6, page 6

A **derivative** is a security that *derives* its value from the value or return of another asset or security.

A physical exchange exists for many options contracts and futures contracts. **Exchange-traded derivatives** are standardized and backed by a clearinghouse.

Forwards and *swaps* are custom instruments and are traded/created by dealers in a market with no central location. A dealer market with no central location is referred to as an **over-the-counter** market. They are largely unregulated markets and each contract is with a counterparty, which may expose the owner of a derivative to default risk (when the counterparty does not honor their commitment).

Some *options* trade in the over-the-counter market, notably bond options.

LOS 56.b: Contrast forward commitments with contingent claims.

CFA® Program Curriculum: Volume 6, page 7

A **forward commitment** is a legally binding promise to perform some action in the future. Forward commitments include forward contracts, futures contracts, and swaps. Forward contracts and futures contracts can be written on equities, indexes, bonds, foreign currencies, physical assets, or interest rates.

A **contingent claim** is a claim (to a payoff) that depends on a particular event. **Options** are contingent claims that depend on a stock price at some future date. While forwards, futures, and swaps have payments that are based on a price or rate outcome whether the movement is up or down, contingent claims only require a payment if a certain threshold price is broken (e.g., if the price is above X or the rate is below Y). It takes two options to replicate the payoffs on a futures or forward contract.

Credit derivatives are contingent claims that depend on a credit event such as a default or ratings downgrade.

LOS 56.c: Define forward contracts, futures contracts, options (calls and puts), swaps, and credit derivatives and compare their basic characteristics.

CFA® Program Curriculum: Volume 6, page 14

Forward Contracts

In a **forward contract**, one party agrees to buy and the counterparty to sell a physical or financial asset at a specific price on a specific date in the future. A party may enter into the contract to speculate on the future price of an asset, but more often a party seeks to enter into a forward contract to hedge an existing exposure to the risk of asset price or interest rate changes. A forward contract can be used to reduce or eliminate uncertainty about the future price of an asset it plans to buy or sell at a later date.

Typically, neither party to the contract makes a payment at the initiation of a forward contract. If the expected future price of the asset increases over the life of the contract, the right to buy at the **forward price** (i.e., the price specified in the forward contract) will have positive value, and the obligation to sell will have an equal negative value. If the expected future price of the asset falls below the forward price, the result is opposite and the right to sell (at an above-market price) will have a positive value.

The party to the forward contract who agrees to buy the financial or physical asset has a **long forward position** and is called the *long*. The party to the forward contract who agrees to sell or deliver the asset has a **short forward position** and is called the *short*.

A *deliverable* forward contract is settled by the short delivering the underlying asset to the long. Other forward contracts are settled in cash. In a **cash-settled forward contract**, one party pays cash to the other when the contract expires based on the difference between the forward price and the market price of the underlying asset (i.e., the **spot price**) at the settlement date. Apart from transactions costs, deliverable and cash-settled forward contracts are economically equivalent. Cash-settled forward contracts are also known as *contracts for differences* or *non-deliverable forwards* (NDFs).

Futures Contracts

A **futures contract** is a forward contract that is standardized and exchange-traded. The primary ways in which forwards and futures differ are that futures are traded in an active secondary market, subject to greater regulation, backed by a clearinghouse, and require a daily cash settlement of gains and losses.

Futures contracts are similar to forward contracts in that both:

■ Can be either deliverable or cash-settled contracts.

■ Have contract prices set so each side of the contract has a value of zero value at the initiation of the contract.

Futures contracts *differ* from forward contracts in the following ways:

■ Futures contracts trade on organized exchanges. Forwards are private contracts and typically do not trade.

■ Futures contracts are standardized. Forwards are customized contracts satisfying the specific needs of the parties involved.

■ A clearinghouse is the counterparty to all futures contracts. Forwards are contracts with the originating counterparty and therefore have counterparty (credit) risk.

■ The government regulates futures markets. Forward contracts are usually not regulated and do not trade in organized markets.

A major difference between forwards and futures is futures contracts have standardized contract terms. For each commodity or financial asset, listed futures contracts specify the quality and quantity of assets required under the contract and the delivery procedure (for deliverable contracts). The exchange sets the minimum price fluctuation (called the tick size), daily price move limit, the settlement date, and the trading times for each contract.

The **settlement price** is analogous to the closing price for a stock but is not simply the price of the final trade of the day. It is an average of the prices of the trades during the last period of trading, called the closing period, which is set by the exchange. This specification of the settlement price reduces the opportunity of traders to manipulate the settlement price. The settlement price is used to calculate the daily gain or loss at the end of each trading day. On its final day of trading the settlement price is equal to the spot price of the underlying asset (i.e., futures prices converge to spot prices as futures contracts approach expiration).

The buyer of a futures contract is said to have gone long or taken a *long position*, while the seller of a futures contract is said to have gone short or taken a *short position*. For each contract traded, there is a buyer (long) and a seller (short). The long has agreed to buy the asset at the contract price at the settlement date, and the short has an agreed to sell at that price. The number of futures contracts of a specific kind (e.g., soybeans for November delivery) that are outstanding at any given time is known as the **open interest**. Open interest increases when traders enter new long and short positions and decreases when traders exit existing positions.

Speculators use futures contracts to gain exposure to changes in the price of the asset underlying a futures contract. In contrast, hedgers use futures contracts to reduce an existing exposure to price changes in the asset (i.e., hedge their asset price risk). An example is a wheat farmer who sells wheat futures to reduce the uncertainty about the price he will receive for his wheat at harvest time.

Each futures exchange has a **clearinghouse**. The clearinghouse guarantees traders in the futures market will honor their obligations. The clearinghouse does this by splitting each trade once it is made and acting as the opposite side of each position. The clearinghouse acts as the buyer to every seller and the seller to every buyer. By doing this, the clearinghouse allows either side of the trade to reverse positions at a future date without having to contact the other side of the initial trade. This allows traders to enter the market knowing that they will be able to reverse or reduce their position. The guarantee of the clearinghouse removes counterparty risk (i.e., the risk that the counterparty to a trade will not fulfill their obligation at settlement) from futures contracts. In the history of U.S. futures trading, the clearinghouse has never defaulted on a contract.

PROFESSOR'S NOTE

The terminology is that you "bought" bond futures if you entered into the contract with the long position. In my experience, this terminology has caused confusion for many candidates. You don't purchase the contract, you enter into it. You are contracting to buy an asset on the long side. "Buy" means take the long side, and "sell" means take the short side in futures.

In the futures markets, **margin** is money that must be deposited by both the long and the short as a performance guarantee prior to entering into a futures contract. Unlike margin in bond or stock accounts, there is no loan involved and, consequently, no interest charges. This provides protection for the clearinghouse. Each day, the margin balance in a futures account is adjusted for any gains and losses in the value of the futures position based on the new settlement price, a process called the mark to market or marking to market. **Initial margin** is the amount that must be deposited in a futures account before a trade may be made. Initial margin per contract is relatively low and equals about one day's maximum price fluctuation on the total value of the assets covered by the contract.

Maintenance margin is the minimum amount of margin that must be maintained in a futures account. If the margin balance in the account falls below the maintenance margin through daily settlement of gains and losses (from changes in the futures price), additional funds must be deposited to bring the margin balance back up to the *initial* margin amount. This is different from maintenance margin in an equity account, which requires investors only to bring the margin backup to the maintenance margin amount. Margin requirements are set by the clearinghouse.

Many futures contracts have **price limits**, which are exchange-imposed limits on how each day's settlement price can change from the previous day's settlement price. Exchange members are prohibited from executing trades at prices outside these limits. If the equilibrium price at which traders would willingly trade is above the upper limit or below the lower limit, trades cannot take place.

Consider a futures contract that has a daily price limit of $0.02 and settled the previous day at $1.04. If, on the following trading day, traders wish to trade at $1.07 because of changes in market conditions or expectations, no trades will take place. The settlement price will be reported as $1.06 (for the purposes of marking-to-market). The contract will be said to have made a **limit move**, and the price is said to be **limit up** (from the previous day). If market conditions had changed such that the price at which traders are willing to trade is below $1.02, $1.02 will be the settlement price, and the price is said to be **limit down**. If trades cannot take place because of a limit move, either up or down, the price is said to be **locked limit** since no trades can take place and traders are locked into their existing positions.

MODULE 56.2: SWAPS AND OPTIONS

Video covering this content is available online.

Swaps are agreements to exchange a series of payments on periodic *settlement dates* over a certain time period (e.g., quarterly payments over two years). At each settlement date, the two payments are *netted* so that only one (net) payment is made. The party with the greater liability makes a payment to the other party. The length of the swap is termed the *tenor* of the swap and the contract ends on the termination date.

Swaps are similar to forwards in several ways:

- Swaps typically require no payment by either party at initiation.

- Swaps are custom instruments.

- Swaps are not traded in any organized secondary market.

- Swaps are largely unregulated.

- Default risk is an important aspect of the contracts.

- Most participants in the swaps market are large institutions.

- Individuals are rarely swaps market participants.

There are swaps facilitators who bring together parties with needs for the opposite sides of swaps. There are also dealers, large banks, and brokerage firms who act as principals in trades just as they do in forward contracts.

In the simplest type of swap, a **plain vanilla interest rate swap**, one party makes *fixed-rate* interest payments on a notional principal amount specified in the swap in return for *floating-rate* payments from the other party. A **basis swap** involves trading one set of floating rate payments for another. In a plain vanilla interest rate swap, the party who wants floating-rate interest payments agrees to pay fixed-rate interest and has the *pay-fixed* side of the swap. The counterparty, who receives the fixed payments and agrees to pay variable-rate interest, has the *pay-floating* side of the swap and is called the *floating-rate payer*. The payments owed by one party to the other are based on a **notional principal** that is stated in the swap contract.

PROFESSOR'S NOTE

The Level I derivatives material focuses on interest rate swaps. Other types of swaps, such as currency swaps and equity swaps, are introduced at Level II.

Options

An **option contract** gives its owner the right, but not the obligation, to either buy or sell an underlying asset at a given price (the **exercise price** or **strike price**). While an option buyer can choose whether to exercise an option, the seller is obligated to perform if the buyer exercises the option.

■ The owner of a **call option** has the right to purchase the underlying asset at a specific price for a specified time period.

■ The owner of a **put option** has the right to sell the underlying asset at a specific price for a specified time period.

 PROFESSOR'S NOTE

To remember these terms, note that the owner of a call can "call the asset in" (i.e., buy it); the owner of a put has the right to "put the asset to" the writer of the put.

The seller of an option is also called the **option writer**. There are four possible options positions:

1. Long call: the buyer of a call option—has the right to buy an underlying asset.

2. Short call: the writer (seller) of a call option—has the obligation to sell the underlying asset.

3. Long put: the buyer of a put option—has the right to sell the underlying asset.

4. Short put: the writer (seller) of a put option—has the obligation to buy the underlying asset.

The price of an option is also referred to as the **option premium**.

American options may be exercised at any time up to and including the contract's expiration date.

European options can be exercised only on the contract's expiration date.

 PROFESSOR'S NOTE

The name of the option does not imply where the option trades—they are just names.

At expiration, an American option and a European option on the same asset with the same strike price are identical. They may either be exercised or allowed to expire. Before expiration, however, they are different and may have different values. In those cases, we must distinguish between the two.

Credit Derivatives

A **credit derivative** is a contract that provides a bondholder (lender) with protection against a downgrade or a default by the borrower. The most common type of credit derivative is a **credit default swap** (CDS), which is essentially an insurance contract against default. A bondholder pays a series of cash flows to a credit protection seller and receives a payment if the bond issuer defaults.

Another type of credit derivative is a **credit spread option**, typically a call option that is based on a bond's yield spread relative to a benchmark. If the bond's credit quality decreases, its yield spread will increase and the bondholder will collect a payoff on the option.

LOS 56.d: Describe purposes of, and controversies related to, derivative markets.

CFA® Program Curriculum: Volume 6, page 39

The *criticism of derivatives* is that they are "too risky," especially to investors with limited knowledge of sometimes complex instruments. Because of the high leverage involved in derivatives payoffs, they are sometimes likened to gambling.

The *benefits of derivatives* markets are that they:

- Provide price information.
- Allow risk to be managed and shifted among market participants.
- Reduce transactions costs.

LOS 56.e: Explain arbitrage and the role it plays in determining prices and promoting market efficiency.

CFA® Program Curriculum: Volume 6, page 47

Arbitrage is an important concept in valuing (pricing) derivative securities. In its purest sense, arbitrage is riskless. If a return greater than the risk-free rate can be earned by holding a portfolio of assets that produces a certain (riskless) return, then an arbitrage opportunity exists.

Arbitrage opportunities arise when assets are mispriced. Trading by arbitrageurs will continue until they affect supply and demand enough to bring asset prices to efficient (no-arbitrage) levels.

There are two arbitrage arguments that are particularly useful in the study and use of derivatives.

The first is based on the **law of one price**. Two securities or portfolios that have identical cash flows in the future, regardless of future events, should have the same price. If A and B have the identical future payoffs and A is priced lower than B, buy A and sell B. You have an immediate profit, and the payoff on A will satisfy the (future) liability of being short on B.

The second type of arbitrage requires an investment. If a portfolio of securities or assets will have a certain payoff in the future, there is no risk in investing in that portfolio. In order to prevent profitable arbitrage, it must be the case that the return on the portfolio is the risk free rate. If the certain return on the portfolio is greater than the risk free rate, the arbitrage would be to borrow at Rf, invest in the portfolio, and keep the excess of the portfolio return above the risk free rate that must be paid on the loan. If the portfolio's certain return is less than Rf, we could sell the portfolio, invest the proceeds at Rf, and earn more than it will cost to buy back the portfolio at a future date.

PROFESSOR'S NOTE

We discuss derivatives pricing based on arbitrage in more detail in our review of Basics of Derivative Pricing and Valuation.

MODULE QUIZ 56.1, 56.2

To best evaluate your performance, enter your quiz answers online.

1. Which of the following statements *most accurately* describes a derivative security? A derivative:
   A. always increases risk.
   B. has no expiration date.
   C. has a payoff based on an asset value or interest rate.

2. Which of the following statements about exchange-traded derivatives is *least accurate*? Exchange-traded derivatives:
   A. are liquid.
   B. are standardized contracts.
   C. carry significant default risk.

3. Which of the following derivatives is a forward commitment?
   A. Stock option.
   B. Interest rate swap.
   C. Credit default swap.

4. A custom agreement to purchase a specific *T*-bond next Thursday for $1,000 is:
   A. an option.
   B. a futures contract.
   C. a forward commitment.

5. Interest rate swaps are:
   A. highly regulated.
   B. equivalent to a series of forward contracts.
   C. contracts to exchange one asset for another.

6. A call option is:
   A. the right to sell at a specific price.
   B. the right to buy at a specific price.
   C. an obligation to buy at a certain price.

7. Derivatives are *least likely* to:
   A. improve liquidity.
   B. provide price information.
   C. prevent arbitrage.

8. Arbitrage prevents:
   A. market efficiency.
   B. earning returns higher than the risk-free rate of return.
   C. two assets with identical payoffs from selling at different prices.

KEY CONCEPTS

LOS 56.a

A derivative's value is derived from the value of another asset or an interest rate.

Exchange-traded derivatives, notably futures and some options, are traded in centralized locations (exchanges) and are standardized, regulated, and are free of default.

Forwards and swaps are custom contracts (over-the-counter derivatives) created by dealers or financial institutions. There is limited trading of these contracts in secondary markets and default (counterparty) risk must be considered.

LOS 56.b

A forward commitment is an obligation to buy or sell an asset or make a payment in the future. Forward contracts, futures contracts, and swaps are all forward commitments.

A contingent claim is an asset that has a future payoff only if some future event takes place (e.g., asset price is greater than a specified price). Options and credit derivatives are contingent claims.

LOS 56.c

Forward contracts obligate one party to buy, and another to sell, a specific asset at a specific price at a specific time in the future.

Interest rate swaps contracts are equivalent to a series of forward contracts on interest rates.

Futures contracts are much like forward contracts, but are exchange-traded, liquid, and require daily settlement of any gains or losses.

A call option gives the holder the right, but not the obligation, to buy an asset at a specific price at some time in the future.

A put option gives the holder the right, but not the obligation, to sell an asset at a specific price at some time in the future.

A credit derivative is a contract that provides a payment if a specified credit event occurs.

LOS 56.d

Derivative markets are criticized for their risky nature. However, many market participants use derivatives to manage and reduce existing risk exposures.

Derivative securities play an important role in promoting efficient market prices and reducing transaction costs.

LOS 56.e

Riskless arbitrage refers to earning more than the risk-free rate of return with no risk, or receiving an immediate gain with no possible future liability.

Arbitrage can be expected to force the prices of two securities or portfolios of securities to be equal if they have the same future cash flows regardless of future events.

ANSWER KEY FOR MODULE QUIZZES

Module Quiz 56.1, 56.2

1. **C** A derivative's value is derived from another asset or an interest rate. (Module 56.1, LOS 56.a)

2. **C** Exchange-traded derivatives have relatively low default risk because the clearinghouse stands between the counterparties involved in most contracts. (Module 56.1, LOS 56.a)

3. **B** An interest rate swap is a forward commitment because both counterparties have obligations to make payments in the future. Options and credit derivatives are contingent claims because one of the counterparties only has an obligation if certain conditions are met. (Module 56.1, LOS 56.b)

4. **C** This type of custom contract is a forward commitment. (Module 56.1, LOS 56.c)

5. **B** A swap is an agreement to buy or sell an underlying asset periodically over the life of the swap contract. It is equivalent to a series of forward contracts. (Module 56.2, LOS 56.c)

6. **B** A call gives the owner the right to call an asset away (buy it) from the seller. (Module 56.2, LOS 56.c)

7. **C** While derivatives prices are the result of potential arbitrage, they do not prevent arbitrage. Derivatives improve liquidity and provide price information. (Module 56.2, LOS 56.d)

8. **C** Arbitrage forces two assets with the same expected future value to sell for the same current price. If this were not the case, you could simultaneously buy the cheaper asset and sell the more expensive one for a guaranteed riskless profit. (Module 56.2, LOS 56.e)

READING
57

Basics of Derivative Pricing and Valuation

EXAM FOCUS

Here the focus is on the pricing and valuation of derivatives based on a no-arbitrage condition. The derivation of the price in a forward contract and calculating the value of a forward contract over its life are important applications of no-arbitrage pricing. Candidates should also understand the equivalence of interest rates swaps to a series of forward rate agreements and how each factor that affects option values affects puts and calls.

MODULE 57.1: FORWARDS AND FUTURES VALUATION

Video covering this content is available online.

LOS 57.a: Explain how the concepts of arbitrage, replication, and risk neutrality are used in pricing derivatives.

CFA® Program Curriculum: Volume 6, page 66

For most risky assets, we estimate current value as the discounted present value of the expected price of the asset at some future time. Because the future price is subject to risk (uncertainty), the discount rate includes a risk premium along with the risk-free rate. There may be costs of owning an asset, such as storage and insurance costs. For financial assets, these costs are very low and not significant. The other important cost of holding an asset is the opportunity cost of the funds that are invested in the asset, which we usually measure as the asset cost times the risk-free rate, compounded over the holding period.

There may also be benefits to holding the asset, either monetary or non-monetary. Dividend payments on a stock or interest payments on a bond are examples of monetary benefits of owning an asset. Non-monetary benefits of holding an asset are sometimes referred to as its **convenience yield**. The convenience yield is difficult to measure and is only significant for some assets, primarily commodities. If an asset is difficult to sell short in the market, owning it may convey benefits in circumstances where selling the asset is advantageous. For example, a shortage of the asset may drive prices up, making sale of the asset in the short term profitable. While the ability to look at a painting or sculpture provides non-monetary benefits to its owner, this is unlikely with corn or other commodities.

The net cost of holding an asset, considering both the costs and benefits of holding the asset, is referred to as the **cost of carry**. Taking into account all of these costs and benefits, we can describe the present value of an asset, based on its expected future price, as:

$S_0 = E(S_T) / (1 + Rf + \text{risk premium})^T + PV$ (benefits of holding the asset for time T) $- PV$ (costs of holding the asset for time T),

where:
S_0 is the current spot price of the asset and $E(S_T)$ is the expected value of the asset at time T, the end of the expected holding period.

We assume that investors are **risk-averse** so they require a positive premium (higher return) on risky assets. An investor who is **risk-neutral** would require no risk premium and, as a result, would discount the expected future value of an asset at the risk-free rate.

In contrast to this model of calculating the current value of a risky asset, the valuation of derivative securities is based on a **no-arbitrage** condition. Arbitrage refers to a transaction wherein an investor purchases one asset (or portfolio of assets) at one price and simultaneously sells an asset or portfolio that has the same future payoff, regardless of future events, at a higher price, realizing a risk-free gain on the transaction. While arbitrage opportunities may be rare, the reasoning is that when they do exist they will be exploited rapidly. Therefore, we can use the no-arbitrage condition to determine the current value (spot price) of an asset or portfolio of assets that have the same future payoffs regardless of future events. Because there are transactions costs of exploiting an arbitrage opportunity, small differences in price may persist because the arbitrage gain is less than the transactions cost of exploiting it.

In markets for traditional securities, we don't often encounter two assets that have the same future payoffs. With derivative securities, however, the risk of the derivative is entirely based on the risk of the underlying asset, so we can construct a portfolio of the underlying asset and a derivative based on it that has no uncertainty about its value at some future date (i.e., a hedged portfolio). Because the future payoff is certain, we can calculate the present value of the portfolio as the future payoff discounted at the risk-free rate. This will be the current value of the portfolio under the no-arbitrage condition, which will force the return on a risk-free (hedged) portfolio to the risk-free rate. This structure, with a long position in the asset and a short position in the derivative security, can be represented as:

asset position at time 0 + short position in a forward contract at time 0 = (payoff on the asset at time T + payoff on the short forward at time T) $/ (1 + Rf)^T$

Because the payoff at time T (expiration of the forward) is from a fully hedged position, its time T value is certain. To prevent arbitrage, the above equality must hold. If the net cost of buying the asset and selling the forward at time t is less than the present value (discounted at Rf) of the certain payoff at time T, an investor can borrow the funds (at Rf) to buy the asset, sell the forward at time t, and earn a risk-free return in excess of Rf. If the net cost is greater than the present value of the certain payoff at time T, an arbitrageur could sell the hedged position (short the asset, invest the proceeds at Rf, and buy the forward). At expiration, the asset can be purchased with the maturity payment on the loan and the excess of that repayment over the forward price is a gain with no net investment over the period.

When the equality holds we say the derivative is currently at its no-arbitrage price. Because we know Rf, the spot price of the asset, and the certain payoff at time T, we can solve for the no-arbitrage price of the derivative based on the no arbitrage price of the forward. Note the investor's risk aversion has not entered into our valuation of the derivative as it did when we described the valuation of a risky asset. For this reason, the determination of the no-arbitrage derivative price is sometimes called **risk-neutral pricing**, which is the same as no-arbitrage pricing or the price under a no-arbitrage condition.

Because we can create a risk-free asset (or portfolio) from a position in the underlying asset that is hedged with a position in a derivative security, we can duplicate the payoff on a derivative position with the risk-free asset and the underlying asset or duplicate the payoffs on the underlying asset with a position in the risk-free asset and the derivative security. This process is called **replication** because we are replicating the payoffs on one asset or portfolio with those of a different asset or portfolio.

As an example of replication and risk-neutral pricing, consider a long position in a stock and a short position in a forward contract at 50 on the stock. Regardless of the price of the stock at the settlement of the forward contract, the stock will be delivered for the forward price of 50. As 50 will be received at the forward settlement date, the value today is 50 discounted at the risk-free rate for the time until settlement of the forward contract. For a share of stock and a short forward at 50 with six months until settlement, we can write:

$$S - F(50) = 50 / (1 + Rf)^{0.5}$$

and replicate a long forward position as

$$F(50) = S - 50 / (1 + Rf)^{0.5}.$$

That is, we can replicate the long forward position by purchasing a share of stock and borrowing the present value of 50 at the risk-free rate so the value at the maturity of the loan will be the stock price minus 50. Alternatively, we could replicate a short stock position by taking a short forward position and borrowing the present value of 50 at the risk-free rate.

Another example of risk-neutral pricing is that combining a risky bond with a credit protection derivative replicates a risk-free bond. So we can write:

risky bond + credit protection = bond valued at the risk-free rate

and see that the no-arbitrage price of credit protection is the value of the bond if it were risk-free minus the price of the risky bond.

As a final example of risk-neutral pricing and replication, consider an investor who buys a share of stock, sells a call on the stock at 40, and buys a put on the stock at 40 withthe same expiration date as the call. The investor will receive 40 at option expiration regardless of the stock price because:

■ If the stock price is 40 at expiration, the put and the call are both worthless at expiration.

■ If the stock price > 40 at expiration, the call will be exercised, the stock will be delivered for 40, and the put will expire worthless.

■ If the stock price is < 40 at expiration, the put will be exercised, the stock will be delivered for 40, and the call will expire worthless.

Thus, for a six-month call and put we can write:

stock + put − call = $40 / (1+Rf)^{0.5}$ and equivalently

call = stock + put − $40 / (1+Rf)^{0.5}$ and

put = call + $40 / (1+Rf)^{0.5}$ − stock

These replications will be introduced later in this reading as the *put-call parity* relationship.

LOS 57.b: Distinguish between value and price of forward and futures contracts.

CFA® Program Curriculum: Volume 6, page 72

Recall that the *value* of futures and forward contracts is zero at initiation. As the expected future price of the underlying asset changes, the value of the futures or forward contract position may increase or decrease with the gains or losses in value of the long position in the contract just opposite to the gains or losses in the short position on the contract.

In contrast to the value of a futures or forward position, the *price* of a futures or forward contract refers to the futures or forward price specified in the contract. As an example of this difference, consider a long position in a forward contract to buy the underlying asset in the future at $50, which is the forward contract price. At initiation of the contract, the value is zero but the contract price is $50. If the expected future value of the underlying asset increases, the value of the long contract position will increase (and the value of the short position will decrease by a like amount). The contract *price* at which the long forward can purchase the asset in the future remains the same. If a new forward contract were now created it would have a zero value, but a higher forward price that reflects the higher expected future value of the underlying asset.

LOS 57.c: Explain how the value and price of a forward contract are determined at expiration, during the life of the contract, and at initiation.

CFA® Program Curriculum: Volume 6, page 73

Because neither party to a forward transaction pays to enter the contract at initiation, the forward contract price must be set so the contract has zero value at initiation. To understand how this price is set, consider an asset that has no storage costs and no benefits to holding it so that the net cost of carry is simply the opportunity cost of the invested funds, which we assume to be the risk-free rate.

Under these conditions the current forward price of an asset to be delivered at time T, $F_0(T)$, must equal the spot price of the asset, S_0, compounded at the risk-free rate for a period of length T (in years) and we can write:

$$F_0(T) = S_0(1 + Rf)^T, \text{ which is equivalent to } \frac{F_0(T)}{S_0} = (1 + Rf)^T$$

If the forward price were $F_0(T)+$, a price greater than $S_0(1 + Rf)^T$, an arbitrageur could take a short position in the forward contract, promising to sell the asset at time T at $F_0(T)+$, and buy the asset at S_0, with funds borrowed at Rf, which requires no cash investment in the position. At time T, the arbitrageur would deliver the asset and receive $F_0(T)+$, repay the loan at a cost of $S_0(1 + Rf)^T$, and keep the positive difference between $F_0(T)+$ and $S_0(1 + Rf)^T$.

If the forward price were $F_0(T)-$, a price less than $S_0(1 + Rf)^T$, a profit could be earned with the opposite transactions, short selling the asset for S_0, investing the proceeds at Rf, and taking a long position in the forward. At time T, the arbitrageur would receive $S_0(1 + Rf)^T$ from investing the proceeds of the short sale, pay $F_0(T)-$ to purchase the asset and cover the short asset position, and keep the difference between $S_0(1 + Rf)^T$ and $F_0(T)-$. This process is the mechanism that ensures $F_0(T)$ is the (no-arbitrage) price in a forward contract that has zero value at T = 0.

When the forward is priced at its no-arbitrage price the value of the forward at initiation,

$$V_0(T) = S_0 - \frac{F_0(T)}{(1 + Rf)^T} = 0, \text{ because } S_0 = \frac{F_0(T)}{(1 + Rf)^T}.$$

During its life, at time t < T, the value of the forward contract is the spot price of the asset minus the present value of the forward price,

$$V_t(T) = S_t - \frac{F_0(T)}{(1 + Rf)^{T-t}}.$$

At expiration at time T, the discounting term is $(1 + Rf)^0 = 1$ and the payoff to a long forward is $S_T - F_0(T)$, the difference between the spot price of the asset at expiration and the price of the forward contract.

LOS 57.d: Describe monetary and nonmonetary benefits and costs associated with holding the underlying asset and explain how they affect the value and price of a forward contract.

CFA® Program Curriculum: Volume 6, page 64

We can denote the present value of any costs of holding the asset from time 0 to expiration at time T as PV_0 (cost) and the present value of any cash flows from the asset and any convenience yield over the holding period as PV_0 (benefit).

Consider first a case where there are costs of holding the asset but no benefits. The asset can be purchased now and held to time T at a total cost of:

$$[S_0 + PV_0 \text{(cost)}](1 + Rf)^T$$

so this is the no-arbitrage forward price. Any other forward price will create an arbitrage opportunity at the initiation of the forward contract.

In a case where there are only benefits of holding the asset over the life of the forward contract, the cost of buying the asset and holding it until the expiration of the forward at time T is:

$$[S_0 - PV_0 \text{(benefit)}](1 + Rf)^T$$

Again, any forward price that is not the no-arbitrage forward price will create an arbitrage opportunity. Note the no-arbitrage forward price is lower the greater the present value of the benefits and higher the greater the present value of the costs incurred over the life of the forward contract.

If an asset has both storage costs and benefits from holding the asset over the life of the forward contract, we can combine these in to a more general formula and express the no-arbitrage forward price (that will produce a value of zero for the forward at initiation) as:

$$[S_0 + PV_0 \text{(cost)} - PV_0 \text{(benefit)}](1 + Rf)^T = F_0(T)$$

Both the present values of the costs of holding the asset and the benefits of holding the asset decrease as time passes and the time to expiration (T − t) decreases, so the value of the forward at any point in time t < T is:

$$V_t(T) = S_t + PV_t\text{(cost)} - PV_t\text{(benefit)} \ - \ \frac{F_0(T)}{(1 + Rf)^{T-t}}$$

At expiration t = T the costs and benefits of holding the asset until expiration are zero, as is T − t, so that the payoff on a long forward position at time T is, again, simply $S_T - F_0(T)$, the difference between the spot price of the asset at expiration and the forward price.

MODULE QUIZ 57.1

To best evaluate your performance, enter your quiz answers online.

1. Derivatives pricing models use the risk-free rate to discount future cash flows because these models:
   A. are based on portfolios with certain payoffs.
   B. assume that derivatives investors are risk-neutral.
   C. assume that risk can be eliminated by diversification.

2. The price of a forward or futures contract:
   A. is typically zero at initiation.
   B. is equal to the spot price at expiration.
   C. remains the same over the term of the contract.

3. For a forward contract on an asset that has no costs or benefits from holding it to have zero value at initiation, the arbitrage-free forward price must equal:
   A. the expected future spot price.
   B. the future value of the current spot price.
   C. the present value of the expected future spot price.

4. The underlying asset of a derivative is *most likely* to have a convenience yield when the asset:
   A. is difficult to sell short.
   B. pays interest or dividends.
   C. must be stored and insured.

MODULE 57.2: FORWARD RATE AGREEMENTS AND SWAP VALUATION

Video covering this content is available online.

LOS 57.e: Define a forward rate agreement and describe its uses.

CFA® Program Curriculum: Volume 6, page 77

A **forward rate agreement** (FRA) is a derivative contract that has a future interest rate, rather than an asset, as its underlying. The point of entering into an FRA is to lock in a certain interest rate for borrowing or lending at some future date. One party will pay the other party the difference (based on an agreed-upon notional contract value) between the fixed interest rate specified in the FRA and the market interest rate at contract settlement.

LIBOR is most often used as the underlying rate. U.S. dollar LIBOR refers to the rates on Eurodollar time deposits, interbank U.S. dollar loans in London.

Consider an FRA that will, in 30 days, pay the difference between 90-day LIBOR and the 90-day rate specified in the FRA (the contract rate). A company that expects to borrow 90-day funds in 30 days will have higher interest costs if 90-day LIBOR 30 days from now increases. A long position in the FRA (pay fixed, receive floating) will receive a payment that will offset the increase in borrowing costs from the increase in 90-day LIBOR. Conversely, if 90-day LIBOR 30 days from now decreases over the next 30 days, the long position in the FRA will make a payment to the short in the amount that the company's borrowing costs have decreased relative to the FRA contract rate.

FRAs are used by firms to hedge the risk of (remove uncertainty about) borrowing and lending they intend to do in the future. A company that intends to borrow funds in 30 days could take a long position in an FRA, receiving a payment if future 90-day LIBOR (and its borrowing cost) increases, and making a payment if future 90-day LIBOR (and its borrowing cost) decreases, over the 30-day life of the FRA. Note a perfect hedge means not only that the firm's borrowing costs will not be higher if rates increase, but also that the firm's borrowing costs will not be lower if interest rates decrease.

For a firm that intends to have funds to lend (invest) in the future, a short position in an FRA can hedge its interest rate risk. In this case, a decline in rates would decrease the return on funds loaned at the future date, but a positive payoff on the FRA would augment these returns so that the return from both the short FRA and loaning the funds is the no-arbitrage rate that is the *price* of the FRA at initiation.

Rather than enter into an FRA, a bank can create the same payment structure with two LIBOR loans, a **synthetic FRA**. A bank can borrow money for 120 days and lend that amount for 30 days. At the end of 30 days, the bank receives funds from the repayment of the 30-day loan it made, and has use of these funds for the next 90 days at an effective rate determined by the original transactions. The effective rate of interest on this 90-day loan depends on both 30-day LIBOR and 120-day LIBOR at the time the money is borrowed and loaned to the third party. This rate is the contract rate on a 30-day FRA on 90-day LIBOR. The resulting cash flows will be the same with either the FRA or the synthetic FRA.

Figure 57.1 illustrates these two methods of "locking in" a future lending or borrowing rate (i.e., hedging the risk from uncertainty about future interest rates).

Figure 57.1: 30-Day FRA on 90-Day LIBOR

(a) Forward rate agreement

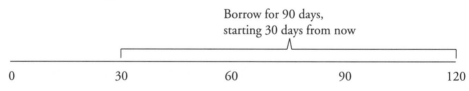

(b) Synthetic FRA

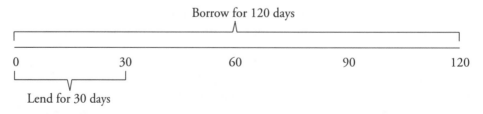

Note that the no-arbitrage price of an FRA is determined by the two transactions in the synthetic FRA, borrowing for 120 days and lending for 30 days.

LOS 57.f: Explain why forward and futures prices differ.

CFA® Program Curriculum: Volume 6, page 80

Forwards and futures serve the same function in gaining exposure to or hedging specific risks, but differ in their degree of standardization, liquidity, and, in many instances, counterparty risk. From a pricing and valuation perspective, the most important distinction is that futures gains and losses are settled each day and the margin balance is adjusted accordingly. If gains put the margin balance above the initial margin level, any funds in excess of that level can be withdrawn. If losses put the margin value below the minimum margin level, funds must be deposited to restore the account margin to its initial (required) level. Forwards, typically, do not require or provide funds in response to fluctuations in value during their lives.

While this difference is theoretically important in some contexts, in practice it does not lead to any difference between the prices of forwards and futures that have the same terms otherwise. If interest rates are constant, or even simply uncorrelated with futures prices, the prices of futures and forwards are the same. A positive correlation between interest rates and the futures price means that (for a long position) daily settlement provides funds (excess margin) when rates are high and they can earn more interest, and requires funds (margin deposits) when rates are low and opportunity cost of deposited funds is less. Because of this, futures prices will be higher than forward prices when interest rates and futures prices are positively correlated, and they will be lower than forward prices when interest rates and futures prices are negatively correlated.

LOS 57.g: Explain how swap contracts are similar to but different from a series of forward contracts.

LOS 57.h: Distinguish between the value and price of swaps.

CFA® Program Curriculum: Volume 6, page 82

In a simple interest-rate swap, one party pays a floating rate and the other pays a fixed rate on a notional principal amount. Consider a one-year swap with quarterly payments, one party paying a fixed rate and the other a floating rate of 90-day LIBOR. At each payment date the difference between the swap fixed rate and LIBOR (for the prior 90 days) is paid to the party that owes the least, that is, a net payment is made from one party to the other.

We can separate these payments into a known payment and three unknown payments which are equivalent to the payments on three forward rate agreements. Let S_n represent the floating rate payment (based on 90-day LIBOR) owed at the end of quarter n and F_n be the fixed payment owed at the end of quarter n. We can represent the swap payment to be received by the fixed rate payer at the end of period n as $S_n - F_n$. We can replicate each of these payments to (or from) the fixed rate payer in the swap with a forward contract, specifically a long position in a forward rate agreement with a contract rate equal to the swap fixed rate and a settlement value based on 90-day LIBOR.

We illustrate this separation below for a one-year fixed for floating swap with a fixed rate of F, fixed payments at time n of F_n, and floating rate payments at time n of S_n.

First payment (90 days from now) = $S_1 - F_1$ which is known at time zero because the payment 90 days from now is based on 90-day LIBOR at time 0 and the swap fixed rate, F, both of which are known at the initiation of the swap.

Second payment (180 days from now) is equivalent to a long position in an FRA with contract rate F that settles in 180 days and pays $S_2 - F_2$.

Third payment (270 days from now) is equivalent to a long position in an FRA with contract rate F that settles in 270 days and pays $S_3 - F_3$.

Fourth payment (360 days from now) is equivalent to a long position in an FRA with contract rate F that settles in 360 days and pays $S_4 - F_4$.

Note that a forward on 90-day LIBOR that settles 90 days from now, based on 90-day LIBOR at that time, actually pays the present value of the difference between the fixed rate F and 90-day LIBOR 90 days from now (times the notional principal amount). Thus, the forwards in our example actually pay on days 90, 180, and 270. However, the amounts paid are equivalent to the differences between the fixed rate payment and floating rate payment that are due when interest is actually paid on days 180, 270, and 360, which are the amounts we used in the example.

Therefore, we can describe an interest rate swap as equivalent to a series of forward contracts, specifically forward rate agreements, each with a forward contract rate equal to the swap fixed rate. However, there is one important difference. Because the forward contract rates are all equal in the FRAs that are equivalent to the swap, these would not be zero value forward contracts at the initiation of the swap. Recall that forward contracts are based on a contract rate for which the value of the forward contract at initiation is zero. There is no reason to suspect that the swap fixed rate results in a zero value forward contract for each of the future dates.

When a forward contract is created with a contract rate that gives it a non-zero value at initiation, it is called an *off-market forward*. The forward contracts we found to be equivalent to the series of swap payments are almost certainly all off-market forwards with non-zero values at the initiation of the swap. Because the swap itself has zero value to both parties at initiation, it must consist of some off-market forwards with positive present values and some off-market forwards with negative present values, so that the sum of their present values equals zero.

Finding the swap fixed rate (which is the contract rate for our off-market forwards) that gives the swap a zero value at initiation is not difficult if we follow our principle of no-arbitrage pricing. The fixed rate payer in a swap can replicate that derivative position by borrowing at a fixed rate and lending the proceeds at a variable (floating) rate. For the swap in our example, borrowing at the fixed rate F and lending the proceeds at 90-day LIBOR will produce the same cash flows as the swap. At each date the payment due on the fixed-rate loan is F_n and the interest received on lending at the floating rate is S_n.

As with forward rate agreements, the price of a swap is the fixed rate of interest specified in the swap contract (the contract rate) and the value depends on how expected future floating rates change over time. At initiation, a swap has zero value because the present value of the fixed-rate payments equals the present value of the expected floating-rate payments. An increase in expected short-term future rates will produce a positive value for the fixed-rate payer in an interest rate swap, and a decrease in expected future rates will produce a negative value because the promised fixed rate payments have more value than the expected floating rate payments over the life of the swap.

MODULE QUIZ 57.2

To best evaluate your performance, enter your quiz answers online.

1. How can a bank create a synthetic 60-day forward rate agreement on a 180-day interest rate?
   A. Borrow for 180 days and lend the proceeds for 60 days.
   B. Borrow for 180 days and lend the proceeds for 120 days.
   C. Borrow for 240 days and lend the proceeds for 60 days.

2. For the price of a futures contract to be greater than the price of an otherwise equivalent forward contract, interest rates must be:
   A. uncorrelated with futures prices.
   B. positively correlated with futures prices.
   C. negatively correlated with futures prices.

3. The price of a fixed-for-floating interest rate swap:
   A. is specified in the swap contract.
   B. is paid at initiation by the floating-rate receiver.
   C. may increase or decrease during the life of the swap contract.

MODULE 57.3: OPTION VALUATION AND PUT-CALL PARITY

Video covering this content is available online.

LOS 57.i: Explain how the value of a European option is determined at expiration.

LOS 57.j: Explain the exercise value, time value, and moneyness of an option.

CFA® Program Curriculum: Volume 6, page 86

Moneyness refers to whether an option is *in the money or out of the money*. If immediate exercise of the option would generate a positive payoff, it is in the money. If immediate exercise would result in a loss (negative payoff), it is out of the money. When the current asset price equals the exercise price, exercise will generate neither a gain nor loss, and the option is *at the money*.

The following describes the conditions for a **call option** to be in, out of, or at the money. S is the price of the underlying asset and X is the exercise price of the option.

■ *In-the-money call options.* If $S - X > 0$, a call option is in the money. $S - X$ is the amount of the payoff a call holder would receive from immediate exercise, buying a share for X and selling it in the market for a greater price S.

- *Out-of-the-money call options.* If S − X < 0, a call option is out of the money.

- *At-the-money call options.* If S = X, a call option is said to be at the money.

The following describes the conditions for a **put option** to be in, out of, or at the money.

- *In-the-money put options.* If X − S > 0, a put option is in the money. X − S is the amount of the payoff from immediate exercise, buying a share for *S* and exercising the put to receive *X* for the share.

- *Out-of-the-money put options.* When the stock's price is greater than the strike price, a put option is said to be out of the money. If X − S < 0, a put option is out of the money.

- *At-the-money put options.* If S = X, a put option is said to be at the money.

> **EXAMPLE:** Moneyness
>
> Consider a July 40 call and a July 40 put, both on a stock that is currently selling for $37/share. Calculate how much these options are in or out of the money.
>
> **PROFESSOR'S NOTE**
>
> A July 40 call is a call option with an exercise price of $40 and an expiration date in July.
>
> **Answer:**
>
> The call is $3 out of the money because S − X = −$3.00. The put is $3 in the money because X − S = $3.00.

We define the **intrinsic value** (or **exercise value**) of an option the maximum of zero and the amount that the option is in the money. That is, the intrinsic value is the amount an option is in the money, if it is in the money, or zero if the option is at or out of the money. The intrinsic value is also the exercise value, the value of the option if exercised immediately.

Prior to expiration, an option has time value in addition to any intrinsic value. The **time value** of an option is the amount by which the **option premium** (price) exceeds the intrinsic value and is sometimes called the *speculative value* of the option. This relationship can be written as:

option premium = intrinsic value + time value

At any point during the life of an option, its value will typically be greater than its intrinsic value. This is because there is some probability that the underlying asset price will change in an amount that gives the option a positive payoff at expiration greater than the (current) intrinsic value. Recall that an option's intrinsic value (to a buyer) is the amount of the payoff at expiration and is bounded by zero.

When an option reaches expiration, there is no time remaining and the time value is zero. This means the value at expiration is either zero, if the option is at or out of the money, or its intrinsic value, if it is in the money.

LOS 57.k: Identify the factors that determine the value of an option and explain how each factor affects the value of an option.

CFA® Program Curriculum: Volume 6, page 87

There are six factors that determine option prices.

1. **Price of the underlying asset.** For call options, the higher the price of the underlying, the greater its intrinsic value and the higher the value of the option. Conversely, the lower the price of the underlying, the less its intrinsic value and the lower the value of the call option. In general, call option values increase when the value of the underlying asset increases.

   For put options this relationship is reversed. An increase in the price of the underlying reduces the value of a put option.

2. **The exercise price.** A higher exercise price decreases the values of call options and a lower exercise price increases the values of call options.

   A higher exercise price increases the values of put options and a lower exercise price decreases the values of put options.

3. **The risk-free rate of interest.** An increase in the risk-free rate will increase call option values, and a decrease in the risk-free rate will decrease call option values.

   An increase in the risk-free rate will decrease put option values, and a decrease in the risk-free rate will increase put option values.

   PROFESSOR'S NOTE

   One way to remember the effects of changes in the risk-free rate is to think about present values of the payments for calls and puts. These statements are strictly true only for in-the-money options, but it's a way to remember the relationships. The holder of a call option will pay in the future to exercise a call option and the present value of that payment is lower when the risk-free rate is higher, so a higher risk-free rate increases a call option's value. The holder of a put option will receive a payment in the future when the put is exercised and an increase in the risk-free rate decreases the present value of this payment, so a higher risk-free rate decreases a put option's value.

4. **Volatility of the underlying.** Volatility is what makes options valuable. If there were no volatility in the price of the underlying asset (its price remained constant), options would always be equal to their intrinsic values and time or speculative value would be zero. An increase in the volatility of the price of the underlying asset increases the values of both put and call options and a decrease in volatility of the price of the underlying decreases both put values and call values.

5. **Time to expiration.** Because volatility is expressed per unit of time, longer time to expiration effectively increases expected volatility and increases the value of a call option. Less time to expiration decreases the time value of a call option so that at expiration it value is simply its intrinsic value.

   For most put options, longer time to expiration will increase option values for the same reasons. For some European put options, however, extending the time to expiration can decrease the value of the put. In general, the deeper a put option is in the money, the higher the risk-free rate, and the longer the current time to expiration, the more likely that extending the option's time to expiration will decrease its value.

To understand this possibility consider a put option at $20 on a stock with a value that has decreased to $1. The intrinsic value of the put is $19 so the upside is very limited, the downside (if the price of the underlying subsequently increases) is significant, and because no payment will be received until the expiration date, the current option value reflects the present value of any expected payment. Extending the time to expiration would decrease that present value. While overall we expect a longer time to expiration to increase the value of a European put option, in the case of a deep in-the-money put, a longer time to expiration could decrease its value.

6. **Costs and benefits of holding the asset.** If there are benefits of holding the underlying asset (dividend or interest payments on securities or a convenience yield on commodities), call values are decreased and put values are increased. The reason for this is most easily understood by considering cash benefits. When a stock pays a dividend, or a bond pays interest, this reduces the value of the asset. Decreases in the value of the underlying asset decrease call values and increase put values.

Positive storage costs make it more costly to hold an asset. We can think of this as making a call option more valuable because call holders can have long exposure to the asset without paying the costs of actually owning the asset. Puts, on the other hand, are less valuable when storage costs are higher.

LOS 57.l: Explain put–call parity for European options.

CFA® Program Curriculum: Volume 6, page 94

Our derivation of **put-call parity** for European options is based on the payoffs of two portfolio combinations: a fiduciary call and a protective put.

A *fiduciary call* is a combination of a call with exercise price X and a pure-discount, riskless bond that pays X at maturity (option expiration). The payoff for a fiduciary call at expiration is X when the call is out of the money, and $X + (S − X) = S$ when the call is in the money.

A *protective put* is a share of stock together with a put option on the stock. The expiration date payoff for a protective put is $(X − S) + S = X$ when the put is in the money, and S when the put is out of the money.

PROFESSOR'S NOTE

When working with put-call parity, it is important to note that the exercise prices on the put and the call and the face value of the riskless bond are all equal to X.

If at expiration S is greater than or equal to X:

■ The protective put pays S on the stock while the put expires worthless, so the payoff is S.

■ The fiduciary call pays X on the bond portion while the call pays $(S − X)$, so the payoff is $X + (S − X) = S$.

If at expiration X is greater than S:

■ The protective put pays S on the stock while the put pays $(X − S)$, so the payoff is $S + (X − S) = X$.

■ The fiduciary call pays X on the bond portion while the call expires worthless, so the payoff is X.

In either case, the payoff on a protective put is the same as the payoff on a fiduciary call. Our no-arbitrage condition holds that portfolios with identical payoffs regardless of future conditions must sell for the same price to prevent arbitrage. We can express the put-call parity relationship as:

$$c + X / (1 + Rf)^T = S + p$$

Equivalencies for each of the individual securities in the put-call parity relationship can be expressed as:

$$S = c − p + X / (1 + Rf)^T$$
$$p = c − S + X / (1 + Rf)^T$$
$$c = S + p − X / (1 + Rf)^T$$
$$X / (1 + Rf)^T = S + p − c$$

Note that the options must be European-style and the puts and calls must have the same exercise price and time to expiration for these relations to hold.

The single securities on the left-hand side of the equations all have exactly the same payoffs as the portfolios on the right-hand side. The portfolios on the right-hand side are the **synthetic** equivalents of the securities on the left. For example, to synthetically produce the payoff for a long position in a share of stock, use the following relationship:

$$S = c − p + X / (1 + Rf)^T$$

This means that the payoff on a long stock can be synthetically created with a long call, a short put, and a long position in a risk-free discount bond.

The other securities in the put-call parity relationship can be constructed in a similar manner.

PROFESSOR'S NOTE

After expressing the put-call parity relationship in terms of the security you want to synthetically create, the sign on the individual securities will indicate whether you need a long position (+ sign) or a short position (– sign) in the respective securities.

> **EXAMPLE:** Call option valuation using put-call parity
>
> Suppose that the current stock price is $52 and the risk-free rate is 5%. You have found a quote for a 3-month put option with an exercise price of $50. The put price is $1.50, but due to light trading in the call options, there was not a listed quote for the 3-month, $50 call. Estimate the price of the 3-month call option.
>
> **Answer:**
>
> Rearranging put-call parity, we find that the call price is:
>
> call = put + stock − present value (X)
>
> $$call = \$1.50 + \$52 - \frac{\$50}{1.05^{0.25}} = \$4.11$$
>
> This means that if a 3-month, $50 call is available, it should be priced at (within transactions costs of) $4.11 per share.

LOS 57.m: Explain put–call–forward parity for European options.

CFA® Program Curriculum: Volume 6, page 98

Put-call-forward parity is derived with a forward contract rather than the underlying asset itself. Consider a forward contract on an asset at time T with a contract price of $F_0(T)$. At contract initiation the forward contract has zero value. At time T, when the forward contract settles, the long must purchase the asset for $F_0(T)$. The purchase (at time=0) of a pure discount bond that will pay $F_0(T)$ at maturity (time = T) will cost $F_0(T) / (1 + Rf)^T$.

By purchasing such a pure discount bond and simultaneously taking a long position in the forward contract, an investor has created a synthetic asset. At time = T the proceeds of the bond are just sufficient to purchase the asset as required by the long forward position. Because there is no cost to enter into the forward contract, the total cost of the synthetic asset is the present value of the forward price, $F_0(T) / (1 + Rf)^T$.

The put-call forward parity relationship is derived by substituting the synthetic asset for the underlying asset in the put-call parity relationship. Substituting $F_0(T) / (1 + Rf)^T$ for the asset price S_0 in $S + p = c + X / (1 + Rf)^T$ gives us:

$$F_0(T) / (1 + Rf)^T + p_0 = c_0 + X / (1 + Rf)^T$$

which is put-call forward parity at time 0, the initiation of the forward contract, based on the principle of no arbitrage. By rearranging the terms, put-call forward parity can also be expressed as:

$$p_0 - c_0 = [X - F_0(T)] / (1 + Rf)^T$$

MODULE 57.4: BINOMIAL MODEL FOR OPTION VALUES

Video covering this content is available online.

LOS 57.n: Explain how the value of an option is determined using a one-period binomial model.

CFA® Program Curriculum: Volume 6, page 100

Recall from Quantitative Methods that a **binomial model** is based on the idea that, over the next period, some value will change to one of two possible values (binomial). To construct a binomial model, we need to know the beginning asset value, the size of the two possible changes, and the probabilities of each of these changes occurring.

One-Period Binomial Model

Consider a share of stock currently priced at $30. The size of the possible price changes, and the probabilities of these changes occurring, are as follows:

U = size of up move = 1.15

D = size of down move = $\dfrac{1}{U} = \dfrac{1}{1.15} = 0.87$

π_U = probability of an up-move = 0.715

π_D = probability of a down-move = $1 - \pi_U = 1 - 0.715 = 0.285$

Note that the down-move factor is the reciprocal of the up-move factor, and the probability of an up-move is one minus the probability of a down-move. The one-period binomial tree for the stock is shown in Figure 57.2. The beginning stock value of $30 is to the left, and to the right are the two possible end-of-period stock values, $34.50 and $26.10.

Figure 57.2: One-Period Binomial Tree

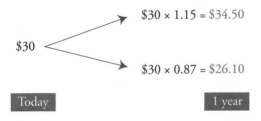

$30 × 1.15 = $34.50

$30

$30 × 0.87 = $26.10

Today

1 year

Study Session 18

The probabilities of an up-move and a down-move are calculated based on the size of the moves and the risk-free rate:

$$\pi_U = \text{risk-neutral probability of an up-move} = \frac{1 + R_f - D}{U - D}$$

$$\pi_D = \text{risk-neutral probability of a down-move} = 1 - \pi_U$$

where:

R_f = risk-free rate

U = size of an up-move

D = size of a down-move

PROFESSOR'S NOTE

These two probabilities are not the actual probability of an up- or down-move. They are risk-neutral pseudo probabilities. The calculation of risk-neutral probabilities is not required for the Level I exam, so you don't need to worry about it.

We can calculate the value of an option on the stock by:

■ Calculating the payoff of the option at maturity in both the up-move and down-move states.

■ Calculating the expected value of the option in one year as the probability-weighted average of the payoffs in each state.

■ Discounting this expected value back to today at the risk-free rate.

> **EXAMPLE: Calculating call option value with a one-period binomial tree**
>
> Use the binomial tree in Figure 3 to calculate the value today of a one-year call option on the stock with an exercise price of $30. Assume the risk-free rate is 7%, the current value of the stock is $30, and the size of an up-move is 1.15.
>
> **Answer:**
>
> First, we have to calculate the parameters—the size of a down-move and the probabilities:
>
> $$D = \text{size of down move} = \frac{1}{U} = \frac{1}{1.15} = 0.87$$
>
> $$\pi_U = \text{risk-neutral probability of an up-move} = \frac{1 + 0.07 - 0.87}{1.15 - 0.87} = 0.715$$
>
> $$\pi_D = \text{risk-neutral probability of a down-move} = 1 - 0.715 = 0.285$$
>
> Next, determine the payoffs to the option in each state. If the stock moves up to $34.50, a call option with an exercise price of $30 will pay $4.50. If the stock moves down to $26.10, the call option will expire worthless. The option payoffs are illustrated in the following figure.
>
> Let the stock values for the up-move and down-move be S_1^+ and S_1^- and for the call values, C_1^+ and C_1^-.

One-Period Call Option With X = \$30

$$\pi_U = 0.715 \nearrow \quad S_1^+ = \$30 \times 1.15 = \$34.50$$
$$C_1^+ = \max (0, \$34.50 - \$30) = \$4.50$$

$$S_0 = \$30$$

$$\pi_D = 0.285 \searrow \quad S_1^- = \$30 \times 0.87 = \$26.10$$
$$C_1^- = \max (0, \$26.10 - \$30) = \$0$$

| Today | | 1 year |

The expected value of the option in one period is:

E(call option value in 1 year) = ($4.50 × 0.715) + ($0 × 0.285) = $3.22

The value of the option today, discounted at the risk-free rate of 7%, is:

$$C_0 = \frac{\$3.22}{1.07} = \$3.01$$

We can use the same basic framework to **value a one-period put option**. The only difference is that the payoff to the put option will be different from the call payoffs.

EXAMPLE: Valuing a one-period put option on a stock

Use the information in the previous example to calculate the value of a put option on the stock with an exercise price of $30.

Answer:

If the stock moves up to $34.50, a put option with an exercise price of $30 will expire worthless. If the stock moves down to $26.10, the put option will be worth $3.90.

The risk-neutral probabilities are 0.715 and 0.285 for an up- and down-move, respectively. The expected value of the put option in one period is:

E(put option value in 1 year) = ($0 × 0.715) + ($3.90 × 0.285) = $1.11

The value of the option today, discounted at the risk-free rate of 7%, is:

$$P_0 = \frac{\$1.11}{1.07} = \$1.04$$

In practice, we would construct a binomial model with many short periods and have many possible outcomes at expiration. However, the one-period model is sufficient to understand the concept and method. Note that the actual probabilities of an up move and a down move do not enter directly into our calculation of option value. The size of the up-move and down-move, along with the risk-free rate, determine the risk-neutral probabilities we use to calculate the expected payoff at option expiration. Remember, the risk-neutral probabilities come from constructing a hedge that creates a certain payoff. Because their calculation is based on an arbitrage relationship, we can discount the expected payoff based on risk-neutral probabilities, at the risk-free rate.

LOS 57.o: Explain under which circumstances the values of European and American options differ.

CFA® Program Curriculum: Volume 6, page 104

The only difference between European and American options is that a holder of an American option has the right to exercise prior to expiration, while European options can only be exercised at expiration. The prices of European and American options will be equal unless the right to exercise prior to expiration has positive value. At expiration, both types of options are, of course, equivalent and they will have the same value, the exercise value. Their exercise value at expiration will either be zero if they are at or out of the money, or the amount that they are in the money.

For a call option on an asset that has no cash flows during the life of the option, there is no advantage to early exercise. During its life, the market value of a call option will be greater than its exercise value (by its time value), so early exercise is not valuable and we sometimes say that such call options are "worth more alive than dead." Because there is no value to early exercise, otherwise identical American and European call options on assets with no cash flows will have the same value.

If the asset pays cash flows during the life of a call option, early exercise can be valuable because options are not adjusted for cash flows on the underlying asset. Consider a call option on a stock that will pay a $3 dividend. The stock price is expected to decrease by $3 on the ex-dividend day which will decrease the value of the call option, so exercising the call option prior to the ex-dividend date may be advantageous because the stock can be sold at its predividend price or held to receive the dividend. Because early exercise may be valuable for call options on assets with cash flows, the price of American call options on assets with cash flows will be greater than the price of otherwise identical European call options.

For put options, cash flows on the underlying do not make early exercise valuable. Actually, a decrease in the price of the underlying asset after cash distributions makes put options more valuable. In the case of a put option that is deep in the money, however, early exercise may be advantageous. Consider the (somewhat extreme) case of a put option at $20 on a stock that has fallen in value to zero. Exercising the put will result in an immediate payment of $20, the exercise value of the put. With a European put option, the $20 cannot be realized until option expiration, so its value now is only the present value of $20. Given the potential positive value of early exercise for put options, American put options can be priced higher than otherwise identical European put options.

MODULE QUIZ 57.3, 57.4

To best evaluate your performance, enter your quiz answers online.

1. At expiration, the exercise value of a put option is:
    A. positive if the underlying asset price is less than the exercise price.
    B. zero only if the underlying asset price is equal to the exercise price.
    C. negative if the underlying asset price is greater than the exercise price.

2. The price of an out-of-the-money option is:
    A. less than its time value.
    B. equal to its time value.
    C. greater than its time value.

3. A decrease in the risk-free rate of interest will:
    A. increase put and call option prices.
    B. decrease put option prices and increase call option prices.
    C. increase put option prices and decrease call option prices.

4. The put-call parity relationship for European options must hold because a protective put will have the same payoff as:
    A. a covered call.
    B. a fiduciary call.
    C. an uncovered call.

5. The put-call-forward parity relationship *least likely* includes:
    A. a risk-free bond.
    B. call and put options.
    C. the underlying asset.

6. In a one-period binomial model, the value of an option is *best* described as the present value of:
    A. a probability-weighted average of two possible outcomes.
    B. a probability-weighted average of a chosen number of possible outcomes.
    C. one of two possible outcomes based on a chosen size of increase or decrease.

7. An American call option is *most likely* to be exercised early when:
    A. the option is deep in the money.
    B. the underlying asset pays dividends.
    C. the risk-free interest rate has increased.

KEY CONCEPTS

LOS 57.a

Valuation of derivatives is based on a no-arbitrage condition with risk-neutral pricing. Because the risk of a derivative is entirely based on the risk of the underlying asset, we can construct a fully hedged portfolio and discount its future cash flows at the risk-free rate.

We can describe three replications among a derivative, its underlying asset, and a risk-free asset:

> risky asset + derivative = risk-free asset
>
> risky asset − risk- free asset = − derivative position
>
> derivative position − risk-free asset = − risky asset

LOS 57.b

The price of a forward or futures contract is the forward price that is specified in the contract.

The value of a forward or futures contract is zero at initiation. Its value may increase or decrease during its life, with gains or losses in the value of a long position just opposite to gains or losses in the value of a short position.

LOS 57.c

If there are no costs or benefits from holding the underlying asset, the forward price of an asset to be delivered at time T is:

$$F_0(T) = S_0 (1 + Rf)^T$$

The value of a forward contract is zero at initiation. During its life, at time t, the value of the forward contract is:

$$V_t(T) = S_t - F_0(T) / (1 + Rf)^{T-t}.$$

At expiration, the payoff to a long forward is $S_T - F_0(T)$, the difference between the spot price of the asset at expiration and the price of the forward contract.

LOS 57.d

If holding an asset has costs and benefits, the no-arbitrage forward price is:

$$F_0(T) = [S_0 + PV_0 (cost) - PV_0 (benefit)] (1 + Rf)^T$$

The present values of the costs and benefits decrease as time passes. The value of the forward at time t is:

$$V_t(T) = S_t + PV_t(cost) - PV_t(benefit) - \frac{F_0(T)}{(1 + Rf)^{T-t}}.$$

At expiration the costs and benefits of holding the asset are zero and do not affect the value a long forward position, which is $S_T - F_0(T)$.

LOS 57.e

A forward rate agreement (FRA) is a derivative contract that has a future interest rate, rather than an asset, as its underlying. FRAs are used by firms to hedge the risk of borrowing and lending they intend to do in the future. A firm that intends to borrow in the future can lock in an interest rate with a long position in an FRA. A firm that intends to lend in the future can lock in an interest rate with a short position in an FRA.

LOS 57.f

Because gains and losses on futures contracts are settled daily, prices of forwards and futures that have the same terms may be different if interest rates are correlated with futures prices. Futures are more valuable than forwards when interest rates and futures prices are positively correlated and less valuable when they are negatively correlated. If interest rates are constant or uncorrelated with futures prices, the prices of futures and forwards are the same.

LOS 57.g

In a simple interest-rate swap, one party pays a floating rate and the other pays a fixed rate on a notional principal amount. The first payment is known at initiation and the rest of the payments are unknown. The unknown payments are equivalent to the payments on off-market FRAs. To replicate a swap with a value of zero at initiation, the sum of the present values of these FRAs must equal zero.

LOS 57.h

The price of a swap is the fixed rate of interest specified in the swap contract. The value depends on how expected future floating rates change over time. An increase in expected short-term future rates will produce a positive value for the fixed-rate payer, and a decrease in expected future rates will produce a negative value for the fixed-rate payer.

LOS 57.i

At expiration, the value of a call option is the greater of zero or the underlying asset price minus the exercise price.

At expiration, the value of a put option is the greater of zero or the exercise price minus the underlying asset price.

LOS 57.j

If immediate exercise of an option would generate a positive payoff, the option is in the money. If immediate exercise would result in a negative payoff, the option is out of the money. An option's exercise value is the greater of zero or the amount it is in the money. Time value is the amount by which an option's price is greater than its exercise value. Time value is zero at expiration.

LOS 57.k

Factors that determine the value of an option:

Increase in:	Effect on call option values	Effect on put option values
Price of underlying asset	Increase	Decrease
Exercise price	Decrease	Increase
Risk-free rate	Increase	Decrease
Volatility of underlying asset	Increase	Increase
Time to expiration	Increase	Increase, except some European puts
Costs of holding underlying asset	Increase	Decrease
Benefits of holding underlying asset	Decrease	Increase

LOS 57.l

A fiduciary call (a call option and a risk-free zero-coupon bond that pays the strike price X at expiration) and a protective put (a share of stock and a put at X) have the same payoffs at expiration, so arbitrage will force these positions to have equal prices: $c + X / (1 + Rf)^T = S + p$. This establishes put-call parity for European options.

Based on the put-call parity relation, a synthetic security (stock, bond, call, or put) can be created by combining long and short positions in the other three securities.

- $c = S + p - X / (1 + Rf)^T$
- $p = c - S + X / (1 + Rf)^T$
- $S = c - p + X / (1 + Rf)^T$
- $X / (1 + Rf)^T = S + p - c$

LOS 57.m

Based on the fact that the present value of an asset's forward price is equal to its spot price, we can substitute the present value of the forward price into the put-call parity relationship at the initiation of a forward contract to establish put-call-forward parity as:

$$c_0 + X / (1 + Rf)^T = F_0(T) / (1 + Rf)^T + p_0$$

LOS 57.n

To determine the value of an option using a one-period binomial model, we calculate its payoff following an up-move and following a down-move, estimate risk-neutral probabilities of an up-move and a down-move, calculate the probability-weighted average of its up-move and down-move payoffs, and discount this value by one period.

LOS 57.o

The prices of European and American options will be equal unless the right to exercise prior to expiration has positive value.

For a call option on an asset that has no cash flows during the life of the option, there is no advantage to early exercise so identical American and European call options will have the same value. If the asset pays cash flows during the life of a call option, early exercise can be valuable and an American call option will be priced higher than an otherwise identical European call option.

For put options, early exercise can be valuable when the options are deep in the money and an American put option will be priced higher than an otherwise identical European put option.

ANSWER KEY FOR MODULE QUIZZES

Module Quiz 57.1

1. **A**   Derivatives pricing models use the risk-free rate to discount future cash flows (risk-neutral pricing) because they are based on constructing arbitrage relationships that are theoretically riskless. (LOS 57.a)

2. **C**   The price of a forward or futures contract is defined as the price specified in the contract at which the two parties agree to trade the underlying asset on a future date. The value of a forward or futures contract is typically zero at initiation, and at expiration is the difference between the spot price and the contract price. (LOS 57.b)

3. **B**   For an asset with no holding costs or benefits, the forward price must equal the future value of the current spot price, compounded at the risk-free rate over the term of the forward contract, for the contract to have a value of zero at initiation. Otherwise an arbitrage opportunity would exist. (LOS 57.c)

4. **A**   Convenience yield refers to nonmonetary benefits from holding an asset. One example of convenience yield is the advantage of owning an asset that is difficult to sell short when it is perceived to be overvalued. Interest and dividends are monetary benefits. Storage and insurance are carrying costs. (LOS 57.d)

Module Quiz 57.2

1. **C**   To create a synthetic 60-day FRA on a 180-day interest rate, a bank would borrow for 240 days and lend the proceeds for 60 days, creating a 180-day loan 60 days from now. (LOS 57.e)

2. **B**   If interest rates are positively correlated with futures prices, interest earned on cash from daily settlement gains on futures contracts will be greater than the opportunity cost of interest on daily settlement losses, and a futures contract will be have a higher price than an otherwise equivalent forward contract that does not feature daily settlement. (LOS 57.f)

3. **A**   The price of a fixed-for-floating interest rate swap is defined as the fixed rate specified in the swap contract. Typically a swap will be priced such that it has a value of zero at initiation and neither party pays the other to enter the swap. (LOS 57.h)

Module Quiz 57.3, 57.4

1. **A** The exercise value of a put option is positive at expiration if the underlying asset price is less than the exercise price. Its exercise value is zero if the underlying asset price is greater than or equal to the exercise price. The exercise value of an option cannot be negative because the holder can allow it to expire unexercised. (Module 57.3, LOS 57.i)

2. **B** Because an out-of-the-money option has an exercise value of zero, its price is its time value. (Module 57.3, LOS 57.j)

3. **C** Interest rates are inversely related to put option prices and directly related to call option prices. (Module 57.3, LOS 57.k)

4. **B** Given call and put options on the same underlying asset with the same exercise price and expiration date, a protective put (underlying asset plus a put option) will have the same payoff as a fiduciary call (call option plus a risk-free bond that will pay the exercise price on the expiration date) regardless of the underlying asset price on the expiration date. (Module 57.3, LOS 57.l)

5. **C** The put-call-forward parity relationship is $F_0(T) / (1 + RFR)^T + p_0 = c_0 + X / (1 + RFR)^T$, where $X / (1 + RFR)^T$ is a risk-free bond that pays the exercise price on the expiration date, and $F_0(T)$ is the forward price of the underlying asset. (Module 57.3, LOS 57.m)

6. **A** In a one-period binomial model, the value of an option is the present value of a probability-weighted average of two possible values after one period, during which its value is assumed to move either up or down by a chosen size. (Module 57.4, LOS 57.n)

7. **B** An American call option might be exercised early to receive a dividend paid by the underlying asset. Otherwise, there is no benefit to the holder from exercising an American call early because the call can be sold instead for its higher market value. (Module 57.4, LOS 57.o)

READING 58

Introduction to Alternative Investments

EXAM FOCUS

"Alternative investments" collectively refers to the many asset classes that fall outside the traditional definitions of stocks and bonds. This category includes hedge funds, private equity, real estate, commodities, infrastructure, and other alternative investments, primarily collectibles. Each of these alternative investments has unique characteristics that require a different approach by the analyst. You should be aware of the different strategies, fee structures, due diligence, and issues in valuing and calculating returns with each of the alternative investments discussed in this topic review.

MODULE 58.1: PRIVATE EQUITY AND REAL ESTATE

Video covering this content is available online.

LOS 58.a: Compare alternative investments with traditional investments.

CFA® Program Curriculum: Volume 6, page 124

Alternative investments differ from traditional investments (publicly traded stocks, bonds, cash) both in the types of assets and securities included in this asset class and in the structure of the investment vehicles in which these assets are held. Managers of alternative investment portfolios may use derivatives and leverage, invest in illiquid assets, and short securities. Many types of real estate investment are considered alternatives to traditional investment as well. Types of alternative investment structures include hedge funds, private equity funds, various types of real estate investments, and some ETFs. Fee structures for alternative investments are different than those of traditional investments, with higher management fees on average and often with additional incentive fees based on performance. Alternative investments as a group have had low returns correlations with traditional investments. Compared to traditional investments, alternative investments exhibit:

■ Less liquidity of assets held.

■ More specialization by investment managers.

■ Less regulation and transparency.

■ More problematic and less available historical return and volatility data.

■ Different legal issues and tax treatments.

LOS 58.b: Describe categories of alternative investments.

CFA® Program Curriculum: Volume 6, page 128

We will examine six categories of alternative investments in detail in this topic review. Here we introduce each of those categories.

1. **Hedge funds.** These funds may use leverage, hold long and short positions, use derivatives, and invest in illiquid assets. Managers of hedge funds use a great many different strategies in attempting to generate investment gains. They do not necessarily hedge risk as the name might imply.

2. **Private equity funds.** As the name suggests, private equity funds invest in the equity of companies that are not publicly traded or in the equity of publicly traded firms that the fund intends to take private. Leveraged buyout (LBO) funds use borrowed money to purchase equity in established companies and comprise the majority of private equity investment funds. A much smaller portion of these funds, venture capital funds, invest in or finance young unproven companies at various stages early in their existence. For our purposes here we will also consider investing in the securities of financially distressed companies to be private equity, although hedge funds may hold these also.

3. **Real estate.** Real estate investments include residential or commercial properties as well as real estate backed debt. These investments are held in a variety of structures including full or leveraged ownership of individual properties, individual real estate backed loans, private and publicly traded securities backed by pools of properties or mortgages, and limited partnerships.

4. **Commodities.** To gain exposure to changes in commodities prices, investors can own physical commodities, commodities derivatives, or the equity of commodity producing firms. Some funds seek exposure to the returns on various commodity indices, often by holding derivatives contracts that are expected to track a specific commodity index.

5. **Infrastructure.** Infrastructure refers to long-lived assets that provide public services. These include economic infrastructure assets such as roads, airports, and utility grids, and social infrastructure assets such as schools and hospitals.

6. **Other.** This category includes investment in tangible collectible assets such as fine wines, stamps, automobiles, antique furniture, and art, as well as patents, an intangible asset.

LOS 58.c: Describe potential benefits of alternative investments in the context of portfolio management.

CFA® Program Curriculum: Volume 6, page 132

Alternative investment returns have had low correlations with those of traditional investments over long periods. The primary motivation for holding alternative investments is their historically low correlation of returns with those of traditional investments, which can reduce an investor's overall portfolio risk. However, the risk measures we use for traditional assets may not be adequate to capture the risk characteristics of alternative investments. Managers often consider measures of risk other than standard deviation of returns, such as worst month or historical frequency of downside returns.

Historical returns for alternative investments have been higher on average than for traditional investments, so adding alternative investments to a traditional portfolio may increase expected returns. The reasons for these higher returns are thought to be that some alternative investments are less efficiently priced than traditional assets (providing opportunities for skilled managers), that alternative investments may offer extra returns for being illiquid, and that alternative investments often use leverage.

While it seems that adding alternative investments to a portfolio will improve both portfolio risk and expected return, choosing the optimal portfolio allocation to alternative investments is complex and there are potential problems with historical returns data and traditional risk measures. *Survivorship bias* refers to the upward bias of returns if data only for currently existing (surviving) firms is included. Since surviving firms tend to be those that had better-than-average returns, excluding the returns data for failed firms results in average returns that are biased upward. *Backfill bias* refers to bias introduced by including the previous performance data for firms recently added to a benchmark index. Since firms that are newly added to an index must be those that have survived and done better than average, including their returns for prior years (without including the previous and current returns for funds that have not been added to the index) tends to bias index returns upward.

LOS 58.d: Describe hedge funds, private equity, real estate, commodities, infrastructure, and other alternative investments, including, as applicable, strategies, sub-categories, potential benefits and risks, fee structures, and due diligence.

LOS 58.f: Describe issues in valuing and calculating returns on hedge funds, private equity, real estate, commodities, and infrastructure.

CFA® Program Curriculum: Volume 6, page 133

PROFESSOR'S NOTE:
We cover these LOS together and slightly out of curriculum order so that we can present the complete analysis of each category of alternative investments to help candidates better understand each category.

Private Equity

The majority of private equity funds invest either in private companies or public companies they intend to take private (leveraged buyout funds), or in early stage companies (venture capital funds). Two additional, but smaller, categories of private equity funds are distressed investment funds and developmental capital funds.

A private equity fund may also charge fees for arranging buyouts, fees for a deal that does not happen, or fees for handling asset divestitures after a buyout.

Private Equity Strategies

Leveraged buyouts (LBOs) are the most common type of private equity fund investment. "Leveraged" refers to the fact that the fund's purchase of the portfolio company is funded primarily by debt. This may be bank debt (leveraged debt), high-yield bonds, or **mezzanine financing**. Mezzanine financing refers to debt or preferred shares that are subordinate to the high-yield bonds issued and carry warrants or conversion features that give investors participation in equity value increases.

PROFESSOR'S NOTE

We will use a similar term, "mezzanine-stage financing," when referring to a late-stage investment in a venture capital company that is preparing to go public via an IPO. Here we are referring to a type of security rather than a type of investment.

Two types of LBOs are **management buyouts** (MBOs), in which the existing management team is involved in the purchase, and **management buy-ins** (MBIs), in which an external management team will replace the existing management team.

In an LBO, the private equity firm seeks to increase the value of the firm through some combination of new management, management incentives, restructuring, cost reduction, or revenue enhancement. Firms with high cash flow are attractive LBO candidates because their cash flow can be used to service and eventually pay down the debt taken on for acquisition.

Venture capital (VC) funds invest in companies in the early stages of their development. The investment often is in the form of equity but can be in convertible preferred shares or convertible debt. While the risk of start-up companies is often great, returns on successful companies can be very high. This is often the case when a company has grown to the point where it is sold (at least in part) to the public via an IPO.

The companies in which a venture capital fund is invested are referred to as its **portfolio companies**. Venture capital fund managers are closely involved in the development of portfolio companies, often sitting on their boards or filling key management roles.

Categorization of venture capital investments is based on the company's stage of development. Terminology used to identify venture firm investment at different stages of the company's life includes the following:

1. The **formative stage** refers to investments made during a firm's earliest period and comprises three distinct phases.

   - **Angel investing** refers to investments made very early in a firm's life, often the "idea" stage, and the investment funds are used for business plans and assessing market potential. The funding source is usually individuals ("angels") rather than venture capital funds.

   - The **seed stage** refers to investments made for product development, marketing, and market research. This is typically the stage during which venture capital funds make initial investments, through ordinary or convertible preferred shares.

   - **Early stage** refers to investments made to fund initial commercial productionand sales.

2. **Later stage** investment refers to the stage of development where a company already has production and sales and is operating as a commercial entity. Investment funds provided at this stage are typically used for expansion of production and/or increasing sales though an expanded marketing campaign.

3. **Mezzanine-stage financing** refers to capital provided to prepare the firm for an IPO. The term refers to the timing of the financing (between private company and public company) rather than the type of financing.

Other Private Equity Strategies

Developmental capital or **minority equity investing** refers to the provision of capital for business growth or restructuring. The firms financed may be public or private. In the case of public companies, such financing is referred to as **private investment in public equities** (PIPEs).

Distressed investing involves buying debt of mature companies that are experiencing financial difficulties (potentially or currently in default, or in bankruptcy proceedings). Investors in distressed debt often take an active role in the turnaround by working with management on reorganization or to determine the direction the company should take. Distressed debt investors are sometimes referred to as *vulture investors*. Note that although distressed debt investing is included in the private equity category, some hedge funds invest in the debt of financially distressed companies as well.

Private Equity Structure and Fees

Similar to hedge funds, private equity funds are typically structured as limited partnerships. **Committed capital** is the amount of capital provided to the fund by investors. The committed capital amount is typically not all invested immediately but is "drawn down" (invested) as securities are identified and added to the portfolio. Committed capital is usually drawn down over three to five years, but the *drawdown period* is at the discretion of the fund manager. Management fees are typically 1% to 3% of committed capital, rather than invested capital.

Incentive fees for private equity funds are typically 20% of profits, but these fees are not earned until after the fund has returned investors' initial capital. It is possible that incentive fees paid over time may exceed 20% of the profits realized when all portfolio companies have been liquidated. This situation arises when returns on portfolio companies are high early and decline later. A **clawback** provision requires the manager to return any periodic incentive fees to investors that would result in investors receiving less than 80% of the profits generated by portfolio investments as a whole.

Private Equity Exit Strategies

The average holding period for companies in private equity portfolios is five years. There are several primary methods of exiting an investment in a portfolio company:

1. **Trade sale:** Sell a portfolio company to a competitor or another strategic buyer.

2. **IPO:** Sell all or some shares of a portfolio company to the public.

3. **Recapitalization:** The company issues debt to fund a dividend distribution to equity holders (the fund). This is not an exit, in that the fund still controls the company, but is often a step toward an exit.

4. **Secondary sale:** Sell a portfolio company to another private equity firm or a group of investors.

5. **Write-off/liquidation:** Reassess and adjust to take losses from an unsuccessful outcome.

Private Equity Potential Benefits and Risks

There is evidence that over the last 20 years returns on private equity funds have been higher on average than overall stock returns. Less-than-perfect correlation of private equity returns with traditional investment returns suggests that there may be portfolio diversification benefits from including private equity in portfolios. The standard deviation of private equity returns has been higher than the standard deviation of equity index returns, suggesting greater risk. As with hedge fund returns data, private equity returns data may suffer from survivorship bias and backfill bias (both lead to overstated returns). Because portfolio companies are revalued infrequently, reported standard deviations of returns and correlations of returns with equity returns may both be biased downward.

Evidence suggests that choosing skilled fund managers is important. Differences between the returns to top quartile funds and bottom quartile funds are significant and performance rank shows persistence over time.

Private Equity Due Diligence

Because of the high leverage typically used for private equity funds, investors should consider how interest rates and the availability of capital may affect any required refinancing of portfolio company debt. The choice of manager (general partner) is quite important and many of the factors we listed for hedge fund due diligence also apply to private equity fund investments. Specifically, the operating and financial experience of the manager, the valuation methods used, the incentive fee structures, and drawdown procedures are all important areas to investigate prior to investing.

Private Equity Company Valuation

Valuation for private equity portfolio companies is essentially the same as valuing a publicly traded company, although the discount rate or multiples used may be different for private companies.

Market/comparables approach: Market or private transaction values of similar companies may be used to estimate multiples of EBITDA, net income, or revenue to use in estimating the portfolio company's value.

Discounted cash flow approach: A dividend discount model falls into this category, as does calculating the present value of free cash flow to the firm or free cash flow to equity.

Asset-based approach: Either the liquidation values or fair market values of assets can be used. Liquidation values will be lower as they are values that could be realized quickly in a situation of financial distress or termination of company operations. Liabilities are subtracted so only the equity portion of the firm's value is being estimated.

EXAMPLE: Portfolio company comparables approach

A private equity fund is valuing a French private manufacturing company. EBITDA and market values for four publicly traded European companies in the same industry are shown in the following table (in millions of euros):

	EBITDA	Market Value
Company 1:	€100	€1,000
Company 2:	€250	€2,000
Company 3:	€250	€1,500
Company 4:	€275	€2,200

The estimated EBITDA for the French company is €175 million. Using an average of the four companies as the industry multiple, estimate the market value for the French company.

Answer:

	EBITDA Multiple
Company 1:	€1,000 / €100 = 10×
Company 2:	€2,000 / €250 = 8×
Company 3:	€1,500 / €250 = 6×
Company 4:	€2,200 / €275 = 8×

The average multiple for these four companies is 8×. Based on the French company's expected EBITDA of €175 million, its estimated value is €175 million × 8 = €1,400 million or €1.4 billion.

Real Estate

Investment in real estate can provide income in the form of rents as well as the potential for capital gains. Real estate as an asset class can provide diversification benefits to an investor's portfolio and a potential inflation hedge because rents and real estate values tend to increase with inflation. Real estate investments can be differentiated according to their underlying assets. Assets included under the heading of real estate investments include:

- Residential property—single-family homes.

- Commercial property—produces income.

- Loans with residential or commercial property as collateral—mortgages ("whole loans"), construction loans.

Residential property is considered a direct investment in real estate. Some buyers pay cash but most take on a mortgage (borrow) to purchase. The issuer (lender) of the mortgage has a direct investment in a whole loan and is said to "hold the mortgage." Issuers often sell the mortgages they originate and the mortgages are then pooled (securitized) as publicly traded mortgage-backed securities (MBS), which represent an indirect investment in the mortgage loan pool. Property purchased with a mortgage is referred to as a *leveraged investment* and the owner's equity is the property value minus the outstanding loan amount. Changes in property value over time, therefore, affect the property owner's equity in the property.

Commercial real estate properties generate income from rents. Homes purchased for rental income are considered investment in commercial property. Large properties (e.g., an office building) are a form of direct investment for institutions or wealthy individuals, either purchased for cash or leveraged (a mortgage loan is taken for a portion of the purchase price). Long time horizons, illiquidity, the large size of investment needed, and the complexity of the investments make commercial real estate inappropriate for many investors. Commercial real estate properties can also be held by a limited partnership in which the partners have limited liability and the general partner manages the investment and the properties, or by a real estate investment trust (REIT).

As with residential mortgages, whole loans (commercial property mortgages) are considered a direct investment, but loans can be pooled into commercial mortgage-backed securities (CMBS) that represent an indirect investment.

Real estate investment trusts (REITs) issue shares that trade publicly like shares of stock. REITs are often identified by the type of real estate assets they hold: mortgages, hotel properties, malls, office buildings, or other commercial property. Income is used to pay dividends. Typically, 90% of income must be distributed to shareholders to avoid taxes on this income that would have to be paid by the REIT before distribution to shareholders.

Two additional assets considered as real estate are timberland and farmland, for which one component of returns comes from sales of timber or agricultural products. Timberland returns also include price changes on timberland, which depend on expectations of lumber prices in the future and how much timber has been harvested. Farmland returns are based on land price changes, changes in farm commodity prices, and the quality and quantity of the crops produced.

Potential Benefits and Risks of Real Estate

Real estate performance is measured by three different types of indices. An **appraisal index**, such as those prepared by the National Council of Real Estate Investment Fiduciaries (NCREIF), is based on periodic estimates of property values. Appraisal index returns are smoother than those based on actual sales and have the lowest standard deviation of returns of the various index methods. A **repeat sales index** is based on price changes for properties that have sold multiple times. The sample of properties sold and thus included in the index is not necessarily random and may not be representative of the broad spectrum of properties available (an example of sample selection bias). **REIT indices** are based on the actual trading prices of REIT shares, similar to equity indices.

Historically, REIT index returns and global equity returns have had a relatively strong correlation (on the order of 0.6) because business cycles affect REITs and global equities similarly. The correlation between global bond returns and REIT returns has been very low historically. In either case diversification benefits can result from including real estate in an investor's portfolio. However, the methods of index construction (e.g., appraisal or repeat sales indices) may be a factor in the low reported correlations, in which case actual diversification benefits may be less than expected.

Real Estate Investment Due Diligence

Property values fluctuate because of global and national economic factors, local market conditions, and interest rate levels. Other specific risks include variation in the abilities of managers to select and manage properties, and changes in regulations. Decisions regarding selecting, financing, and managing real estate projects directly affect performance. The degree of leverage used in a real estate investment is important because leverage amplifies losses as well as gains.

Distressed properties investing has additional risk factors compared to investing in properties with sound financials and stable operating histories. *Real estate development* has additional risk factors including regulatory issues such as zoning, permitting, and environmental considerations or remediation, and economic changes and financing decisions over the development period. The possible inability to get long-term financing at the appropriate time for properties initially developed with temporary (short-term) financing presents an additional risk.

Real Estate Valuation

Three methods are commonly used to value real estate:

- The **comparable sales approach** bases valuation on recent sales of similar properties. Values for individual properties include adjustments for differences between the characteristics of the specific property and those of the properties for which recent sales prices are available, such as age, location, condition, and size.

■ The **income approach** estimates property values by calculating the present value of expected future cash flows from property ownership or by dividing the net operating income (NOI) for a property by a capitalization (cap) rate. The cap rate is a discount rate minus a growth rate and is estimated based on factors such as general business conditions, property qualities, management effectiveness, and sales of comparable properties. Note that dividing by a cap rate of 12.5% is the same as using a multiple of 8 times NOI (1 / 0.125 = 8).

■ The **cost approach** estimates the replacement cost of a property. The cost of land and the cost of rebuilding at current construction costs are added to estimate replacement cost.

Value estimates for real estate investment trusts can be income based or asset based. The income-based approach is similar to the income approach for a specific property and uses some measure of cash flow and a cap rate based on the factors we noted previously for the income approach. One measure of cash flow for a REIT is funds from operations (FFO). FFO is calculated from net income with depreciation added back (because depreciation is a non-cash charge) and with gains from property sales subtracted and losses on property sales added (because these gains and losses are assumed to be nonrecurring). A second measure of cash flow is adjusted funds from operations (AFFO), which is FFO with recurring capital expenditures subtracted. AFFO is similar to free cash flow. The asset-based approach provides an estimate of the net asset value of the REIT by subtracting total liabilities from the total value of the real estate assets and dividing by the number of shares outstanding.

MODULE QUIZ 58.1

To best evaluate your performance, enter your quiz answers online.

1. Compared to managers of traditional investments, managers of alternative investments are likely to have fewer restrictions on:
   A. holding cash.
   B. buying stocks.
   C. using derivatives.

2. Compared to alternative investments, traditional investments tend to:
   A. be less liquid.
   B. be less regulated.
   C. require lower fees.

3. In which category of alternative investments is an investor *most likely* to use derivatives?
   A. Real estate.
   B. Commodities.
   C. Collectibles.

4. Diversification benefits from adding hedge funds to an equity portfolio may be limited because:
   A. correlations tend to increase during periods of financial crisis.
   B. hedge fund returns are less than perfectly correlated with global equities.
   C. hedge funds tend to perform better when global equity prices are declining.

©2018 Kaplan, Inc.

5.   A private equity valuation approach that uses estimated multiples of cash flows to value a portfolio company is:
   A.   the asset-based approach.
   B.   the discount cash flow approach.
   C.   the market/comparables approach.

6.   In a leveraged buyout, covenants in leveraged loans can:
   A.   restrict additional borrowing.
   B.   require lenders to provide transparency.
   C.   provide protection for the general partners.

7.   Direct commercial real estate ownership *least likely* requires investing in:
   A.   large amounts.
   B.   illiquid assets.
   C.   a short time horizon.

8.   A real estate property valuation would *least likely* use:
   A.   an income approach.
   B.   an asset-based approach.
   C.   a comparable sales approach.

MODULE 58.2: HEDGE FUNDS, COMMODITIES, AND INFRASTRUCTURE

Video covering this content is available online.

Hedge Funds

Hedge funds employ a large number of different strategies. Hedge fund managers have more flexibility than managers of traditional investments. Hedge funds can use leverage, take short equity positions, and take long or short positions in derivatives. The complex nature of hedge fund transactions leads managers to trade through **prime brokers**, who provide many services including custodial services, administrative services, money lending, securities lending for short sales, and trading. Hedge fund managers can negotiate various service parameters with the prime brokers, such as margin requirements.

Hedge fund return objectives can be stated on an **absolute basis** (e.g., 10%) or on a **relative basis** (e.g., returns 5% above a specific benchmark return) depending on the fund strategy. Hedge funds are *less regulated* than traditional investments. Like private equity funds, hedge funds are typically set up as limited partnerships, with the investors as the limited (liability) partners. A hedge fund limited partnership may not include more than a proscribed number of investors, who must possess adequate wealth, sufficient liquidity, and an acceptable degree of investment sophistication. The management firm is the general partner and typically receives both a management fee based on the value of assets managed and an incentive fee based on fund returns.

Hedge fund investments are less liquid than traditional, publicly traded investments. Restrictions on redemptions may include a **lockup period** and/or a **notice period**. A lockup period is a time after initial investment during which withdrawals are not allowed. A notice period, typically 30 to 90 days, is the amount of time a fund has after receiving a redemption request to fulfill the request. Additional fees may be charged at redemption. All of these, of course, discourage redemptions. Hedge fund managers often incur significant transactions costs when they redeem shares. Redemption fees can offset these costs. Notice periods allow time for managers to reduce positions in an orderly manner. Redemptions often increase when hedge fund performance is poor over a period, and the costs of honoring redemptions may further decrease the value of partnership interests. This is an additional source of risk for hedge fund investors.

A **fund-of-funds** is an investment company that invests in hedge funds, giving investors diversification among hedge fund strategies and allowing smaller investors to access hedge funds in which they may not be able to invest directly. Fund-of-funds managers charge an additional layer of fees beyond the fees charged by the individual hedge funds in the portfolio.

Hedge Fund Strategies

Similar to categorizing alternative investments, classifying hedge funds can also be challenging. According to Hedge Fund Research, Inc., there are four main classifications of hedge fund strategies:

1. **Event-driven strategies** are typically based on a corporate restructuring or acquisition that creates profit opportunities for long or short positions in common equity, preferred equity, or debt of a specific corporation. Subcategories are:

   - **Merger arbitrage:** Buy the shares of a firm being acquired and sell short the firm making the acquisition.

   - **Distressed/restructuring:** Buy the (undervalued) securities of firms in financial distress when analysis indicates value will be increased by a successful restructuring; possibly short overvalued security types at the same time.

   - **Activist shareholder:** Buy sufficient equity shares to influence a company's policies with the goal of increasing company value.

   - **Special situations:** Invest in the securities of firms that are issuing or repurchasing securities, spinning off divisions, selling assets, or distributing capital.

2. **Relative value strategies** involve buying a security and selling short a related security with the goal of profiting when a perceived pricing discrepancy between the two is resolved.

   - **Convertible arbitrage fixed income:** Exploit pricing discrepancies between convertible bonds and the common stock of the issuing companies.

   - **Asset-backed fixed income:** Exploit pricing discrepancies among various mortgage-backed securities (MBS) or asset-backed securities (ABS).

   - **General fixed income:** Exploit pricing discrepancies between fixed income securities of various types.

   - **Volatility:** Exploit pricing discrepancies arising from differences between returns volatility implied by options prices and manager expectations of future volatility.

   - **Multi-strategy:** Exploit pricing discrepancies among securities in asset classes different from those previously listed and across asset classes and markets.

3. **Macro strategies** are based on global economic trends and events and may involve long or short positions in equities, fixed income, currencies, or commodities.

4. **Equity hedge fund strategies** seek to profit from long or short positions in publicly traded equities and derivatives with equities as their underlying assets.

    – **Market neutral:** Use technical or fundamental analysis to select undervalued equities to be held long, and to select overvalued equities to be sold short, in approximately equal amounts to profit from their relative price movements without exposure to market risk.

    – **Fundamental growth:** Use fundamental analysis to find high-growth companies. Identify and buy equities of companies that are expected to sustain relatively high rates of capital appreciation.

    – **Fundamental value:** Buy equity shares that are believed to be undervalued based on fundamental analysis. Here it is the hedge fund structure, rather than the type of assets purchased, that results in classification as an alternative investment.

    – **Quantitative directional:** Buy equity securities believed to be undervalued and short securities believed to be overvalued based on technical analysis. Market exposure may vary depending on relative size of long and short portfolio positions.

    – **Short bias:** Employ predominantly short positions in overvalued equities, possibly with smaller long positions, but with negative market exposure overall.

Many hedge funds tend to specialize in a specific strategy at first and over time may develop or add additional areas of expertise, becoming multi-strategy funds.

Hedge Fund Potential Benefits and Risks

Hedge fund returns have tended to be better than those of global equities in down equity markets and to lag the returns of global equities in up markets. Different hedge fund strategies have the best returns during different time periods. Statements about the performance and diversification benefits of hedge funds are problematic because of the great variety of strategies used. Less-than-perfect correlation with global equity returns may offer some diversification benefits, but correlations tend to increase during periods of financial crisis.

Hedge Fund Due Diligence

Selecting hedge funds (or funds of funds) requires significant investigation of the available funds. This may be somewhat hampered by a lack of transparency by funds that consider their strategies and systems to be proprietary information. The fact that the regulatory requirements for hedge fund disclosures are minimal presents additional challenges. A partial list of factors to consider when selecting a hedge fund or a fund-of-funds includes an examination of the fund's:

■ Investment strategy.

■ Investment process.

- Source of competitive advantages.

- Historical returns.

- Valuation and returns calculation methods.

- Longevity.

- Amount of assets under management.

- Management style.

- Key person risk.

- Reputation.

- Growth plans.

- Systems for risk management.

- Appropriateness of benchmarks.

The analysis of these factors is challenging because a lack of persistence in returns may mean that funds with better historical returns will not provide better-than-average returns in the future. Additionally, many of the items for due diligence, such as reputation, risk management systems, and management style, are difficult to quantify in a way that provides clear choices for potential investors. Further, previously profitable strategies to exploit pricing inefficiencies are likely to become less profitable as more funds pursue the same strategy.

Hedge Fund Valuation

Hedge fund values are based on market values for traded securities in their portfolios but must use model (estimated) values for non-traded securities. For traded securities it is most conservative to use the prices at which a position could be closed: bid prices for long positions and ask prices for short positions. Some funds use the average of the bid and ask prices instead. In the case of illiquid securities, quoted market prices may be reduced for the degree of illiquidity, based on position size compared to the total value of such securities outstanding and their average trading volume. Some funds calculate a "trading NAV" using such adjustments for illiquidity. Trading NAV is different from the calculated net asset value required by accounting standards, which is based on either market or model prices.

Commodities

While it is possible to invest directly in commodities such as grain and gold, the most commonly used instruments to gain exposure to commodity prices are derivatives. Commodities themselves are physical goods and thus incur costs for storage and transportation. Returns are based on price changes and not on income streams.

Futures, forwards, options, and swaps are all available forms of commodity derivatives. Futures trade on exchanges; some options trade on exchanges while others trade over the counter; and forwards and swaps are over-the-counter instruments originated by dealers. Futures and forwards are contractual obligations to buy or sell a commodity at a specified price and time. Options convey the right, but not the obligation, to buy or sell a commodity at a specified price and time. Other methods of exposures to commodities include the following:

- **Exchange-traded funds** (commodity ETFs) are suitable for investors who are limited to buying equity shares. ETFs can invest in commodities or commodity futures and can track prices or indices.

- **Equities that are directly linked to a commodity** include shares of a commodity producer, such as an oil producer or a gold mining firm, and give investors exposure to price changes of the produced commodity. One potential drawback to commodity-linked equities is that the price movements of the stock and the price movements of the commodity may not be perfectly correlated.

- **Managed futures funds** are actively managed. Some managers concentrate on specific sectors (e.g., agricultural commodities) while others are more diversified. Managed future funds can be structured as limited partnerships with fees like those of hedge funds (e.g., 2 and 20) and restrictions on the number, net worth, and liquidity of the investors. They can also be structured like mutual funds with shares that are publicly traded so that retail investors can also benefit from professional management. Additionally, such a structure allows a lower minimum investment and greater liquidity compared to a limited partnership structure.

- **Individual managed accounts** provide an alternative to pooled funds for high net worth individuals and institutions. Accounts are tailored to the needs of the specific investor.

- **Specialized funds in specific commodity sectors** can be organized under any of the structures we have discussed and focus on certain commodities, such as oil and gas, grains, precious metals, or industrial metals.

Potential Benefits and Risks of Commodities

Returns on commodities over time have been lower than returns on global stocks or bonds. Sharpe ratios for commodities as an asset class have been low due to these lower returns and the high volatility of commodities prices. As with other investments, speculators can earn high returns over short periods when their expectations about short-term commodity price movements are correct and they act on them.

Historically, correlations of commodity returns with those of global equities and global bonds have been low, typically less than 0.2, so that adding commodities to a traditional portfolio can provide diversification benefits. Because commodity prices tend to move with inflation rates, holding commodities can act as a hedge of inflation risk. To the extent that commodities prices move with inflation the real return over time would be zero, although futures contracts may offer positive real returns.

Commodity Prices and Investments

Spot prices for commodities are a function of supply and demand. Demand is affected by the value of the commodity to end-users and by global economic conditions and cycles. Supply is affected by production and storage costs and existing inventories. Both supply and demand are affected by the purchases and sales of nonhedging investors (speculators).

For many commodities, supply is inelastic in the short run because of long lead times to alter production levels (e.g., drill oil wells, plant crops, or decide to plant less of them). As a result, commodity prices can be volatile when demand changes significantly over the economic cycle. Production of some commodities, especially agricultural commodities, can be significantly affected by the weather, leading to high prices when production is low and low prices when production is high. Costs of extracting oil and minerals increase as more expensive methods or more remote areas are used. To estimate future needs, commodities producers analyze economic events, government policy, and forecasts of future supply. Investors analyze inventory levels, forecasts of production, changes in government policy, and expectations of economic growth in order to forecast commodity prices.

Commodity Valuation

Wheat today and wheat six months from today are different products. Purchasing the commodity today will give the buyer the use of it if needed, while contracting for wheat to be delivered six months from today avoids storage costs and having cash tied up. An equation that considers these aspects is:

futures price ≈ spot price (1 + risk-free rate) + storage costs − convenience yield

Convenience yield is the value of having the physical commodity for use over the period of the futures contract. If this equation does not hold, an arbitrage transaction is possible.

If there is little or no convenience yield, futures prices will be higher than spot prices, a situation termed **contango**. When the convenience yield is high, futures prices will be less than spot prices, a situation referred to as **backwardation**.

Three sources of commodities futures returns are:

1. **Roll yield**—The yield due to a difference between the spot price and futures price, or a difference between two futures prices with different expiration dates. Futures prices converge toward spot prices as contracts get closer to expiration. Roll yield is positive for a market in backwardation and negative for a market in contango.

2. **Collateral yield**—The interest earned on collateral required to enter into a futures contract.

3. **Change in spot prices**—The total price return is a combination of the change in spot prices and the convergence of futures prices to spot prices over the term of the futures contract.

Infrastructure

Infrastructure investments include transportation assets such as roads, airports, ports, and railways, as well as utility assets, such as gas distribution facilities, electric generation and distribution facilities, and waste disposal and treatment facilities. Other categories of infrastructure investments are communications (e.g., broadcast assets and cable systems) and social (e.g., prisons, schools, and health care facilities).

Investments in infrastructure assets that are already constructed are referred to as **brownfield investments** and investments in infrastructure assets that are to be constructed are referred to as **greenfield investments**. In general, investing in brownfield investments provides stable cash flows and relatively high yields, but offers little potential for growth. Investing in greenfield investments is subject to more uncertainty and may provide relatively lower yields, but offers greater growth potential.

In addition to categorizing infrastructure investments by type or whether or not construction of the assets is complete, they may be categorized by their geographic location.

Investment in infrastructure can be made by constructing the assets and either selling or leasing them to the government or by directly operating the assets. Alternatively, investment in infrastructure can be made by purchasing existing assets from the government to lease back to the government or operate directly.

Infrastructure assets typically have a long life and are quite large in cost and scale so direct investment in them has low liquidity. However, more liquid investments backed by infrastructure assets are available through ETFs, mutual funds, private equity funds, or master limited partnerships (MLPs). Publicly traded vehicles for investing in infrastructure are a small part of the overall universe of infrastructure investments and are relatively concentrated in a few categories of assets.

Investing in infrastructure assets can provide diversification benefits, but investors should be aware that they are often subject to regulatory risk, risk from financial leverage, and the possibility that cash flows will be less than expected. Investors who construct infrastructure assets have construction risk. When the assets are owned and operated by a private owner, operational risk must also be considered.

Other Alternative Investments

Various types of tangible collectibles are considered investments, including rare wines, art, rare coins and stamps, valuable jewelry and watches, and sports memorabilia. There is no income generation but owners do get enjoyment from use, as with a collectible automobile. Storage costs may be significant, especially with art and wine. Specialized knowledge is required, the markets for many collectibles are illiquid, and gains result only from increases in the prices of these assets.

LOS 58.e: Describe, calculate, and interpret management and incentive fees and net-of-fees returns to hedge funds.

CFA® Program Curriculum: Volume 6, page 139

The total fee paid by investors in a hedge fund consists of a **management fee** and an **incentive fee**. The management fee is earned regardless of investment performance and incentive fees are a portion of profits. The most common fee structure for a hedge fund is "2 and 20" or "2 plus," 2% of the value of the assets under management plus an incentive fee of 20% of profits.

Profits can be (1) any gains in value, (2) any gains in value in excess of the management fee, or (3) gains in excess of a **hurdle rate**. A hurdle rate can be set either as a percentage (e.g., 4%) or a rate plus a premium (e.g., LIBOR + 2%). A *hard hurdle rate* means that incentive fees are earned only on returns in excess of the benchmark. A *soft hurdle rate* means that incentive fees are paid on all profits, but only if the hurdle rate is met.

Another feature that is often included is called a **high water mark**. This means that the incentive fee is not paid on gains that just offset prior losses. Thus incentive fees are only paid to the extent that the current value of an investor's account is above the highest value after fees previously recorded. This feature ensures that investors will not be charged incentive fees twice on the same gains in their portfolio values.

Investors in funds of funds incur additional fees from the managers of the funds of funds. A common fee structure from funds of funds is "1 and 10." A 1% management fee and a 10% incentive fee are charged in addition to any fees charged by the individual hedge funds within the fund-of-funds structure.

Fee calculations for both management fees and incentive fees can differ not only by the schedule of rates but also method of fee determination. Management fees may be calculated on either the beginning-of-period or end-of-period values of assets under management. Incentive fees may be calculated net of management fees (value increase less management fees) or independent of management fees. Although the most common hedge fund fee rates tend to be the "2 and 20" and "1 and 10" for funds of funds, fee structures can vary. Price breaks to investors, competitive conditions, and historical performance can influence negotiated rates.

Fee structures and their impact on investors' results are illustrated in the following example.

EXAMPLE: Hedge fund fees

BJI Funds is a hedge fund with a value of $110 million at initiation. BJI Funds charges a 2% management fee based on assets under management at the beginning of the year and a 20% incentive fee with a 5% soft hurdle rate, and it uses a high water mark. Incentive fees are calculated on gains net of management fees. The ending values before fees are as follows:

- Year 1: $102.2 million
- Year 2: $118.0 million

Calculate the total fees and the investor's net return for both years.

Answer:

Year 1:

Management fee: $110.0 million × 2% = $2.2 million

Gross value end of year (given): $102.2 million

Return net of management fee $= \dfrac{\$102.2 \text{ million} - \$2.2 \text{ million}}{\$110.0 \text{ million}} - 1 = -9.1\%$

There is no incentive fee because the return is less than the hurdle rate.

Total fees = $2.2 million

Ending value net of fees = $102.2 million – $2.2 million = $100.00 million

---

Year 2:

Management fee: $100.0 million $\times$ 2% = $2.0 million

Gross value end of year (given): $118.0 million

Return net of management fee $= \dfrac{\$118.0 \text{ million} - \$2.0 \text{ million}}{\$100.0 \text{ million}} - 1 = +16.0\%$

Incentive fee = ($118.0 million – $2.0 million – $110.0 million) $\times$ 20% = $1.2 million

Note that the incentive fee is calculated based on gains in value above $110 million because that is the high water mark.

Total fees = $2.0 million + $1.2 million = $3.2 million

Net return $= \dfrac{\$118.0 \text{ million} - \$3.2 \text{ million}}{\$100.0 \text{ million}} - 1 = +14.8\%$

LOS 58.g: Describe risk management of alternative investments.

CFA® Program Curriculum: Volume 6, page 176

Risk management of alternative investments requires additional understanding of the unique set of circumstances for each category. We can summarize some of the more important risk considerations as follows:

- Standard deviation of returns may be a misleading measure of risk for two reasons. First, returns distributions are not approximately normal; they tend to be leptokurtic (fat tails) and negatively skewed (possibility of extreme negative outcomes). Second, for alternative assets that use appraisal or models to estimate values, returns are smoothed so that standard deviation of returns (and correlations with returns of traditional investments) will be understated. Even market-based returns can have these same limitations when transactions are infrequent. These problems can bias Sharpe measures upward and make estimates of beta misleading as well. Investors should consider downside risk measures such as **value at risk (VaR)**, which is an estimate of the size of a potential decline over a period that will occur, for example, less than 5% of the time; or the **Sortino ratio**, which measures risk as downside deviation rather than standard deviation. For publicly traded securities, such as REITs and ETFs, market returns are used and standard definitions of risk are more applicable.

- Use of derivatives introduces operational, financial, counterparty, and liquidity risk.

- Performance for some alternative investment categories is primarily determined by management expertise and execution, so risk is not just that of holding an asset class but also risk of management underperformance.

- Hedge funds and private equity funds are much less transparent than traditional investments as they release less information and may consider their strategies to be proprietary information.

- Many alternative investments are illiquid. Returns should reflect a premium for lack of liquidity to compensate investors for liquidity risk or the inability to redeem securities at all during lockup periods.

■ When calculating optimal allocations, indices of historical returns and standard deviations may not be good indicators of future returns and volatility.

■ Correlations vary across periods and are affected by events.

Due Diligence

A listing of key items for due diligence for alternative investments includes six major categories: organization, portfolio management, operations and controls, risk management, legal review, and fund terms.

1. **Organization:** Experience, quality, and compensation of management and staff; analysis of all their prior and current fund results; alignment of manager and investor interests; and reputation and quality of third-party service providers used.

2. **Portfolio management:** Management of the investment process; target markets, asset types, and strategies; investment sources; operating partners' roles; underwriting; environmental and engineering review; integration of asset management, acquisitions, and dispositions; and the process for dispositions.

3. **Operations and controls:** Reporting and accounting methods; audited financial statements; internal controls; frequency of valuations; valuation approaches; insurance; and contingency plans.

4. **Risk management:** Fund policies and limits; portfolio risk and key factors; and constraints on leverage and currencies and hedging of related risks.

5. **Legal review:** Fund legal structure; registrations; and current and past litigation.

6. **Fund terms:** Fees, both management and incentive, and expenses; contractual terms; investment period; fund term and extensions; carried interest; distributions; conflicts; rights of limited partners; and termination procedures for key personnel.

 MODULE QUIZ 58.2

To best evaluate your performance, enter your quiz answers online.

1. An investor who chooses a fund-of-funds as an alternative to a single hedge fund is *most likely* to benefit from:
   A. lower fees.
   B. higher returns.
   C. more due diligence.

2. A high water mark of £150 million was established two years ago for a British hedge fund. The end-of-year value before fees for last year was £140 million. This year's end-of-year value before fees is £155 million. The fund charges "2 and 20." Management fees are paid independently of incentive fees and are calculated on end-of-year values. What is the total fee paid this year?
   A. £3.1 million.
   B. £4.1 million.
   C. £6.1 million.

3. Standard deviation is *least likely* an appropriate measure of risk for:
   A. hedge funds.
   B. publicly traded REITs.
   C. exchange-traded funds.

4. A hedge fund that operates as an activist shareholder is *most likely* engaging in:
   A. a macro strategy.
   B. a relative value strategy.
   C. an event-driven strategy.

5. Which component of the return on a long futures position is related to differences between spot prices and futures prices?
   A. Roll yield.
   B. Price return.
   C. Collateral yield.

6. Greenfield investments in infrastructure are *most accurately* described as investments in assets:
   A. that are operating profitably.
   B. that have not yet been constructed.
   C. related to environmental technology.

KEY CONCEPTS

LOS 58.a

"Traditional investments" refers to long-only positions in stocks, bonds, and cash. "Alternative investments" refers to some types of assets such as real estate, commodities, and various collectables, as well as some specific structures of investment vehicles. Hedge funds and private equity funds (including venture capital funds) are often structured as limited partnerships; real estate investment trusts (REITs) are similar to mutual funds; and ETFs can contain alternative investments as well.

Compared to traditional investments, alternative investments typically have lower liquidity; less regulation and disclosure; higher management fees and more specialized management; potential diversification benefits; more use of leverage, use of derivatives; potentially higher returns; limited and possibly biased historical returns data; problematic historical risk measures; and unique legal and tax considerations.

LOS 58.b

Hedge funds are investment companies that use a variety of strategies and may be highly leveraged, use long and short positions, and use derivatives.

Private equity funds usually invest in the equity of private companies or companies wanting to become private, financing their assets with high levels of debt. This category also includes venture capital funds, which provide capital to companies early in their development.

Real estate as an asset class includes residential and commercial real estate, individual mortgages, and pools of mortgages or properties. It includes direct investment in single properties or loans as well as indirect investment in limited partnerships, which are private securities, and mortgage-backed securities and real estate investment trusts, which are publicly traded.

Commodities refer to physical assets such as agricultural products, metals, oil and gas, and other raw materials used in production. Commodities market exposure can provide an inflation hedge and diversification benefits.

Infrastructure refers to long-lived assets that provide public services and are often built or operated by governments. Various types of collectibles, such as cars, wines, and art, are considered alternative investments as well.

LOS 58.c

The primary motivation for adding alternative investments to a portfolio is to reduce portfolio risk based on the less-than-perfect correlation between alternative asset returns and traditional asset returns. For many alternative investments, the expertise of the manager can be an important determinant of returns.

LOS 58.d

Hedge Funds

- *Event-driven* strategies include merger arbitrage, distressed/restructuring, activist shareholder, and special situations.

- *Relative value* strategies seek profits from unusual pricing issues.

- *Macro hedge* strategies are "top down" strategies based on global economic trends.

- *Equity hedge* strategies are "bottom up" strategies that take long and short positions in equities and equity derivatives. Strategies include market neutral, fundamental growth, fundamental value, quantitative directional, short bias, and sector specific.

In periods of financial crisis, the correlation of returns between global equities and hedge funds tends to increase, which limits hedge funds' effectiveness as a diversifying asset class.

Due diligence factors for hedge funds are investment strategy, investment process, competitive advantages, track record, longevity of fund, and size (assets under management). Other qualitative factors include management style, key person risk, reputation, investor relations, growth plans, and management of systematic risk.

Private Equity

Leveraged buyouts (LBOs) and *venture capital* are the two dominant strategies. Other strategies include developmental capital and distressed securities.

Types of LBOs include management buyouts, in which the existing management team is involved in the purchase, and management buy-ins, in which an external management team replaces the existing management.

Stages of venture capital investing include the formative stage (composed of the angel investing, seed, and early stages); the later stage (expansion); and the mezzanine stage (prepare for IPO).

Methods for exiting investments in portfolio companies include trade sale (sell to a competitor or another strategic buyer); IPO (sell some or all shares to investors); recapitalization (issue portfolio company debt); secondary sale (sell to another private equity firm or other investors); or write-off/liquidation.

Private equity has some historical record of potential diversification benefits. An investor must identify top performing private equity managers to benefit from private equity.

Due diligence factors for private equity include the manager's experience, valuation methods used, fee structure, and drawdown procedures for committed capital.

Real Estate

Reasons to invest in real estate include potential long-term total returns, income from rent payments, diversification benefits, and hedging against inflation.

Forms of real estate investing:

	Public (Indirect)	**Private (Direct)**
Debt	■ Mortgage-backed securities ■ Collateralized mortgage obligations	■ Mortgages ■ Construction loans
Equity	■ Real estate corporation shares ■ Real estate investment trust shares	■ Sole ownership ■ Joint ventures ■ Limited partnerships ■ Commingled funds

Real estate investment categories include residential properties, commercial real estate, REITs, mortgage-backed securities, and timberland and farmland.

Historically, real estate returns are highly correlated with global equity returns but less correlated with global bond returns. The construction method of real estate indexes may contribute to the low correlation with bond returns.

Due diligence factors for real estate include global and national economic factors, local market conditions, interest rates, and property-specific risks including regulations and abilities of managers. Distressed properties investing and real estate development have additional risk factors to consider.

Commodities

The most common way to invest in commodities is with derivatives. Other methods include exchange-traded funds, equities that are directly linked to a commodity, managed futures funds, individual managed accounts, and specialized funds in specific commodity sectors.

Beyond the potential for higher returns and lower volatility benefits to a portfolio, commodity as an asset class may offer inflation protection. Commodities can offset inflation, especially if commodity prices are used to determine inflation indices.

Spot prices for commodities are a function of supply and demand. Global economics, production costs, and storage costs, along with value to user, all factor into prices.

Infrastructure

Infrastructure investments may be classified as greenfield (assets to be built) or brownfield (existing assets).

Liquidity is low for direct investments in infrastructure because the assets are long-lived and tend to be large-scale. However, some liquid investment vehicles exist that are backed by infrastructure assets.

LOS 58.e

The total fee for a hedge fund consists of a management fee and an incentive fee. Other fee structure specifications include hurdle rates and high water marks. Funds of funds incur an additional level of management fees. Fee calculations for both management fees and incentive fees can differ by the schedule and method of fee determination.

LOS 58.f

Hedge funds often invest in securities that are not actively traded and must estimate their values, and invest in securities that are illiquid relative to the size of a hedge fund's position. Hedge funds may calculate a trading NAV that adjusts for the illiquidity of these securities.

A private equity portfolio company may be valued using a market/comparables approach (multiple-based) approach, a discounted cash flow approach, or an asset-based approach.

Real estate property valuation approaches include the comparable sales approach, the income approach (multiples or discounted cash flows), and the cost approach. REITs can be valued using an income-based approach or an asset-based approach.

A commodity futures price is approximately equal to the spot price compounded at the risk-free rate, plus storage costs, minus the convenience yield.

LOS 58.g

Risk management of alternative investments requires understanding of the unique circumstances for each category.

- Standard deviation of returns may be misleading as a measure of risk.
- Use of derivatives introduces operational, financial, counterparty, and liquidity risks.
- Performance for some alternative investment categories depends primarily on management expertise.
- Hedge funds and private equity funds are less transparent than traditional investments.
- Many alternative investments are illiquid.
- Indices of historical returns and standard deviations may not be good indicators of future returns and volatility.
- Correlations vary across periods and are affected by events.

Key items for due diligence include organization, portfolio management, operations and controls, risk management, legal review, and fund terms.

Study Session 19

ANSWER KEY FOR MODULE QUIZZES

Module Quiz 58.1

1. **C** Traditional managers can hold cash and buy stocks but may be restricted from using derivatives. (LOS 58.a)

2. **C** Traditional investments typically require lower fees, are more regulated, and are more liquid than alternative investments. (LOS 58.a)

3. **B** Commodities investing frequently involves the use of futures contracts. Derivatives are less often employed in real estate or collectibles investing. (LOS 58.b)

4. **A** Adding hedge funds to traditional portfolios may not provide the expected diversification to an equity portfolio because return correlations tend to increase during periods of financial crisis. (LOS 58.c)

5. **C** The market/comparables approach uses market or private transaction values of similar companies to estimate multiples of EBITDA, net income, or revenue to use in estimating the portfolio company's value. (LOS 58.f)

6. **A** Debt covenants in leveraged buyout loans may restrict additional borrowing by the acquired firm. Covenants restrict and require borrowers' actions, not lenders' actions. Covenants in leveraged loans provide protection for the lenders, not the general partners. (LOS 58.d)

7. **C** Commercial real estate ownership requires long time horizons and purchasing illiquid assets that require large investment amounts. (LOS 58.d)

8. **B** The three approaches to valuing a property are income, comparable sales, and cost. An asset-based approach can be used for real estate investment trusts, but not for valuing individual real estate properties. (LOS 58.f)

Module Quiz 58.2

1. **C** A fund-of-funds manager is expected to provide more due diligence and better redemption terms. Funds of funds charge an additional layer of fees. Investing in fund-of-funds may provide more diversification but may not necessarily provide higher returns. (LOS 58.d)

2. **B** Management fee is £155 million × 0.02 = £3.1 million.

   Incentive fee is (£155 million – £150 million) × 0.20 = £1.0 million.

   Total fee is £3.1 million + £1.0 million = £4.1 million. (LOS 58.e)

3. **A** Hedge funds may hold illiquid assets that may use estimated values to calculate returns. Risk as measured by standard deviation could be understated. For publicly traded securities, such as REITs and ETFs, standard definitions of risk are more applicable. (LOS 58.g)

4. **C** Activist shareholder strategies are a subcategory of event-driven strategies. (LOS 58.d)

5. **A** Roll yield results from a difference between the spot and futures prices. (LOS 58.f)

6. **B** Greenfield investments refer to infrastructure assets that are yet to be constructed. (LOS 58.d)

TOPIC ASSESSMENT: DERIVATIVES AND ALTERNATIVE INVESTMENTS

You have now finished the Derivatives and Alternative Investments topic sections. The following Topic Assessment provides immediate feedback on how effective your study has been for this material. The number of questions on this test is equal to the number of questions for the topic on one-half of the actual Level I CFA exam. Questions are more exam-like than typical Module Quiz or QBank questions; a score of less than 70% indicates that your study likely needs improvement. These tests are best taken timed; allow 1.5 minutes per question.

After you've completed this Topic Assessment, you may additionally log in to your Schweser.com online account and enter your answers in the Topic Assessments product. Select "Performance Tracker" to view a breakdown of your score. Select "Compare with Others" to display how your score on the Topic Assessment compares to the scores of others who entered their answers.

1. Which of the following derivatives positions replicates investing at the risk-free rate?
   A. Holding an asset and a short position in a forward contract on the asset.
   B. Holding an asset and a long position in a forward contract on the asset.
   C. Selling an asset short and holding a short position in a forward contract on the asset.

2. Compared to an asset with no net cost of carry, holding costs that are greater than benefits:
   A. increase the no-arbitrage price of the forward contract.
   B. decrease the no-arbitrage price of the forward contract.
   C. have no effect on the no-arbitrage price of the forward contract.

3. The value of a call option on a stock is *most likely* to decrease as a result of:
   A. an increase in asset price volatility.
   B. a decrease in the risk-free rate of interest.
   C. a decrease in the exercise price of the option.

4. In which of the following ways is an interest rate swap different from a series of forward rate agreements (FRAs)?
   A. The FRAs that replicate an interest rate swap may be off-market contracts.
   B. The fixed rate is known at initiation for an interest rate swap but not for a series of FRAs.
   C. An interest rate swap may have a nonzero value at initiation, while FRAs must have a value of zero at initiation.

5. It is *least likely* that a forward contract:
   A. has counterparty risk.
   B. can be settled in cash.
   C. requires a margin deposit.

6. With respect to European and American options, cash flows from the underlying asset may make:
   A. a European put more valuable than an otherwise identical American put.
   B. an American put more valuable than an otherwise identical European put.
   C. an American call more valuable than an otherwise identical European call.

7. Cash flows related to futures margin *least likely* include:
   A. interest on the margin loan.
   B. deposits to meet margin calls.
   C. interest received on collateral.

8. Survivorship bias in reported hedge fund index returns will *most likely* result in index:
   A. returns and risk that are biased upward.
   B. returns and risk that are biased downward.
   C. risk that is biased downward and returns that are biased upward.

9. A hedge fund with a 2 and 20 fee structure has a hard hurdle rate of 5%. If the incentive fee and management fee are calculated independently and the management fee is based on beginning-of-period asset values, an investor's net return over a period during which the gross value of the fund has increased 22% is *closest* to:
   A. 16.4%.
   B. 16.6%.
   C. 17.0%.

10. The *least appropriate* measure of risk for alternative investments is:
    A. value at risk (VaR).
    B. the Sortino ratio.
    C. variance of returns.

11. The type of real estate index that *most likely* exhibits sample selection bias is:
    A. REIT index.
    B. appraisal index.
    C. repeat sales index.

12. With respect to mezzanine-stage financing in venture capital investing and mezzanine financing of a leveraged buyout:
    A. mezzanine-stage financing refers to a type of security but mezzanine financing does not.
    B. mezzanine financing refers to a type of security but mezzanine-stage financing does not.
    C. both terms refer to financing by issuance of securities that have both debt and equity characteristics.

13. A hedge fund that engages primarily in distressed debt investing and merger arbitrage is *best* described as using:
    A. a macro strategy.
    B. an event-driven strategy.
    C. a relative value strategy.

TOPIC ASSESSMENT ANSWERS: DERIVATIVES AND ALTERNATIVE INVESTMENTS

1. **A** Holding an asset and a short position in a forward contract on the asset replicates investing at the risk- free rate because the future payoff is certain. (Study Session 18, Module 57.1, LOS 57.a)

2. **A** Costs of holding the underlying asset that are greater than the benefits increase the no-arbitrage price of a forward contract. (Study Session 18, Module 57.1, LOS 57.d)

3. **B** A decrease in the risk-free rate of interest will decrease call values. The other changes will tend to increase the value of a call option. (Study Session 18, Module 57.3, LOS 57.k)

4. **A** An interest rate swap may be replicated by a series of off-market FRAs (i.e., FRAs with nonzero values at initiation), if their present values sum to zero at initiation. The fixed rate is known at initiation for either an interest rate swap or a series of FRAs. Parties to both FRAs and interest rate swaps may agree to off-market prices at initiation. (Study Session 18, Module 57.2, LOS 57.g)

5. **C** Forward contracts typically do not require a margin deposit. They are custom instruments that may require settlement in cash or delivery of the underlying asset, and they have counterparty risk. (Study Session 18, Module 56.1, LOS 56.c)

6. **C** For call options, early exercise is valuable only if the underlying asset pays a cash flow during the life of the option. If early exercise is valuable, an American call can be more valuable than an otherwise identical European call. Cash flows on the underlying asset do not make early exercise of a put option valuable. A European option cannot be more valuable than an otherwise identical American option. (Study Session 18, Module 57.4, LOS 57.o)

7. **A** Futures margin is satisfied by posting collateral and does not involve a loan. A futures investor may post interest-bearing securities as collateral and earn interest (collateral yield) on these securities. Faced with a margin call, a futures investor must either post additional margin to restore the account to the initial margin requirement or close the position. (Study Session 18, Module 56.1, LOS 56.c and Study Session 19, Module 58.2, LOS 58.f)

8. **C** Surviving firms are more likely to have had good past returns and have taken on less risk than the average fund, leading to upward bias in index returns and downward bias in index risk measures. (Study Session 19, Module 58.2, LOS 58.f)

9. **B** The management fee is 2% of the beginning asset value, which reduces an investor's gross return by 2% to 22 − 2 = 20%. The incentive fee is 20% of the excess gross return over the hurdle rate, or 0.20(0.22 − 0.05) = 3.4%. The investor return net of fees is 22% − 2% − 3.4% = 16.6%. (Study Session 19, Module 58.2, LOS 58.e)

10. **C** Because returns distributions of alternative investments are often leptokurtic and negatively skewed, variance is not an appropriate risk measure. Value at risk (VaR) and the Sortino ratio based on downside deviations from the mean are measures of downside risk that are more appropriate for alternative investments. (Study Session 19, Module 58.2, LOS 58.g)

11. **C** A repeat sales index includes prices of properties that have recently sold. Because these properties may not be representative of overall property values (may be biased toward properties that have declined or increased the most in value of the period), there is the risk of sample selection bias. An appraisal index or a REIT index is generally constructed for a sample of representative properties or REIT property pools. (Study Session 19, Module 58.1, LOS 58.f)

12. **B** Mezzanine financing in an LBO refers to the issue of securities that have both debt and equity features so that they are on the balance sheet between debt and equity. Mezzanine-stage financing refers to financing of different types that is employed during the period just prior to an IPO of a firm funded by venture capital. (Study Session 19, Module 58.1, LOS 58.d)

13. **B** Event-driven strategies attempt to capitalize on unique events or opportunities such as distressed debt or mergers and acquisitions. Relative value strategies involve taking long and short positions in related securities to exploit pricing inefficiencies. Macro strategy funds make directional trades on markets, currencies, interest rates, or other factors. (Study Session 19, Module 58.2, LOS 58.d)

APPENDIX

RATES, RETURNS, AND YIELDS

A **holding period return** (HPR), or holding period yield (HPY), can be for a period of any length and is simply the percentage increase in value over the period, which is calculated as:

HPR = ending value / beginning value – 1

1. If an investor puts $2,000 into an account and 565 days later it has grown in value to $2,700, the 565-day HPY is 2,700 / 2,000 – 1 = 35%.

2. If an investor buys a share of stock for $20/share, receives a $0.40 dividend, and sells the shares after nine months, the nine-month HPY is (22 + 0.40) / 20 – 1 = 12%.

An HPR for a given period is also the **effective yield** for that period.

An **effective annual yield** is the HPR for a one-year investment or the HPY for a different period converted to its annual equivalent yield.

3. If the six-month HPR is 2%, the effective annual yield is $1.02^2 – 1 = 4.040\%$.

4. If the 125-day HPR is 1.5%, the effective annual yield is $1.015^{365/125} – 1 = 4.443\%$.

5. If the two-year HPR (two-year effective rate) is 9%, the effective annual yield is $1.09^{1/2} – 1 = 4.4031\%$.

Compounding Frequency

Sometimes the "rate" on an investment is expressed as a **simple annual rate** (or *stated rate*)—the annual rate with no compounding of returns. The number of compounding periods per year is called the **periodicity** of the rate. For a periodicity of one, the stated rate and the effective annual rate are the same. When the periodicity is greater than one (more than one compounding period per year), the effective annual rate is the effective rate for the sub-periods, compounded for the number of sub-periods.

6. A bank CD has a stated annual rate of 6% with annual compounding (periodicity of 1); the effective annual rate is 6% and a $1,000 investment will return $1,000(1.06) = $1,060 at the end of one year.

7. A bank CD has a stated annual rate of 6% with semiannual compounding (periodicity of 2); the effective annual rate is $(1 + 0.06 / 2)^2 = 1.03^2 – 1 = 6.09\%$ and a $1,000 investment will return $1,000 (1.0609) = $1,060.90 at the end of one year.

8. A bank CD has a stated annual rate of 6% with quarterly compounding (periodicity of 4); the effective annual rate is $(1 + 0.06 / 4)^4 = 1.015^4 – 1 = 6.136\%$ and a $1,000 investment will return $1,000(1.06136) = $1,061.36 at the end of one year.

Note that increasing compounding frequency increases the effective annual yield for any given stated rate. In the limit, as compounding periods get shorter (more frequent), compounding is *continuous*. A stated rate of $r\%$, with continuous compounding, results in an effective annual return of $e^r - 1$.

9. A bank CD has a stated annual rate of 6%, continuously compounded; its effective annual yield is $e^{0.06} - 1 = 6.184\%$ and a $1,000 investment will return $1,061.84 at the end of one year.

Bond Quotations and Terminology

The **stated (coupon) rate** on a bond is the total cash coupon payments made over one year as a percentage of face value.

10. A bond with a face value of $1,000 that pays a coupon of $50 once each year (an annual-pay bond) has a stated (coupon) rate of $50 / 1,000 = 5\%$ and we say it has a periodicity of 1.

11. A bond with a face value of $1,000 that pays a coupon of $25 twice each year (a semiannual-pay bond) has a stated (coupon) rate of $(25 + 25) / 1,000 = 5\%$ and we say it has a periodicity of 2.

12. A bond with a face value of $1,000 that pays a coupon of $12.50(1.25%) four times each year (a quarterly-pay bond) has a coupon rate of $(12.50 + 12.50 + 12.50 + 12.50) / 1,000 = 5\%$ and we say it has a periodicity of 4.

The **current yield** on a bond is the stated (coupon) rate divided by the bond price as a percentage of face value or, alternatively, the sum of the coupon payments for one year divided by the bond price.

13. A bond with a stated coupon rate of 5% that is selling at 98.54% of face value has a current yield of $5 / 98.54 = 5.074\%$.

14. A bond that is trading at $1,058 and makes annual coupon payments that sum to $50 has a current yield of $50 / 1,058 = 4.726\%$.

The **yield to maturity** (YTM) of a bond, on an *annual basis*, is the effective annual yield and is used for bonds that pay an annual coupon. For bonds that pay coupons semiannually, we often quote the YTM on a *semiannual basis*, that is, two times the effective semiannual yield. To compare the yields of two bonds, we must calculate their YTMs on the same basis.

15. A bond with a YTM of 5% on a semiannual basis has a YTM on an annual basis (effective annual yield) of $(1 + 0.05 / 2)^2 - 1 = 5.0625\%$.

16. A bond with a YTM of 5% on an annual basis has a YTM on a semiannual basis of $(1.05^{1/2} - 1) \times 2 = 4.939\%$.

Note that in quantitative methods, the term **bond equivalent yield** (BEY) is used to refer to the YTM on a semiannual basis, whereas in corporate finance, BEY is used to refer to an annualized holding period return based on a 365-day year, [i.e., BEY = HPY $\times$ (365 / days in holding period)].

Internal Rate of Return (IRR)

The internal rate of return is the discount rate that makes the PV of a series of cash flows equal to zero. This calculation must be done with a financial calculator. We use the IRR for calculating the return on a capital project, the YTM on a bond, and the money weighted rate of return for a portfolio.

17. For the YTM of an annual-pay bond (YTM on an annual basis) on a coupon date with N years remaining until maturity, we calculate the annual IRR that satisfies:

$$-\text{bond price} + \frac{\text{coupon 1}}{1 + \text{IRR}} + \frac{\text{coupon 2}}{(1 + \text{IRR})^2} + ... + \frac{\text{coupon N} + \text{face value}}{(1 + \text{IRR})^N} = 0$$

18. For the YTM of a semiannual-pay bond on a coupon date with N years remaining until maturity, we calculate the IRR that satisfies:

$$-\text{bond price} + \frac{\text{coupon 1}}{1 + \dfrac{\text{IRR}}{2}} + \frac{\text{coupon 2}}{\left(1 + \dfrac{\text{IRR}}{2}\right)^2} + ... + \frac{\text{coupon 2N} + \text{face value}}{\left(1 + \dfrac{\text{IRR}}{2}\right)^{2N}} = 0$$

After solving for IRR / 2, which is the IRR for semiannual periods, we must multiply it by 2 to get the bond's YTM on a semiannual basis.

19. For a capital project, the (annual) IRR satisfies:

$$-\text{initial outlay} + \frac{CF_1}{1 + \text{IRR}} + \frac{CF_2}{(1 + \text{IRR})^2} + ... + \frac{CF_N}{(1 + \text{IRR})^N} = 0$$

where annual cash flows (CF) can be positive or negative (when a future expenditure is required). Note that if the sign of the cash flows changes more than once, there may be more than one IRR that satisfies the equation.

Money Market Securities

For some money market securities, such as U.S. T-bills, price quotations are given on a bond discount (or simply discount) basis. The bond discount yield (BDY) is the percentage discount from face value of a T-bill, annualized based on a 360-day year, and is therefore not an effective yield but simply an annualized discount from face value.

20. A T-bill that will pay $1,000 at maturity in 180 days is selling for $984, a discount of $1 - 984 / 1,000 = 1.6\%$. The annualized discount is $1.6\% \times 360 / 180 = 3.2\%$.

21. A 120-day T-bill is quoted at a BDY of 2.83%, its price is $[1 - (0.0283 \times 120 / 360)] \times 1,000 = \$990.57$. Its 120-day *holding period return* is $1,000 / 990.57 - 1 = 0.952\%$. Its *effective annual yield* is $(1,000 / 990.57)^{365/120} - 1 = 2.924\%$.

LIBOR (London Interbank Offered Rate) is an add-on rate quoted for several currencies and for several periods of one year or less, as an annualized rate.

22. HPY on a 30-day loan at a quoted LIBOR rate of 1.8% is $0.018 \times 30 / 360 = 0.15\%$ so the interest on a $10,000 loan is $10,000 \times 0.0015 = \$15$.

A related yield is the **money market yield** (MMY), which is HPY annualized based on a 360-day year.

23. A 120-day discount security with a maturity value of $1,000 that is priced at $995 has a money market yield of $(1{,}000 / 995 - 1) \times 360 / 120 = 1.5075\%$.

Forward rates are rates for a loan to be made in a future period. They are quoted based on the period of the loan. For loans of one year, we write 1y1y for a 1-year loan to be made one year from today and 2y1y for a 1-year loan to be made two years from today.

Spot rates are discount rates for single payments to be made in the future (such as for zero-coupon bonds).

24. Given a 3-year spot rate expressed as a compound annual rate (S_3) of 2%, a 3-year bond that makes a single payment of $1,000 in three years has a current value of $1{,}000 / (1 + 0.02)^3 = \$942.32$.

An N-year spot rate is the geometric mean of the individual annual forward rates:

$$S_N = [(1 + S_1)(1 + 1y1y)(1 + 2y1y)\ldots(1 + Ny1y)]^{\,1/N} - 1$$

and the annualized forward rate for M − N periods, N periods from now is:

$$Ny(M - N)y = \left[\frac{(1 + S_M)^M}{(1 + S_N)^N}\right]^{\frac{1}{M-N}} - 1$$

25. Given $S_5 = 2.4\%$ and $S_7 = 2.6\%$, $5y2y = [(1.026)^7 / (1.024)^5]^{1/2} - 1 = 3.1017\%$, which is approximately equal to $(7 \times 2.6\% - 5 \times 2.4\%) / 2 = 3.1\%$.

FORMULAS

for an annual-coupon bond with N years to maturity:

$$\text{price} = \frac{\text{coupon}}{(1 + \text{YTM})} + \frac{\text{coupon}}{(1 + \text{YTM})^2} + \dots + \frac{\text{coupon} + \text{principal}}{(1 + \text{YTM})^N}$$

for a semiannual-coupon bond with N years to maturity:

$$\text{price} = \frac{\text{coupon}}{\left(1 + \dfrac{\text{YTM}}{2}\right)} + \frac{\text{coupon}}{\left(1 + \dfrac{\text{YTM}}{2}\right)^2} + \dots + \frac{\text{coupon} + \text{principal}}{\left(1 + \dfrac{\text{YTM}}{2}\right)^{N \times 2}}$$

bond value using spot rates:

$$\text{no-arbitrage price} = \frac{\text{coupon}}{\left(1 + S_1\right)} + \frac{\text{coupon}}{\left(1 + S_2\right)^2} + \dots + \frac{\text{coupon} + \text{principal}}{\left(1 + S_N\right)^N}$$

full price between coupon payment dates:

(Bond value at last coupon date based on the current YTM) $\times (1 + \text{YTM}/\#)^{t/T}$

where # is the number of coupon periods per year, t is the number of days from the last coupon payment date until the date the bond trade will settle, and T is the number of days in the coupon period.

flat price = full price − accrued interest

$$\text{current yield} = \frac{\text{annual cash coupon payment}}{\text{bond price}}$$

forward and spot rates: $(1 + S_2)^2 = (1 + S_1)(1 + 1y1y)$

option-adjusted spread: OAS = Z-spread − option value

$$\text{modified duration} = \frac{\text{Macaulay duration}}{1 + \text{YTM}}$$

$$\text{approximate modified duration} = \frac{V_- - V_+}{2\,V_0\,\Delta\text{YTM}}$$

$$\text{effective duration} = \frac{V_- - V_+}{2\,V_0\,\Delta\text{curve}}$$

money duration = annual modified duration × full price of bond position

money duration per 100 units of par value =

   annual modified duration × full bond price per 100 of par value

price value of a basis point: PVBP = [(V_− − V_+) / 2]

$$\text{approximate convexity} = \frac{V_- + V_+ - 2\,V_0}{(\Delta\text{YTM})^2\,V_0}$$

$$\text{approximate effective convexity} = \frac{V_- + V_+ - 2\,V_0}{(\Delta\text{curve})^2\,V_0}$$

$$\%\Delta \text{ full bond price} = -\text{annual modified duration}(\Delta YTM) + \frac{1}{2}\text{ annual convexity}(\Delta YTM)^2$$

$$\text{duration gap} = \text{Macaulay duration} - \text{investment horizon}$$

$$\text{return impact} \approx -\text{duration} \times \Delta\text{spread} + \tfrac{1}{2}\text{convexity} \times (\Delta\text{spread})^2$$

$$\text{risky asset} + \text{derivative} = \text{risk-free asset}$$

$$\text{risky asset} - \text{risk-free asset} = -\text{ derivative position}$$

$$\text{derivative position} - \text{risk-free asset} = -\text{ risky asset}$$

$$\text{no-arbitrage forward price: } F_0(T) = S_0(1 + Rf)^T$$

$$\text{payoff to long forward at expiration} = S_T - F_0(T)$$

$$\text{value of forward at time } t: V_t(T) = S_t + PV_t(\text{cost}) - PV_t(\text{benefit}) - \frac{F_0(T)}{(1 + Rf)^{T-t}}$$

$$\text{intrinsic value of a call} = \text{Max}[0, S - X]$$

$$\text{intrinsic value of a put} = \text{Max}[0, X - S]$$

$$\text{option value} = \text{intrinsic value} + \text{time value}$$

$$\text{put-call parity: } c + X / (1 + Rf)^T = S + p$$

$$\text{put-call-forward parity: } F_0(T) / (1 + Rf)^T + p_0 = c_0 + X / (1 + Rf)^T$$

INDEX

A

absolute basis, 193
add-on yield, 25
adjustable-rate mortgage (ARM), 69
affirmative covenants, 4, 123
agency bonds, 23
agency RMBS, 71
alternative investments, 183
amortizing loan, 8
annualized holding period rate of return, 90
appraisal index, 191
approximate modified duration, 96
at par, 3
average life variability, 76

B

backup lines of credit, 25
backwardation, 198
balloon payment, 8, 79
bankruptcy remote vehicles, 5
basis points, 10
bearer, 4
benchmark bonds, 23
benchmark spread, 56
best efforts offering, 21
bilateral loan, 24
binomial model, 171
bond equivalent yield, 216
bond indenture, 3
bridge financing, 25
broken PAC, 76
brownfield investments, 199
bullet, 8

C

call option, 12, 165
cap, 10
capital-indexed bonds, 11
capital market securities, 2, 20
carrying value, 91
cash flow yield, 101
cash-settled forward contract, 144
central bank funds market, 28
central bank funds rates, 28
certificates of deposit (CDs), 28
change in spot prices, 198
clawback, 188
clean price, 41
CMBS-level call protection, 79
CMBS structure, 78
collateral, 6

collateralized debt obligations (CDO), 81
collateralized mortgage obligations (CMO), 74
collateral manager, 81
collateral trust bonds, 6
collateral yield, 198
commercial mortgage-backed securities (CMBS), 77
commercial paper, 25
commercial real estate, 190
committed capital, 187
commodities, 196
comparable sales approach, 191
conditional prepayment rate (CPR), 73
constant-yield price trajectory, 39
contango, 198
contingency provision, 11
convenience yield, 155, 198
conventional bonds, 3
conversion price, 14
conversion ratio, 14
conversion value, 14
convertible mortgage, 70
convexity, 104
corporate bonds, 26
corporate credit ratings, 119
corporate family ratings, 119
corporations, 2
cost approach, 192
cost of carry, 156
covered bonds, 6
credit enhancement, 6, 77
credit-linked coupon bond, 10
credit-linked note (CLN), 27
credit migration risk, 118
credit rating, 119
credit risk, 117
credit spread, 127
credit tranching, 68
currency option bond, 3
current yield, 46, 216

D

debentures, 6
debt service coverage ratio, 78
default risk, 117
deferred coupon bond, 11
developed markets, 20
developmental capital, 187
dirty price, 41
discount, 3
discount margin, 48
distressed investing, 187
domestic bonds, 4

downgrade risk, 118
dual-currency bond, 3
duration, 95
duration gap, 108

E

effective annual yield, 215
effective convexity, 104
effective duration, 98
effective yield, 45, 215
embedded options, 12
emerging markets, 20
enterprise value, 130
equipment trust certificates, 6
equity hedge fund strategies, 195
Eurobonds, 4
event-driven strategies, 194
exercise value, 166
expected loss, 117

F

fiduciary call, 168
fixed-rate mortgage, 69
flat price, 41
floaters, 10
floating-rate notes, 10
floating-rate note yields, 48
floor, 10
foreign bonds, 4
forward contract, 144
forward price, 144
forward rate agreement (FRA), 161
forward rates, 52
forward yield curve, 52
four Cs of credit analysis, 121
fully amortizing, 8, 70
fund-of-funds, 194

G

general obligation bonds, 131
global bonds, 4
greenfield investments, 199
grey market, 21
G-spread, 56
guarantee certificate, 27

H

haircut, 29
high water mark, 200
high yield, 128
holding period return, 215
hurdle rate, 199

Notes

Notes

Notes

Notes

Notes

Notes

Notes

Notes